MATTERS OF
THE MIND

MATTERS OF THE MIND

Latter-day Saint Helps for Mental Health

Edited by

Marleen S. Williams, Ph.D.
W. Dean Belnap, M.D.
John P. Livingstone, Ed.D.

DESERET
BOOK

Salt Lake City, Utah

Chapter 20, "How Does Serious and Persistent Mental Illness Affect Families?" © 2008 Dawn Fox and Jay Fox

Library of Congress Cataloging-in-Publication Data

Matters of the mind : Latter-day Saint helps for mental health / edited by Marleen S. Williams, W. Dean Belnap, and John P. Livingstone.
    p. cm.
  Includes bibliographical references and index.
  ISBN 978-1-59038-870-9 (paperbound)
  1. Mormons—Mental health. 2. Mental illness—Religious aspects—Mormons. 3. Mental illness—Religious aspects—Christianity. 4. Mentally ill—Religious life. I. Williams, Marleen. II. Belnap, W. Dean (Wilford Dean), 1926– III. Livingstone, John P.
  RC455.4.R4M38 2008
  616.89—dc22   2008008696

Printed in the United States of America
Sheridan Books, Chelsea, MI

10 9 8 7 6 5 4 3 2 1

Contents

IV. Coping with Mental Illness

Acknowledgments

We thank our spouses, Robert Williams, Mary Elen Belnap, and Linda Livingstone, for their constant support, encouragement, and help with this book. We also thank our research assistants, Anna Cariello and Brooke Burdge, for their careful scholarship and research. Community members and leaders, family members of individuals with mental illness, and those who experience these illnesses contributed to focus groups that helped us to generate topics for the book. Their input was very helpful. We appreciate the dedicated professionals who contributed chapters. Their expertise and commitment to improving the lives of others has made this book possible.

Introduction

How This Book Can Help You

This book was written to give you a more accurate understanding of mental illnesses. The information it contains will give you a greater knowledge of the difficulties experienced by those who have mental illnesses and teach you how to respond with compassion and empathy. If you are experiencing mental illness, this book can help you understand your own illness and be more compassionate and patient with yourself. You will also learn ways to help yourself manage and recover from the illness.

The chapters in this book will inform you about the causes of many mental illnesses. You will find ideas for managing brain problems, as well as ideas for reducing stress which can make them worse. You will learn how to strengthen spiritual, social, and emotional skills that will help you cope. You will also learn about how mental illnesses can be treated and where to find competent help.

Many of the symptoms of mental illness may resemble normal human experiences. It is important that a professional who has been trained to recognize mental illnesses make an accurate diagnosis. This book is not intended to train you how to diagnose mental illnesses. It can help you, however, recognize when a person may be experiencing a mental illness and know when and how to seek professional help. Early, appropriate treatment can reduce much suffering for both those who suffer from mental illness and those who love them.

The names used in case illustrations are fictional, but the facts represent examples of typical mental health problems. Any resemblance to real individuals, living or dead, is purely coincidental.

Section I

Understanding Mental Illness

1

What Is Mental Illness?

Marleen S. Williams

An accurate understanding of mental illness can help reduce the suffering that is caused by mental illness. Both those who suffer from mental illness and those who love them suffer much more when others do not understand mental illness. For many people, the term *mental illness* brings to mind strange and frightening images, such as those often portrayed in film and other media. These dramatic portrayals may be the only information many people have about mental illnesses. Historically, people with mental illnesses have often been scorned, blamed, banished from society, imprisoned, and mistreated. Many people still believe that mental illness is a rare problem that happens to other people and their families. They may believe that if they are good and do what is right, they can never be affected by mental illness.

Many individuals and their families who suffer from the effects of mental illness are faithful, religious people who try to do the best they can to keep God's commandments. Just as other medical diseases and disorders can afflict those who keep commandments and live righteous lives, mental illnesses can strike any person.

In these latter days we have been blessed by new discoveries that have improved our understanding of the causes and treatments of many serious diseases. Science has made advances in our understanding of viruses, genetics, body functions, and many other fields. These have improved our health and given us a longer life expectancy.

The brain is an organ of the body and, like other organs, is subject to disease and malfunction. Until recently, however, it has been difficult to explore how our brain affects thoughts, moods, behaviors, and our ability to understand and interpret information from the five senses. Science has made great progress in the past twenty-five years. Neuroimaging allows us to watch the brain as it works, discover what is happening when it does not work properly, and explore ways of correcting problems. There is still much we do not know, but these scientific advances have given us a much better understanding of what mental illness is and what it is not.

The term *mental illness* refers to many different kinds of mental problems. Most of these problems are related to difficulties in the brain's ability to function properly. Some of these disorders are easy to recognize as being related to problems in the brain. When a person has a stroke and loses the ability to speak, it is usually easy to see the connection between the medical problem and the difficulty in speaking. However, the brain performs many other complex functions. It organizes thoughts, experiences and interprets emotions, pays attention to some things while tuning out others, plans behaviors and activities, and processes and makes sense of information that enters the brain through the five senses. It may be difficult, however, for the casual observer to see the connection between what happens when the brain cannot function properly and what we call *mental illnesses*. This book can help you better understand how these brain problems can contribute to mental problems.

Recognizing Mental Illnesses

It is important to recognize mental illnesses and know how they differ from the everyday challenges we all face. People without mental illnesses may temporarily experience many problems that are similar to mental illnesses. When the brain is working properly, however, we have more resources for helping ourselves through the challenges of mortal life. This makes it much easier to change a bad mood, cheer up, solve our problems, or just carry on through difficult experiences. Psychological and spiritual resources are usually sufficient to manage normal problems. These normal challenges, however, are not as severe, disabling, or chronic as those experienced by people with mental illnesses. There are changes in how the brain works when a person has a mental illness. These changes reduce many of the resources that we normally use in the brain to overcome life's challenges. People with mental illnesses cannot simply will themselves to snap out of it.

The other sections of this book will help you understand problems in the brain that contribute to many mental illnesses.

Causes of Mental Illnesses

The causes of mental illnesses are complex. Most mental illnesses result from an interaction of many challenges. Biological problems, stress, and coping skills all influence how the brain works. When a person becomes overloaded with these challenges, mental illness may result. This diagram can help you understand how challenges can interact.

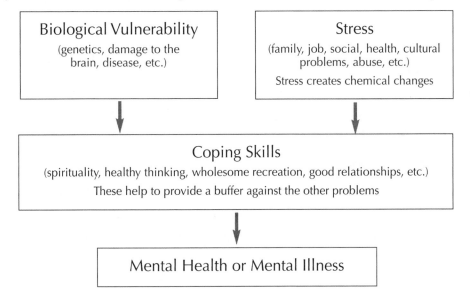

Individuals differ regarding which challenges create the greatest risk for developing a mental illness. If biological problems are high, a person can become ill even when having little stress, good coping skills, solid social support, and a strong, loving family. Another person may not have as many biological problems but may be pushed over the edge by excessive stress, trauma, or few resources for coping with challenges.

You can understand this interaction of biological, psychological, social, and spiritual concerns by thinking of it as a continuum rather than as separate causes.

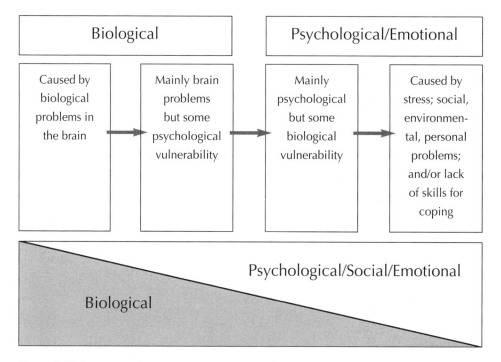

Dual Diagnosis

Dual diagnosis means a person has a drug or alcohol problem *and* a mental illness. The term is also sometimes used to refer to other compulsive problems, such as pornography and other sexual addictions when they occur with a mental illness.

It is much more difficult to recover from dual-diagnosis problems. This double-trouble problem affects much more of a person's life than a mental illness alone. It also requires much more complex treatment. It is often difficult to tell which came first—the mental illness or the addiction. For some people, substance abuse, pornography use, or other compulsive behaviors begin as a way of comforting the pain of a mental illness. They may not even realize they have a treatable mental illness. They only know that they temporarily feel better when they comfort themselves with alcohol, drugs, or compulsive behaviors. This is true of many teenagers who begin abusing drugs and alcohol and using pornography.

Others may develop a mental illness as a result of using drugs or alcohol. Chemical changes in the brain from substance abuse can create problems that are similar to many mental illnesses. Sometimes the symptoms of mental illness stop when a person stops using drugs or alcohol. Sometimes, however, the damage to the brain is permanent and the symptoms continue. (For more about addictions, see chapter 18, "Cognitive Disorders.")

Early recognition and treatment of mental illness can help to prevent many dual-diagnosis problems. Comforting the distress of mental illness with drugs, alcohol, pornography, overeating, or other compulsive problems prevents people from getting treatment because they may feel better for a short time. The mental illness continues to cause them pain and problems, however, and it becomes easy to increase the use of addictive substances or compulsive behaviors. People become caught in a dangerous cycle from which it is difficult to escape.

2

A Look at Your Brain

Marleen S. Williams and W. Dean Belnap

The brain is one of the remarkable achievements of creation. This three-pound mass of soft mortal tissue is the executive organ for the rest of the body. It is through our brain that we are able to command and use our mortal body. Exactly how the brain works has been a mystery throughout history. In the past twenty-five years, however, our knowledge has greatly advanced. In these latter days, God has revealed to us through science a much greater understanding of this remarkable creation. This chapter offers a brief but helpful understanding of what goes on inside your brain and how brain functioning contributes to mental illnesses.

The development of neuroimaging allows us to watch the brain at work without actually cutting into the skull or the brain. Modern technologies can help us understand problems in the brain with little discomfort to the patient and little risk.

Structure of the Brain

The brain may look like a uniform mass of mortal material, but different parts of the brain perform highly specialized functions. The top part of the brain, called the cerebrum, is divided into two equal sides, or hemispheres. Although they look alike, each side has its own specific function. Some of the functions of the left side include language, logic, arithmetic, and verbal interpretation. Some functions of the right side include geometry, nonverbal processing, visual recognition, auditory processing, and spatial skills. The left brain deals more with details, and the right brain looks more at the big picture. This generalization is usually true for right-handed individuals but can be different for those who are left-handed.

The two brain hemispheres communicate with each other through a thick bundle of nerve fibers that carry information back and forth across the brain. We also know that the right side of the brain controls the left side of the body, and the left side of the brain controls the right side of the body. Therefore, a stroke or injury to the right hemisphere can leave the left side of the body paralyzed.

Even though parts of the brain have specialized functions, it is important to understand that the brain works together as a whole. Injury or malfunction of one part can affect how other parts work as well.

There are also other structures inside the brain that control different functions in the body. The illustrations in this chapter show some of the parts of the brain that are often affected by mental illnesses.

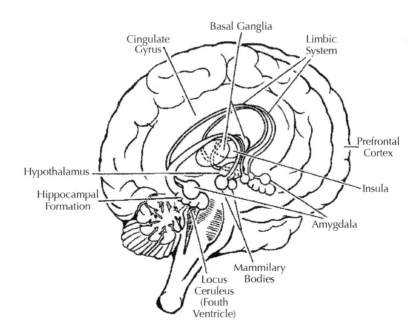

The accompanying illustration shows the prefrontal cortex, or *executive* part of the brain. It has many connections with other parts of the brain. It both receives information from and sends commands to other parts of the brain.

The limbic system is a collection of structures that help humans experience emotions. It has connections to the prefrontal cortex, which helps in interpreting these emotions. The limbic system also supports the basal ganglia. The basal ganglia are a group of structures that help with primitive, instinctive drives, such as self-preservation, fear of death, reproduction, and appetite. These help to keep the human race alive. The connections to the prefrontal cortex help us to make decisions about these drives and appetites. This is one of the ways we humans differ from God's other creations.

With a healthy functioning brain, we have the capacity to choose and make moral decisions. We have the ability to choose to override primitive instincts, if necessary, for moral reasons. It is in the prefrontal cortex that we evaluate whether we think the thought is good or bad. This information is then sent to the left prefrontal cortex for decision making.

How Brain Structures Work Together

All of these parts of the brain are made up of cells called *neurons.* These neurons communicate back and forth with each other through electrochemical energy created by chemicals in the brain. These chemicals create electrical responses that allow the different parts of the brain to communicate and integrate information. You could think of your brain as a complex electrical switchboard. Many of the connections in the brain are present, or hardwired, at birth, but many of the connections between cells have not yet formed. Many of these connections are made by our experiences in mortality.

The accompanying illustration shows a neuron. Each neuron has branches called *dendrites* that connect with other neurons. Many of these dendrite connections are made by what we learn and what we experience. These help to

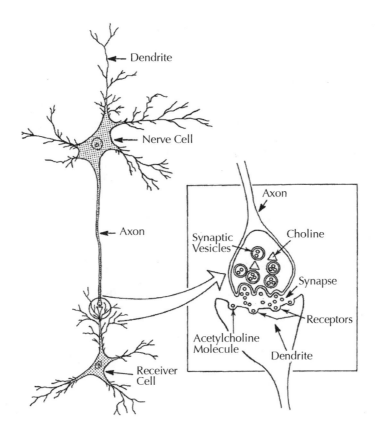

make *pathways* between things we learn. Neurons also communicate with each other through the *axon* on the neuron. The connection between the neurons is called a *synapse.* Chemicals called *neurotransmitters* travel back and forth across the synapse to help move messages along to the next neuron. This diagram shows the neurotransmitter acetylcholine moving across the synapse between an axon and a dendrite. The dendrite has receptors that receive the acetylcholine. This helps to create the electrical impulse that makes the next neuron in the pathway fire, or become active in transmitting the message.

When the neurotransmitter activates the receptor, the electrical impulse travels through that neuron until it repeats the process with the connection at the synapse of the next neuron in the pathway. This happens with incredible speed throughout the brain.

Why Mental Illness Is Sometimes Called a Chemical Imbalance

For various reasons, the brain may not work properly. Sometimes the problems are genetic. They can also be caused by illness or injury to the brain. Excessive stress or emotional trauma can also upset the delicate functioning of the brain. Sometimes the body does not manufacture enough necessary brain chemicals. This is similar to when the pancreas fails to produce enough insulin, resulting in diabetes. In other cases, the neuron releases enough of the neurotransmitter but reabsorbs it too quickly for the receptor to be activated. In some illnesses, such as schizophrenia, receptors may be so overly responsive to the neurotransmitter dopamine that the neurons are overactivated. This results in psychotic symptoms, such as hallucinations and delusions. Medications that block the transmission of dopamine stop the hallucinations, delusions, and many other psychotic symptoms.

The accompanying illustration shows how these problems occur as the brain tries to send messages from one neuron to another.

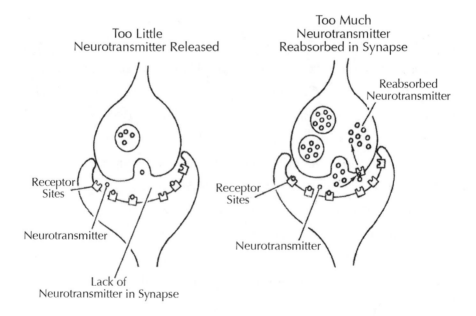

Mental illnesses affect many parts of the brain. Normally, all parts of the brain send their messages to the frontal and prefrontal cortex for evaluation and decision making. Serotonin is one of the main neurotransmitters used by this part of the brain. The primary chemical of the limbic system is dopamine, and the chemicals of the basal ganglia are choline and gamma-aminobutyric acid (GABA). An increase of these chemicals leads to a decrease in the serotonin in the frontal and prefrontal cortex of the brain. This contributes to symptoms of depression and anxiety, which make it hard for people to think clearly, make decisions, and concentrate. This also helps explain why depression and anxiety often occur together.

Medications used to treat this chemical imbalance help by restoring the brain to normal functioning. These medications work differently in the brain than do addictive drugs and chemicals. You cannot become addicted to most of these medications. Rather than altering normal brain processes, they help the brain to work like a normal, healthy, well-functioning brain.

Other mental illnesses may involve many neurotransmitters. More severe illnesses, such as schizophrenia, involve problems in many parts of the brain and with many brain chemicals. Medications that help these illnesses target many chemicals, such as neurotransmitters, hormones, and other brain messengers.

To learn more about this remarkable organ, see chapter 18, "Cognitive Disorders." Other chapters on specific mental illnesses can also help you understand what happens in the brain when mental illnesses occur.

Taking Care of Your Brain

From this information you can see why it is important to take good care of your brain. It is a wonderful gift that allows your spirit to use your body and to understand the temporal world. Here are some things you can do to care for your brain:

Eat healthy foods.

Get adequate sleep, rest, and appropriate recreation.

Get good medical care, especially if you have a high fever or a disease that could harm the brain.

Wear a helmet when riding a bike, playing sports, or doing other activities that could lead to a brain injury.

Keep the Word of Wisdom. Alcohol, tobacco, illegal drugs, and misuse of prescription medication all affect the way the brain works. They can also lead to permanent brain damage.

Avoid exposure to things like violence and pornography, which have been shown to have an addictive potential. Because these things can create powerful emotional responses, they can affect the parts of the brain that play a role in creating addictions.

Use your brain. Studies show that people who regularly engage in thinking activities keep their brains working better as they age.

Learn how to think in healthy ways. This helps to strengthen healthy connections and associations in the brain.

Unfortunately, despite all we do to protect our brains, things can still go wrong. As you read this book, you will learn more about the brain and how it affects and is affected by mental illness.

3

The Brain and Medical Treatment for Mental Disorders

W. Dean Belnap

Typically, the first step in the diagnosis and treatment of mental health disorders should be a visit to your primary care physician, who may be a family practitioner, internist, or pediatrician. Your doctor may not have in-depth training in the field of mental illness. He can, however, assess your symptoms, test for any underlying medical issues that may cause or contribute to the problem, and then decide on a course of action. If your physician believes a simple medication is all that is required, then you may not need to seek further help.

Realize, however, that merely taking medication is not the key to success. Proper follow-up with your physician affords a much better chance of a positive outcome. Why? Because medications require monitoring for effectiveness and negative reactions. So keeping the doctor informed of your response to the medication is critical. In the event the prescribed medication does not produce the desired results, you may want to discuss the possibility of your doctor referring you to a mental health professional, such as a psychiatrist, clinical psychologist, counseling therapist, or social worker.

Communication is your first line of defense. Lack of communication, on the other hand, is a sure way to failure. Unfortunately, doctors and their mentally ill patients often talk *past* one another. A few years ago the nation's chief advocacy and support organization for mental health disorders, the

National Institute of Mental Health, conducted a survey of doctor and patient issues concerning communication. About 50 percent of primary care physicians said they always inquired about mental health when a patient saw them for another medical problem. The rest said they sometimes asked. Nearly one-third of patients surveyed, however, said their doctors never asked them about their mental health.

Doctors also said they usually gave patients detailed instructions about medications, emphasizing the need to continue the medication even after the symptoms improved. However, many patients denied being told anything. Either physicians were not doing all they thought they were doing, or patients were not listening and remembering. Whether patients in the survey were listening or not, they complained that doctors were not listening to them. They said physicians did not usually encourage them to tell their story or to ask questions about their treatment.

What Can You Learn from This?

If there is an information void between you and your doctor, we encourage you to bridge this gap by doing the following:

Write questions and take them with you to the appointment.

Ask open-ended questions.

Take notes during visits with your doctor and during the course of your treatment on feelings, mood changes, drug reactions, and so forth.

Take someone with you to take notes.

Express your feelings or fears.

Listen, repeat instructions, and ask for clarification if you do not understand what is being said or if you feel the doctor is talking over your head.

Remember, in the treatment of mental illness, communication between the patient and the professional is paramount to success. If you have used the steps above and still find your experience fraught with misunderstanding, then it's time to find another professional who is willing to talk through all the issues.

Under New Management—Let's All Work Together

Many mental health care professionals recommend a kind of shared treatment. Just as a person who has had a stroke may have the support of a primary care physician, neurologist, speech therapist, physical therapist, vocational therapist, and nurse practitioner, those with mental disorders may require the same type of multidisciplinary team approach. This may include the primary care physician, in conjunction with a psychiatrist, psychologist, social worker, and psychiatrically trained nurses. Shared treatment can be especially useful for patients with debilitating mental illness because the nature, and perhaps the severity of the illness, can disengage the initiative of a person and make it difficult to take care of himself. The interdisciplinary team of professionals can guide the person and their family to the appropriate environment for treatment. This can be in an out-patient clinic, a residential placement that offers longer term care, or an acute psychiatric in-patient hospital.

Mental health management can be done a number of ways, but an example would be the use of a nurse or other professional as a case manager who would oversee the following:

Advise the physician about the progress of treatment.

Periodically check with the patient to see if he is taking the prescribed medication, experiencing any side effects, keeping appointments, or showing signs of relapse.

Coordinate therapy with other team members.

Find ways to support family members, if necessary.

Managed team care may be as simple as a psychiatrist working in conjunction with a counseling psychologist. Regardless of how the team support is approached, you are an important part of the equation. Look for the therapeutic intervention to do the following:

Define the problem.
Offer reassurance and support.
Set realistic goals.
Plot a clear plan of how the therapy will proceed, and then follow
    through.

Two general reviews covering dozens of studies have found that mentally ill patients and their families who are involved in disease-management programs are more likely to comply with treatment and are eventually more satisfied with the results.

Treating Mental Illness with Medication

A number of fields have been involved in the study of medications used for brain disease, which include biochemistry, physiology, neurology, and psychiatry. All of these disciplines have helped in understanding how medications work in the brain and how they can correct the lack of proper communication between the cells that determine our mood and how we process information, think, react to fear, contemplate the future, and assess relationships. Therefore, psychopharmacology becomes an imperative part of treatment to restore normal functioning and communication between brain cells.

No two people are alike

Medications are often the first choice in a treatment regime, especially if the diagnosis is intense anxiety, severe depression, delusional thinking, excessive sleepiness, or suicidal urges. However, it is important to note that no two people are the same. Unique life experiences, temperament, and biological differences mean that the same medication that works wonders for one may fail to ease the symptoms of another. The same principle applies to the side effects experienced by different patients. The prescribing physician may need to try one or two different medications to find the one that works best for an individual patient. In some cases, a doctor may prescribe a combination of medications to treat the combined symptoms of illness. For instance, two patients may be diagnosed with depression, but one must also be treated for anxiety while another may have depression with distorted thinking. Common sense dictates that the same medication may not work for both and that a combination of medications may be needed to treat either diagnosis.

Choosing a medication

Medications used for the treatment of mental illness are formulated to target the functioning of a particular neurotransmitter within the communication pathways of the brain. Different symptoms, or more accurately, different mental disorders involve different neurotransmitters, so drugs are designed to selectively affect a brain area specific to the symptom. The choices within the science of psychopharmacology constitute an ever-changing landscape, with newer and more definitive research developing medications that work better and with fewer side effects.

The charts on the next few pages have been designed to give an overview of the newest and best medications to treat each indicated illness. Please note that while these drugs are listed in categories, it is possible that a cluster of symptoms may require combining medications.

Anxiety is the most common of all mental disorders. A physician may prescribe antianxiety medications to treat one of the subtypes of the illness, such as general anxiety, separation anxiety, panic disorder, or obsessive-compulsive disorder. Another type of anxiety is called post-traumatic stress disorder (PTSD). The symptoms of this illness can be relieved by using venlafaxine

MEDICATIONS FOR ANXIETY

Generic Name	Brand Name

Benzodiazepines

Generic Name	Brand Name
alprazolam	Xanax
clonazepam	Klonopin
diazepam	Valium
lorazepam	Ativan

Other Antianxiety Agents

Generic Name	Brand Name
buspirone	BuSpar
duloxetine	Cymbalta
hydroxyzine	Atarax
venlafaxine	Effexor

(Effexor), listed above. Selective serotonin reuptake inhibitors (SSRIs), listed on the next page, and atypical neuroleptics, which are listed on the page describing antipsychotics, have also been effective medications for PTSD.

Issues of anxiety may also be part of a diagnosis involving depression, bipolar disorder, schizophrenia, or other psychiatric disabilities. The medications on the SSRI list are highly addictive and are used short term—two to three weeks, in the acute stage of the illness. They usually act quickly to control symptoms, at which point the doctor should change the treatment to a medication used over the long term with no habit-forming or addictive characteristics. There is a good chance anxiety symptoms will recur after drug therapy is discontinued. Do not decide on your own to discontinue a medication. Consult closely with your physician or therapy team.

We have not included older classes of antidepressants. Tricyclics and

MEDICATIONS FOR DEPRESSION

Generic Name	Brand Name

Selective Serotonin Reuptake Inhibitors (SSRIs)

Generic Name	Brand Name
citalopram	Celexa
escitalopram	Lexapro
fluoxetine	Prozac
fluvoxamine	Luvox
paroxetine	Paxil
sertraline	Zoloft

Other Classes

Generic Name	Brand Name
bupropion	Wellbutrin
duloxetine	Cymbalta
mirtazapine	Remeron
venlafaxine	Effexor

monoamine oxidase inhibitors are generally no longer recommended because of their annoying and serious side effects.

It is important to address some of the recent concerns over the use of antidepressants and their relationship to suicide. Because rumors and misinformation abound, we have chosen to address the subject point by point, acknowledging that we obtained most of our information with help from a Harvard Medical School study.[1] Study results vary, but a consistent trend suggests that all antidepressants, when compared to the effects of a placebo, seem to double the risk of suicidal thinking, from 1–2 percent to 2–4 percent in both children and adults. A few theories may explain the trend:

In a small percentage of patients, antidepressants may actually have the paradoxical effect of making moods worse.

Self-injury may result from an antidepressant side effect known as akathisia—an extremely uncomfortable form of inner restlessness.

Before the full effects of the medication are realized, severely depressed people recover enough energy to act on previous suicidal thoughts before mood improves or hope returns.

Giving SSRI antidepressants to a person with bipolar disorder may trigger mania or irritability, increasing the risk of self-destructive behavior. Psychiatrists are very cautious in prescribing SSRIs to patients with more than one diagnosis of mental illness. In such cases psychiatrists prefer to use the "Other Classes" of antidepressants listed on the accompanying chart. These medications help patients avoid aggressive and violent behavior.

If you or a loved one feels suicidal, you can turn to many places for help. Experts recommend the following steps:

Talk with your doctor or mental health professional. Often, treatment eases or entirely eliminates suicidal urges. In some cases, hospitalization is necessary until a sense of equilibrium returns.

Call 1–800–SUICIDE (784–2433) or a local hotline and speak with a crisis counselor.

Discuss your feelings with trusted family members, friends, or religious advisers, who can assist you in getting help.

The Harvard Medical School study referred to previously did not report any cases of completed suicides. So far, no evidence from controlled research links suicide to antidepressant use. Additionally, depression in itself increases the risk of suicide.

Patients on antidepressants should be watched carefully the first six to eight weeks to limit the risk of suicide. After the medication has had time to take its full effect, the incidence of suicide is less than that of the general public.

MEDICATIONS FOR MOOD STABILIZATION (BIPOLAR DISORDER)

Generic Name	Brand Name
carbamazepine	Tegretol
divalproex	Depakote, Depakene
gabapentin	Neurontin
lamotrigine	Lamictal
lithium carbonate	Eskalith, Lithonate
topiramate	Topamax

There is also some concern that sexual arousal and response can be adversely affected by the use of SSRIs. That is true. A doctor will be able to advise on ways to reverse this problem.

While lithium is probably the most prescribed of the medications listed below, others listed also stabilize the mood and manic-depressive symptoms of bipolar disorder. In some cases where there are dual symptoms of mania *and* distorted or psychotic thinking, it may be necessary to use antipsychotic drugs in conjunction with mood stabilizers.

According to Harvard University Medical School, "You may need to stay on some medications or combination of medications indefinitely to keep your mood stable. The likelihood of having a relapse when you go off medication is great, especially if you've had two or more episodes of mania or depression. Experts now believe that the more episodes of depression or mania you've experienced, the more intense and frequent your subsequent episodes may be. Therefore, for people with bipolar disorder, maintenance therapy is the best strategy."[2]

The drugs listed below are second-generation medications that are safer replacements for older antipsychotics. In correct dosages, they can reduce delusions, hallucinations, bizarre behavior, aggressive impulses, and thought disorders by as much as 95 percent. Side effects include Parkinsonian symptoms of tremors and rigidity and restless overactivity, known as akathisia. Some of these drugs can be used to treat bipolar disorder but in much smaller doses.

MEDICATIONS FOR SCHIZOPHRENIA
Antipsychotics

Generic Name	Brand Name
aripiprazole	Abilify
clozapine	Clozaril
olanzapine	Zyprexa
quetiapine	Seroquel
risperidone	Risperdal
ziprasidone	Geodon

Medications for attention-deficit/hyperactivity disorder, often called psychomotor stimulants, offer dramatic improvement in children and adolescents, as well as in those whose symptoms continue into adulthood. They act on the brain's currents by converting the brain chemical dopamine into norepinephrine. The chemical conversion slows cyclical brain rhythm to a normal speed and allows messages to process all the way to the prefrontal cortex of the brain and then throughout the entire nervous system. This helps people to *think before they act.*

Methylphenidate (Ritalin) has always had the drawback of requiring two to three doses per day. This has led to marked contrasts of brain function during the course of the day. Long-lasting chemical modification of short-acting Ritalin led to the formation of Methylin. Two other modified chemicals improved the quality of Ritalin (Concerta and Focalin). They, like Methylin,

MEDICATIONS FOR ADHD
Psychostimulants

Generic Name	Brand Name
d- and l- amphetamine	Adderall
dexmethylphenidate	Concerta, Focalin
methylphenidate	Ritalin, Methylin
	Metadate
pemoline	Cylert

Nonstimulants

Generic Name	Brand Name
buspirone	BuSpar
duloxetine	Cymbalta
hydroxyzine	Atarax
venlafaxine	Effexor

lasted 12 hours instead of 4. Moreover, Adderall can be structured to an extended release of 12–13 hours.

Because methylphenidate and dexedrine derivatives can be addictive in high dosages, the FDA designates them as controlled substances. In prescribed dosages to treat ADHD, they are no more addictive than cough medicine. Time-released forms of these medications provide a more even, or steady, level to the drug over a twelve-hour period. This has alleviated problems with taking two to three pills a day, with subsequent problems of medication highs and lows.

In recent years, a new product called atomoxetine (Strattera) has been introduced as a medication for ADHD. It is not a controlled substance and has proven to be highly effective in treating adolescents and adults.

Though not a medication, neurofeedback (neurotherapy) may be the most promising treatment for ADHD and a significant alternative to medication. Neurofeedback is a type of biofeedback that uses a magneto-electroencephalograph (EEG) to monitor brain waves. The brain controls psychological and physiological components of behavior. A person is not conscious of these processes. Normally, when someone tries to read or concentrate on a project or task, the amount of *beta* waves in the brain increase. These are the fastest waves in the brain and help keep a person attentive. A person with ADHD who tries to concentrate produces slower *theta* waves, which have the opposite effect. The goal of neurofeedback is to show the brain's waves at work and to teach the person how to increase the use of beta waves. The result is a significant reduction of ADHD and the negative behaviors associated with it.

Neurofeedback, previously called biofeedback, has been helpful in treating such brain problems as epilepsy and addictive disorders. In the past, professional training of therapists and the lack of accuracy of electroencephalographic instruments affected the treatment of mental illness. Advanced professional certification and modern sophisticated instrumentation have led to success in treating many with ADHD by neurofeedback.

Despite favorable outcomes in studies that use neurofeedback, there may be some drawbacks to this treatment:

The treatment may be less effective for the very young and the very old. Children should be mature enough to understand what they must accomplish during the treatment. The older people get, the more difficult it is for them to make needed changes on the EEG.

ADHD children are different, but all should be helped early. They have a hard time fitting in and are the recipients of a great deal of negative attention. As they grow, lack of self-esteem and feelings of worthlessness become a big issue. It is important that the diagnosis be made by someone with expertise in ADHD. Other problems may mimic symptoms of ADHD and the problem may be incorrectly diagnosed.

Other issues may mitigate dosage or indicate the use of one medication or therapy over another:

Age. As people age, the body tends to break down drugs more slowly. Older patients may need a lower dosage. Another problem is that mental illness in the elderly can be mistaken for dementia or, in other cases, dementia or other medical problems can disguise the symptoms of mental illness.

With the exception of medications for ADHD, the effects of other psychotherapeutic drugs have not been studied as much in children, and their usage will need to be evaluated on a case-by-case basis. A combined therapy of medication and counseling works well for children.

Drug reactions to other medications. Not all medications can safely be used with other medications. Monoamine oxidase inhibitors (MAOIs) cannot be used in conjunction with SSRIs. Blood pressure medications react adversely with some of the drugs listed on previous pages. Patients must be carefully screened to assure that any medications they are currently taking can be used together with a new medication. This would include over-the-counter herbal compounds and nutritional supplements.

Spiritual Intervention—Faith Really Can Work a Miracle

Many large universities have formed departments to study the relationship among mind, body, and spirituality. Beginning in 2002 with Harvard and the University of Pennsylvania, more than one hundred university medical centers have started such programs. Scientific studies using neuroimaging techniques show positive healing changes in the brain as a result of spiritual interventions for mental health problems. Doctors and health practitioners are beginning to understand what we as Latter-day Saints have known all along—that faith in a loving higher power can be an enormous asset as we look to a future free of the illnesses we have discussed in this book.

Notes

1. *Understanding Depression*; see also *Coping with Anxiety and Phobias*. To purchase these reports, go to health.harvard.edu/special_health_reports/Understanding_Depression.htm, and health.harvard.edu/special_health_reports/Coping_with_Anxiety_and_Phobias.htm respectively, or call 877–649–9457.

2. *Understanding Depression*, 25. See health.harvard.edu/special_health_reports/Understanding_Depresstion.htm

Section II

Mental Illness and Latter-day Saints

4

Finding the Right Therapist for You and Your Family

S. Brent Scharman

Michael Murphy (not his real name) couldn't stop crying. He was twenty-eight years old and a college graduate with a decent job in a local bank. He'd completed a successful mission in Georgia. He was still single but actively involved in the ups and downs of dating. He was optimistic about the future most of the time—that is, until about six months ago.

For no reason that was apparent to him, he had begun to sink into a feeling of hopelessness that nearly overwhelmed him at times. He'd begun to cry periodically, which was uncharacteristic for him. He'd lost his zest for life. Nothing seemed fun any more. His sleeping was spotty. He'd lost ten pounds. He still got to work and was quite successful at putting on a happy face, but those closest to him knew this took a lot of effort on his part.

Michael went to the family doctor, who had known him for many years. The doctor was somewhat surprised at Michael's condition because of his stable history. Nevertheless, he diagnosed major depression after all appropriate tests failed to show any clear explanation for the problem. He also prescribed medication and recommended that Michael get some counseling to help him explore causes and solutions for what he was going through. Generally independent, Michael took a few weeks to decide to pursue counseling. Having made the decision, he was faced with the next challenge—whom to see?

For a period of time, Michael was one of the many people whose lives are filled with pain, disappointment, and confusion. He needed help.

Trials Are a Common Part of Life

Not long before his death in 2007, President James E. Faust caught the attention of Church members by showing the deep empathy the First Presidency feels for those facing challenges. He said, "This message is to all, but especially to those who feel they have had more trials, sorrows, pricks, and thorns than they can bear and in their adversity are almost drowned in the waters of bitterness."[1] He added, "There seems to be a full measure of anguish, sorrow, and often heartbreak for everyone, including those who earnestly seek to do right and be faithful."[2]

Elder Joseph B. Wirthlin reminds us that the gospel provides a "harbor of enduring safety and security,"[3] but Church members are, nevertheless, subject to the same physical, emotional, and social challenges that are common to all mankind. Many of these trials will be resolved in time through prayer, scripture reading, personal insight, consultation with family and friends, and use of self-help materials. But sometimes, despite our best efforts, our struggles continue.

Do I Have to Talk to Somebody Else?

You don't have to talk to somebody else, but there may be some advantages in doing so. Counseling, as a problem-solving process, has endured over time because it is beneficial. Some resist counseling for fear of becoming dependent on the therapist. This is an appropriate concern, and both the counselor and the client play a part in making certain it doesn't happen. A client requesting help could naturally come to feel dependent on the counselor who's offering help. A well-trained counselor is aware of this possibility and is guided by ethical standards to help the client move through the temporary period of dependence to more confident independence. Done properly, counseling strengthens by helping individuals learn to problem solve through use of personal insight, guidance from others, and divine inspiration.

Church Leaders Are a Common Source of Support

When additional help from others is desired or needed, consultation with an ecclesiastical leader has been shown to be one of the most commonly used methods of solving problems, as well as one of the most effective. This is true for all people of faith, whether members of the Church or not.

Peterson and Seligman point out some of the advantages of using faith-based support. They state: "Research . . . suggests that . . . ministers may be particularly effective because they are more accessible than secular professional service providers (i.e., they are available day and night); they ground their work in a value system that their constituents find familiar and useful; they address issues that are often ignored by secular service providers (e.g., forgiveness); they often provide a wider range of supports (e.g., psychological, educational, economic); and their services are free. In addition, the fact that they are located within the community makes ministers and churches accountable to the people to whom they provide assistance."[4]

Direction for Latter-day Saints

The Church Handbook of Instructions states, "The stake president and bishop are entitled to the discernment and inspiration necessary to be spiritual advisers and temporal counselors to ward members who need such help."[5] It is not the role of a bishop, however, to act as a therapist to those in his ward who are experiencing social and emotional challenges. It is his role to listen, provide spiritual direction, teach gospel concepts, call to repentance, act as a common judge, provide support, and organize ward resources as appropriate to assist those requesting help. Bishops come from a variety of professional and personal backgrounds and are wonderfully gifted at drawing on their life experience, common sense, and inspiration to benefit their ward members.

At times, additional support may be needed and the help of a professional may be desired or even required for legal reasons. At such times it is critical that professionals be selected who will work in harmony with gospel teachings and principles. For those seeking professional assistance, many qualified resources are available.

Practical Factors When Considering Professional Help

Many people who enter counseling call an agency and visit with whoever is assigned. This is appropriate when using a reputable agency. Reputable resources can be identified with help from any of the following:

> Ecclesiastical leaders who may have developed a resource list
>
> Trusted family and friends who may have had a good experience with a certain professional
>
> Yellow Pages—look under counselors, marriage counseling, and professions by name
>
> State professional organizations, such as the Utah Psychological Association or the National Association of Social Workers
>
> Web sites for online searches, such as Marriage Counselors in Montana or Psychiatrists in Iowa

LDS Family Services

LDS Family Services has been established to be a resource to Church leaders and members. Your bishop can tell you how to contact the nearest Family Services office, where you will receive cost-effective, confidential help (reporting of some issues, such as sexual abuse of a minor, may be required). There is a fee for services. Fees can be paid by an individual, a family, insurance, fast offerings, or a combination of all four. There is no charge for services to those requesting counseling because of unwed pregnancy or same-gender attraction.

Locations and contact information can also be found by accessing lds.org and then clicking on "Home and Family," then "Marriage, Family & Individual Counseling," and finally, "How to contact us."

Though no referral from a bishop is required, a Family Services counselor will encourage you to sign a release-of-information form so that he or she can correlate with your bishop or stake president. As a client, you would determine if you wanted the counselor to initiate this correlation, and you would give input into what you did and did not want to be shared. Experience has shown that correlation between the counselor and priesthood leader increases the likelihood of positive long-term outcomes because, when the counseling sessions end, the individual may benefit from an understanding relationship with the bishop as long as he remains in his calling. Data gathered in 2005 and 2006 showed that the average person receiving services attended six to seven sessions. Family Services' policy is that a therapist may offer twelve sessions and request permission for additional visits as needed.

Other Resources

Competent professionals, both LDS and non-LDS, work in other settings, including hospitals, agencies, and private practice. Look for assistance from one who is licensed, who is receiving supervision, or who has had experience providing the services you are requesting, such as marriage counseling, help with an eating disorder, or treatment of depression. Commonly, services will be received from a psychiatrist, psychologist, social worker, marriage and family counselor, or licensed professional counselor.

Mental Health Professions

You will want to make certain that the person you see has the following:

Academic training from an accredited program that has led to a master's or doctoral degree

Supervised clinical experience in addition to the textbook learning

Licensure that requires some period of time, often two years, of supervised experience following graduation

Licensed therapists often show their degrees on their office walls and will generally refer to their licensed status in their advertisements or publications. A business card will always state licensure status. Following is a brief description of various mental health professionals:

Psychiatrists receive a traditional medical degree and then complete an internship and residency in psychiatry, where they focus on the relationship of the brain, emotions, and behavior. They are experts in prescribing medication for conditions related to mental health. Some psychiatrists do traditional counseling, though it is becoming the exception.

Psychologists practice with a Ph.D. or Ed.D. and specialize in research and testing, as well as a full range of psychological services, including psychotherapy. In a few states, psychologists are authorized to prescribe medication when supervised by an M.D.

Licensed Professional Counselors have a master's degree and provide counseling services.

Licensed Clinical Social Workers have a master's degree and provide a full range of social work services. In addition, Doctoral-level Social Workers (DSWs), provide social work services and often teach in university settings.

Licensed Marriage and Family Therapists, LMFTs, may have either a master's or doctoral degree. As their title implies, their specialized training is in providing marriage counseling and in seeing entire families.

When deciding what counselor to see, it is appropriate to ask counselors if they have had experience with your specific concern. A psychologist may be excellent at treating depression but may not have had training as a marriage counselor. A social worker may be great with eating disorders but may not have had experience doing family counseling. A marriage and family counselor may be exceptional working with a struggling couple but may have had less experience in diagnosing panic attacks.

It would be a mistake to focus on the differences in the various professions because the similarities outweigh the differences. For example, if a sixteen-year-old male who is skipping school, failing in half his classes, experimenting with marijuana, and refusing to go to church were brought to a therapist from any background, the therapist would probably do most of the following:

Provide a safe setting in which to talk

Attempt to establish a relationship that elicits cooperation

Develop a diagnostic impression to determine whether factors may be influencing the boy's behavior, such as being depressed or having a learning disability

Be open to the possibility of benefits from medication, which should prompt a referral to a medical doctor

Explore family relationships and the way in which the boy's behavior may have meaning in the family; is the unruly behavior an attempt to bring divorcing parents together?

Develop a treatment plan with measurable objectives

Clarify who will be involved in the counseling

Hold weekly sessions initially and move to less-frequent contact as progress is made

Give practical homework assignments

Make any needed contacts with other relevant individuals, such as
 prior counselors, doctors, or teachers (with written approval)
Explore the possibility of the counselor consulting with the client's
 bishop (if the counselor and client are LDS)

It is an accepted part of standard practice today to utilize a teamwork
approach to treatment. It would be common, for example, for a social worker
to see weekly a client who is struggling with difficulties in school and refer
her to a psychologist for testing to determine mental ability or check for
attention deficit disorder. In addition, a referral to a psychiatrist to assess the
possible benefits of medication would demonstrate good practice. The ultimate form of teamwork, in an LDS context, is when the bishop is included in
the network of those providing input and direction.

You will likely find differences in the fees charged by the providers. The
fees tend to represent the degree of training received. Costs are less in many
settings, such as a community mental health center or a United Way agency.
Some centers charge a sliding fee that depends on income. Insurance companies will cover some counseling expenses. You should always check with your
insurance company before beginning counseling because many companies
have a panel of providers from which they expect you to choose your therapist.

Any individual or agency should respond to your requests for information about training, fees, and availability of services.

Ethical Standards

There is a natural tendency for LDS members to prefer counseling services from an LDS counselor. In many parts of the world this desire is easily
fulfilled. Of course, it is not practical in many others. Each profession is governed by a set of ethical principles and codes of conduct that attempt to assure
that all individuals will be treated fairly and appropriately when receiving services. For example, the Principles and Code of the American Psychological

Association state, "Psychologists accord appropriate respect to the fundamental rights, dignity, and worth of all people. They respect the rights of individuals to privacy, confidentiality, [and] self-determination. . . . Psychologists are aware of cultural, individual, and role differences, including those due to age, gender, race, ethnicity, national origin, [and] religion."[6]

In their training, those from each profession are taught to be sensitive to and non-judgmental of the values and religious choices of clients. They are cautioned against telling clients to make choices that would violate their religious standards and further complicate their lives.

While it is difficult to monitor what may be said in a confidential counseling session, these ethical guidelines raise a critical point. Each individual, couple, or family entering a professional relationship has the responsibility to monitor what takes place and assess whether what is said is professionally and morally sound. It may take time to assess a counselor's professional skill, but you will know quickly whether things are being said or done that make you feel uncomfortable or inappropriately challenge your values.

One caution should be mentioned. Clients often enter counseling with the assumption that the counselor will be positive and supportive at all times. While that is frequently the case, it is not at all uncommon for a counselor to feel a need to push or confront a client in order to help him face some issue he may have been avoiding. This may be uncomfortable but needed. An example would be the client who needs to be pushed to take some social risks in order to build her dating confidence or the client who needs to acknowledge that his drinking is out of control.

Choosing a counselor is like choosing a family doctor or dentist. It often takes time and a little experimentation until you find just the right person. Don't hesitate to do a little therapist shopping so that you find someone with the right mix of professional skill, bedside manner, and sensitivity to values.

Questions for Non-LDS Resources

If you're thinking of beginning counseling with a non-LDS therapist and are concerned that his opinions may have a negative bias, here are some questions you could ask:

Have you provided treatment to other LDS people?

Do you consider yourself a counselor who would respect the personal and religious values of a client?

If requested, would you be willing to consult with my ecclesiastical leader?

Would you consider a discounted fee if payment came from church funds?

Do you have any questions regarding LDS doctrine, lifestyle, sociality, or priorities?

There Will Always Be a Need

We live in challenging times. Personal and family problems abound. Counseling can be a valuable resource. President Harold B. Lee commented on the challenges that would be part of life in our generation. He said, "Members may need counseling more than clothing, and members who, through bishops, are referred to an agency in our social services program should feel no more hesitancy in asking for help of this kind than [they] should in requesting help through the priesthood welfare program."[7] This is a sad comment relevant to the prevalence of problems, a positive comment about the appropriateness of receiving professional help, and a comforting statement that assistance could be requested without guilt.

End of the Story

Michael Murphy, the successful but depressed twenty-eight-year-old we were introduced to at the beginning of this chapter, eventually recovered. He took an antidepressant for a year and then phased off it without a return of symptoms. In addition, he spent several months with a professional counselor who helped him understand that even though things had seemed all right, he was really feeling stressed out about being twenty-eight and unmarried. Michael had coped with being passed over for a promotion at the bank by saying, "It was no big deal." But in reality, it had been quite devastating—his first real professional disappointment.

Initially, Michael was embarrassed by his symptoms. As part of getting better, he had to acknowledge that, while he was exceptionally talented, everything wasn't always going to go exactly as he wanted. While his good work habits and high expectations would help him succeed in life, he would need to adjust to the reality that he wouldn't always be able to control outcomes, especially when the agency of others was involved.

This wasn't news to him. As a missionary, he had taught lessons on the importance of agency and choice. But it was the first time he'd had to deal with it on an emotional level over issues that were highly significant to him. In retrospect, he wasn't glad to have gone through this experience, but he was glad to have learned some important insights about himself. He summarized his thoughts about the role of counseling in his recovery this way:

"Making the decision to go to counseling was difficult. Frankly, I was embarrassed by it. But I have to say it was good to be in a setting once a week where I felt totally safe and where I could examine what I was thinking and feeling without being judged. I lucked out with a counselor who listened, didn't overreact and make things worse, had some good suggestions, occasionally made me talk about things I would rather have avoided, and made me work at figuring things out. I might have figured all this out on my own in time, but I think therapy helped me work it out more quickly. It wasn't always easy, but I can see that it's paying off."

Notes

1. James E. Faust, "Refined in Our Trials," *Ensign,* Feb. 2006, 3.

2. Faust, "Refined in Our Trials," 3.

3. Joseph B. Wirthlin, "Finding a Safe Harbor," *Ensign,* May 2000, 61.

4. Neighbors, Jackson, Bowman and Guirn. *Stress, Coping and Black Mental Health,* quoted in Peterson & Seligman, *Character Strength and Virtues,* 619.

5. *Church Handbook of Instructions,* 1:25.

6. "Ethical Principles of Psychologists and Code of Conduct," *American Psychologist* 47 (December 1992): 1599.

7. Seminar for Regional Representatives of the Twelve, Oct. 1, 1970, in *LDS Family Services: Agency Plan and Operations Guide,* 13.

5

Mental Illness and Spirituality

Marleen S. Williams and W. Dean Belnap

Many medical researchers acknowledge that what we call *conscience,* or the capacity to understand and make moral decisions, is programmed into the brain. However, it cannot be explained solely in terms of biological functioning. The prefrontal cortex of the brain, which is unique to human beings, is the source of not only consciousness but also where moral decision making takes place. Many who have studied this uniquely human ability have concluded that its creation could not have occurred accidentally but rather that the creative and cohesive power of the brain was designed by God.[1]

The American Psychological Association established a division for psychologists who study religion and mental health. Many published books and studies show the benefits of having a meaningful, personal religious life. Spiritually based therapies are frequently used to help those who struggle with mental illness.[2]

Latter-day Saints have always been taught that we are dual beings. We have both a body and a spirit. However, God has not yet revealed to us exactly how the spirit interacts with the body. We know that it gives us mortal life and that our spirit has considerable power to direct our body. We do not know, however, exactly how the body and the spirit work together. We can know by simple observation that disease or damage to the body can limit the spirit's ability to command the body.

If a person has an injury that damages the spinal cord, for example, that person may be paralyzed and, therefore, the spirit is unable to command the body to move. The spirit may have a strong desire to move the body, but the damage to the body prevents it from moving. Similarly, if the brain is damaged or diseased, the spirit may not be able to command it to work properly.

Does this mean that what we call our *mind* is just a product of biochemistry, brain structures, and nerve cells? Definitely not! This does not explain all that we think, feel, and are. Elder Neal A. Maxwell offered a beautiful explanation:

"Our genes, circumstances, and environments matter very much, and they shape us significantly. Yet there remains an inner zone in which we are sovereign, unless we abdicate. In this zone lies the essence of our individuality and our personal accountability."[3]

We know that we have a spirit that enlivens our bodies. Our spirit existed long before our mortal body was created (Moses 6:36, 51; Abraham 3:18, 22–23). Each spirit has a personality and a unique identity (D&C 138:53; Abraham 3:22). Our spirits and bodies interact and influence each other (Alma 34:34–36; D&C 88:15; Romans 8:1, 4, 13). Our spirit will be joined forever with our body in the resurrection (2 Nephi 9:12; Alma 34:34; D&C 88:28).

People with mental illnesses can have psychological, emotional, and spiritual problems that can make biological problems worse. However, biological problems can also make psychological, emotional, and spiritual problems worse. The freedom to command the brain may be diminished if the brain is damaged, diseased, or unable to function normally. A person may not have the ability to understand and process information accurately. This makes it much harder to make decisions based in reality, or to *will* the brain to work properly.

Trusting God's Righteous Judgment

It is difficult to determine whether a person with a mental illness has full ability to think through choices, understand options and consequences, and truly use agency effectively to make decisions. We may not always be able to understand how much of a person's behavior is caused by biological brain problems and how much is voluntarily chosen, but we can trust that an all-knowing God can. He *does* accurately know when the ability to choose is impaired by disease and problems that occur in the brain. God fully understands the infirmities of the mortal body and will take these into account. Meanwhile, we have some instruction to help us understand how he will judge us.

Elder M. Russell Ballard stated, "When he does judge us, I feel he will take all things into consideration: our genetic and chemical makeup, our mental state, our intellectual capacity, the teachings we have received, the traditions of our fathers, our health, and so forth."[4]

We have further understanding from Elder Maxwell: "God thus takes into merciful account not only our desires and our performance, but also the degrees of difficulty which our varied circumstances impose upon us."[5]

Joseph Smith, in speaking of the last days, explained that the righteous will not escape tribulation. Even those who live faithful lives will experience disease and other afflictions. He said:

"Yet many of the righteous shall fall prey to disease, to pestilence, etc., by reason of the weakness of the flesh, and yet be saved in the Kingdom of God. So that it is an unhallowed principle to say that such and such have transgressed because they have been preyed upon by disease or death, for all flesh is subject to death; and the Savior has said, 'Judge not, lest ye be judged.'"[6]

The Prophet admonished us that we not judge but that we trust God's judgments.

"While one portion of the human race is judging and condemning the other without mercy, the Great Parent of the universe looks upon the whole of the human family with a fatherly care and paternal regard. . . . He is a wise Lawgiver, and will judge all men, not according to the narrow, contracted notions of men, but, 'according to the deeds done in the body whether they be good or evil.' . . . We need not doubt the wisdom and intelligence of the Great Jehovah; He will award judgment or mercy to all nations according to their several deserts, their means of obtaining intelligence, the laws by which they are governed, the facilities afforded them of obtaining correct informa-tion, and His inscrutable designs in relation to the human family; and when the designs of God shall be made manifest, and the curtain of futurity be withdrawn, we shall all of us eventually have to confess that the Judge of all the earth has done right."[7]

Nephi promises us that "the keeper of the gate is the Holy One of Israel; and he employeth no servant there; and there is none other way save it be by the gate; for he cannot be deceived, for the Lord God is his name" (2 Nephi 9:41). We are promised that all of his judgments will be just (Omni 1:22; Mosiah 3:18; 16:1; 29:12; D&C 137:8–9).

Much is still to be revealed concerning how the brain and spirit work together. Until we have a perfect understanding, we must trust in God and walk by faith.

Spiritual Help in Coping with Mental Illness

Because we do not have answers to all of the questions about mental ill-ness, it can be easy to try to fill in the gaps with folklore or false traditions. It is important that we do not assume more than has been revealed about why people have particular trials or problems in mortality. When watching the painful struggles of others, we, because of human nature, often want to find out "what they did wrong" to deserve such a fate. People often hope to pre-vent a similar problem in their own life.

The truth, however, is that we do not usually know why a particular person has a particular challenge. Job experienced inaccurate judgment by his friends. They believed that bad things happened only to people who had sinned. They continued to challenge him to repent of whatever he had done wrong, saying his trials would disappear. Job kept his integrity and faith, despite not understanding the reasons for his painful challenges (Job 13–27). He did all he could to live a faithful life despite severe trials.

In mortality, bad things often happen to good people. We must be careful when we assign spiritual meaning to the trials and difficulties of others. Often, the *why* is not revealed to us in mortality. Trusting that God is loving, patient, and kind, and that he does not delight in punishing his children can help us have a more correct interpretation of the seeming unfairness of life.

Mental illness and many of the problems that come with it are surely one of life's more difficult and painful challenges. We may not always be able to make sense of suffering with the limited knowledge we have in mortality. In such cases, faith in God and a strong spiritual understanding of what *has* been revealed to us become even more important and can help us cope with the pain of what we do not understand. The world may not have enough answers for us, but the Lord has given us words of comfort:

"Peace I leave with you, my peace I give unto you: *not as the world giveth, give I unto you. Let not your heart be troubled, neither let it be afraid*" (John 14:27; emphasis added).

President Spencer W. Kimball spoke of the importance of continuing to exercise faith in Christ when we struggle with seemingly unanswerable questions and unsolvable problems. Challenges are not always taken from our lives because relief would interfere with the plan of salvation.

"If all the sick for whom we pray were healed, if all the righteous were protected and the wicked destroyed, the whole program of the Father would be annulled and the basic principle of the gospel, free agency, would be ended. No man would have to live by faith. . . . In the face of apparent tragedy we must put our trust in God, knowing that despite our limited view his purposes will not fail. With all its troubles life offers us the tremendous privilege to grow in knowledge and wisdom, faith and works, preparing to return and share God's glory."[8]

When afflictions are not taken from us, we can use them to develop our faith. When we or a loved one suffer from the biological problems that can lead to mental illness, it takes great faith to endure what may be a long battle in mortality. However, we can trust that Christ's grace is sufficient for us and for our loved one. We can trust that God does have a plan for our eventual happiness, even if all health problems are not solved in mortality. Elder Dallin H. Oaks gives us further counsel on this subject:

"Not all problems are overcome and not all needed relationships are fixed in mortality.

"The work of salvation goes on beyond the veil of death, and we should not be too apprehensive about incompleteness within the limits of mortality."[9]

Trusting Christ

Sometimes healing in mortality may come from receiving greater spiritual understanding of our problems or being given enough strength to endure and grow from them. Christ has promised that if we will take our problems to him, he can comfort us: "Come unto me . . . and ye shall find rest unto your souls" (Matthew 11:28–29). We can trust that he does understand what we are experiencing. Alma teaches:

"And he shall go forth, suffering pains and afflictions and temptations of every kind; and this that the word might be fulfilled which saith he will take upon him the pains and the sicknesses of his people. And he will take upon him death, that he may loose the bands of death which bind his people; and he will take upon him their infirmities, that his bowels may be filled with mercy, according to the flesh, that he may know according to the flesh how to succor his people according to their infirmities" (Alma 7:11–12).

Because he took upon himself the "pains and the sicknesses of his people," we can trust that he knows how to help us. He can help us through the scriptures, the Holy Ghost, and the teachings of the gospel to know what we can do to improve our lives and make our challenges easier. He can also bless us with wisdom to properly use the medical knowledge and treatments available to us in these latter days. We can trust that all of our mortal problems can eventually work for our eternal good if we remain faithful (D&C 90:24; 100:15; 105:40; 122:7).

As we draw close to Christ during painful mortal experiences, we can gain strength from understanding the Atonement. Christ's atonement was an infinite atonement (2 Nephi 9:7; Alma 34:10). He atoned not only for our sins, from which we repent, but also for our illnesses, sorrows, and losses in mortality. Because he overcame the world (John 16:33), we have justifiable reason to never lose hope.

"Wherefore, whoso believeth in God might with surety hope for a better world, yea, even a place at the right hand of God, which hope cometh of faith, maketh an anchor to the souls of men, which would make them sure and steadfast" (Ether 12:4).

Notes

1. "Spirituality and Healing in Medicine," conference held at Harvard University, December 2–3, 2006, under the direction of Herbert Benson, M.D., and Christina M. Puchalski, M.D.

2. Richards and Bergin, *A Spiritual Strategy for Counseling and Psychotherapy;* Richards and Bergin, *Handbook of Psychotherapy and Religious Diversity;* Miller, *Integrating Spirituality into Treatment.*

3. Neal A. Maxwell, "According to the Desire of [Our] Hearts," *Ensign,* Nov. 1996, 21.

4. M. Russell Ballard, "Suicide: Some Things We Know, and Some We Do Not," *Ensign,* Oct. 1987, 8.

5. Maxwell, "According to the Desire of [Our] Hearts," 21.

6. *Encyclopedia of Joseph Smith's Teachings,* 360.

7. Smith, *Teachings,* 218.

8. Kimball, *Teachings of Presidents of the Church: Spencer W. Kimball,* 15, 20–21.

9. Dallin H. Oaks, "Powerful Ideas," *Ensign,* Nov. 1995, 26.

6

Perspectives on Suicide and Mental Illness

Marleen S. Williams

One of the most painful problems related to mental illness is suicide. Sometimes a person's ability to think clearly is distorted to the point that the person can see no solution or end to suffering. Thinking may be confused or not based in reality. Sometimes a person may end his own life. For family and loved ones, this can be extremely painful and difficult. Those who are left behind experience great grief and confusion, often with no way to resolve questions and concerns. God has revealed little information about those who take their own life, but some excellent LDS resources provide help and comfort. These resources include the following:

M. Russell Ballard, "Suicide: Some Things We Know, and Some We Do Not," *Ensign,* Oct. 1987, 6–9.

"Q&A: Questions and Answers," *New Era,* Jan. 1990, 14–18.

Karen Athay Packer, "The Broken Bowl," *Ensign,* Sept. 1992, 52–54.

Ezra Taft Benson, "Do Not Despair," *Ensign,* Oct. 1986, 65–67.

Steven C. Yamada, "Coping with Suicide," in *Helping and Healing Our Families,* 239–42.

Alexander B. Morrison, *Valley of Sorrow.*

mentalhealthlibrary.info (this is an online resource sponsored by the Mental Health Resource Foundation).

If you struggle with suicidal thoughts, it is important to get help. Tell a family member, a trusted friend, your bishop, your doctor, or a licensed mental health professional. Most communities have a telephone crisis service that can help you get some support. You do not have to struggle alone. Talking with others can help you see your situation more clearly. Other people can help you explore real solutions to problems. If you isolate yourself or shut others out, it is easy to lose sight of choices and solutions that could help you feel better.

Many people who have thought of ending their life have received help, have found solutions to problems, and have led rewarding and happy lives. Suicide will close off many options, but it will not end your existence. Your spirit is eternal, and suicide is not a solution to your distress.

If someone you know is considering suicide, it is important to recognize the signs and take action. If the person is unable to think clearly, you may have to act in the person's behalf. Keeping the person alive is the most important concern. Chapter 3, "The Brain and Medical Treatment for Mental Disorders," and chapter 19, "Mental Health and the Law," list some warning signs, as well as helps for knowing how to respond and get help. Chapter 8, "Latter-day Saint Readings and Resources," gives additional information that can help you.

7

Spiritual Sources of Support for Emotional Distress

Timothy B. Smith

God knows us, our situations, and our limitations. With that understanding, we can have complete faith that we receive needed help in our struggles, which may include emotional distress and prolonged mental illness. As we turn to him, we can find many spiritual sources of support. This chapter reviews some of those sources, but almost all doctrines and principles of the gospel can be related to our emotional well-being. Studying those doctrines and applying them to the particulars of our situation is the most fruitful strategy for dealing with emotional distress.[1]

Foundational Doctrines of Divinity

The reality of God. God is our Father, and he is close to us (Galatians 4:6). Recognizing reality provides much more than an abstract appreciation or vague hope in the hereafter. Feeling the presence of God provides peace now.[2] That peace is not an absence of trouble. Illness and limitations may or may not be removed, but when we have a sense of God's presence, we no longer feel alone. The Creator of the universe is on our side. "If God be for us, who [or what] can be against us?" (Romans 8:31; see vv. 38–39).

The Atonement of Jesus Christ. Heavenly Father's plan provided a Savior to forgive our sins, strengthen our weaknesses, and heal our hearts (Alma 34:9). On our behalf, Jesus Christ experienced agony and humiliation. There is no pain too deep for his healing touch.[3] Filled with mercy, he pleads our cause before the Father when we ask that his sacrifice be applied to our lives (D&C 45:3–5). His atonement not only provides forgiveness for our willful acts of disobedience but also changes our natures and draws us back to God (John 17).

Elder Boyd K. Packer said: "For some reason, we think the Atonement of Christ applies *only* at the end of mortal life to redemption from the Fall, from spiritual death. It is much more than that. It is an ever-present power to call upon in everyday life. When we are racked or harrowed up or tormented by guilt or burdened with grief, He can heal us . . . [and] we can experience 'the peace of God, which passeth all understanding.'"[4]

To receive this gift and change of heart, we must believe the Atonement to be true, seek after it with all our strength (Moroni 10:32), and continually turn our thoughts to Christ.[5] When performed in the name of Jesus Christ, priesthood ordinances and blessings can invoke the Atonement on our behalf and provide healing or additional strength to endure.

The Holy Ghost is the Comforter. We sense God's presence and the power of Christ's atonement through the Holy Ghost (D&C 20:27), sometimes referred to as the Comforter. The Comforter not only fills us with hope and love (Moroni 8:26) but also teaches all truth "of things as they really are, and of things as they really will be" (Jacob 4:13). Accordingly, with the Comforter's influence we can see ourselves and our situations more accurately.

We are not merely physical bodies with neurotransmitters and hormones but, more profoundly, spiritual children of heaven influenced by the very powers of eternity within us. Situations we face in this life are temporary, even if they last ninety years. With the Comforter reminding us of truths such as these, we can know what to do and where to go (D&C 79:2). Through tender impressions and feelings, the Comforter guides us softly to peaceable things if we will listen (D&C 39:9).

Doctrines That Provide Perspective

Painful experiences do occur. Deep hurts and unbelievable suffering do occur in this life. At times, everything we love or hoped for may be taken from us. Like Alma and Amulek, tied up and forced to watch the cruel murder of innocent women and children (possibly including friends and family of Amulek), we may experience the most painful situations imaginable. Even the Savior trembled at the depth and breadth of suffering (D&C 19:18). When our cup of gall is filled to overflowing, many times we still must drink.[6]

Pain can increase our reliance upon God and upon others. Intense or prolonged suffering can overwhelm our ability to cope. In such circumstances, we rely more upon help from God and from other people. Interdependence with others and dependence upon God are central to his plan. Through the process of admitting our weaknesses and then seeking assistance, we become stronger (Ether 12:27).

Reliance upon God includes dealing with circumstances we would not choose. Few children learning to ride a bicycle avoid scrapes and bruises, but they usually get back on the bike, knowing that their parent will let go again. Trust in the Lord does not depend upon our personal deliverance from pain. Complete trust is when we continue to do what God asks, even when we must deal with circumstances we would not choose (Isaiah 12:2). Like Jonah, we may not wish to go to Nineveh, but if to Nineveh we must go, it may be better for us there than we had imagined. Even when faced with truly terrible circumstances amid the flames of adversity, "our God whom we serve is able to deliver us from the burning fiery furnace. . . . But *if not*" and we are burned anyway, we will still do what he asks (Daniel 3:17–18; emphasis added).[7]

We may experience pain, but complete trust in God can heal us from even more damaging feelings of powerlessness and despair, rage and desires for retribution, doubt and cynicism. Though bruised, we figuratively get back on the bicycle and learn to act rather than be acted upon (2 Nephi 2:26).

A correct understanding of God's attributes. The Restoration has revealed glorious truths about God and thus about ourselves and our connection with Divinity. The Prophet Joseph Smith taught, "If men do not comprehend the character of God, they do not comprehend themselves."[8] Contrary to the popular emphasis on self-exploration, we best learn about our true nature through the ministry of Jesus Christ.[9] Such teachings provide hope and purpose to our days as we catch glimpses of possibilities that we then work to make reality.

Because our perceptions and trust of others have been influenced by how we were treated as children, it is common to attribute to God those characteristics modeled by imperfect caretakers. If our parents were harsh or distant, we may ascribe those qualities to God without realizing it. Particularly when we have been mistreated, we need to separate our childhood experiences from the attributes of God that are correctly taught in the scriptures.

Disobedience to God's laws brings spiritual and emotional pain. If we were to jump from a high place expecting to defy the law of gravity, a moment of excitement would be followed by eventual disappointment upon impact. Spiritual laws have similarly predictable consequences. When we act in ways that attempt to defy God's laws, the feelings we experience may be intense. At first, we may enjoy feeling that way. But feelings are temporary. Upon the impact of consequences, we feel empty or worse. Our spiritual natures revile against disobedience. Guilt can weigh us down,[10] and tactics to avoid feeling guilty can numb our other feelings too. If we persist, we can become "past feeling" (1 Nephi 17:45).

The truth can make us free. Human tendency is to defend against blatant honesty. We minimize some problems. We exaggerate the consequences of other problems such that we may feel overwhelmed. Spirituality partly means living truthfully. Too often we act upon false or partially accurate beliefs. We rarely are completely honest with ourselves. We tend to assume that our motivations are good, when in fact they may be partly selfish. We tend to blame others when we would have acted similarly given their situation. We tend to beat ourselves up over faults that deserve our increased attention rather than our cheap self-criticism.

Honesty means keeping things in perspective—neither exaggerating nor minimizing. It means being open to new experiences and ways of seeing things. Overcoming distress partly entails a more accurate explanation of our circumstances and consequences, seeking out correct information rather than defending against anything that contradicts our current perceptions.

Cultural norms inconsistent with divine principles can lead to distress. In the scriptures, we learn that much suffering is associated with false beliefs and immoral practices within world cultures. For example, women may be mistreated by men based on cultural norms or may be misled by society's devaluation of motherhood. Behaviors such as these are the "traditions of [our] fathers" (Alma 17:15) that restrict our spirits, constrain our potential, and minimize our collective dignity. Therefore, part of our mortal experience is to replace values commonly accepted within our society with those that are consistent with divine principles.

Satanic lies are increasingly taught openly and believed widely. Some false principles are subtle half-truths, only exposed through applications of prophetic teachings to contemporary cultures. Following are some examples of worldly values, followed by gospel values in parentheses:

Hurried lives; time is more valuable than money (but relationships are even more valuable)

Fears of social rejection (we never stand alone when we stand with God, and most often other people care for us more than we assume)

Youthful physical appearance (aging is part of life and need not be negatively stigmatized)

College education, career development (lifelong education,
   character development)

Control (influence, flexible to others' circumstances)

Admiration for the elaborate and ornate (beauty everywhere, often
   in simplicity)

Freedom (agency)

Tolerance of differences (the Golden Rule)

Teenagers are rebellious (not usually if they are listened to and
   respected) and just have to explore the world on their own
   (identity is developed best through following good examples
   and though mentoring, rather than by experiencing negative
   consequences firsthand)

Elder Richard G. Scott has suggested careful examination of our beliefs
and values relative to gospel standards and elimination of culturally accepted
practices that are contrary to the teachings of the Savior.[11] Many of our disap-
pointments and anxieties may be attributable to our fears or unmet expectations based on cultural, rather than on gospel, standards. By aligning our
hopes and beliefs with the teachings of Jesus Christ, we can reduce difficulties that arise from placing too much of our hearts elsewhere.

Doctrines Regarding Our Behavior

Elder Franklin D. Richards declared, "As we incorporate the gospel principles or standards into our lives, we have the confidence and respect of our
fellowmen, enjoy love and harmony in our family relationships, and are
blessed with peace of mind."[12]

Love and service. A common symptom of nearly all forms of emotional
distress is a decreased ability to think about or feel anything else. Our condition forces itself upon our awareness, often relentlessly. In a negative,
downward spiral, rumination (being stuck thinking the same thing over and

over) provides little relief and usually adds to the desperate nature of our situation.

We must certainly consider our own needs and do our best to meet them, but we cannot be whole without loving other people. When we love others, we recognize their needs and seek to meet them. We do so naturally, without motivations of guilt or compulsion. We find happiness in their happiness. They in turn feel more disposed to assist us. In a positive, upward spiral, we receive not only the satisfaction of giving but also the kindness and assistance from those who love us in return. Elder Richard G. Scott stated:

"Love is a potent healer. Realizing that, Satan would separate you from the power of the love of God, kindred, and friends that want to help. He would lead you to feel that the walls are pressing in around you and there is no escape or relief. He wants you to believe you lack the capacity to help yourself and that no one else is really interested. If he succeeds, you will be driven to further despair and heartache. His strategy is to have you think you are not appreciated, loved, or wanted so that you in despair will turn to self-criticism, and in the extreme to even despising yourself and feeling evil when you are not. . . . If you have such thoughts, *break through those helpless feelings by reaching out in love to another in need.* That may sound cruel and unfeeling when you long so much for healing, but it is based upon truth. Paul taught, 'Bear ye one another's burdens, and so fulfill the law of Christ.'"[13]

The more we love, the more we heal—in every respect.

Self-restraint. We are by nature emotional, but when emotions prevent us from seeing God (or the divine in us or in others), our feelings need to be tempered and replaced with feelings that are less intense or self-centered. "See that ye bridle all your passions, that ye may be filled with love" (Alma 38:12).

Popular beliefs encourage us to do what we feel like doing. Such actions provide some satisfaction, but those feelings usually disappear after we have obtained what we sought (leaving us to seek something else in a repetitive cycle). Self-respect comes as we restrain our selfish desires and act accordingly.

Family relationships. This life is a parallel of our premortal life, where we existed with God's family, and we can continue in families after this life. Hence, we come closest to heaven when we form and maintain strong family relationships. Even in circumstances in which the family relationships we have known in this life have been destructive, every effort to correct those situations and to subsequently establish more healthy patterns with others (remarriage following divorce, adoption, and so forth) will be worth the effort, which is often extensive and long-term.

Forgiving others. Having the Spirit with us can help us overlook offense and be resilient to the actions of others. But when we are hurt, the best strategy is to deal with the situation (informing authorities of criminal actions, openly communicating our perceptions, protecting ourselves and others from imminent harm, and so forth), seek healing, and then let go. Emotional pain is toxic enough without harboring resentment.

The consequences of not forgiving can be just as devastating and permanent as the original offense. Perhaps this is why the Lord said, "But I say unto you, Love your enemies, bless them that curse you, do good to them that hate you, and pray for them which despitefully use you, and persecute you" (Matthew 5:44). Efforts to deal with the situation might need to be strong and intense but are still much healthier than the alternatives of remaining hurt or attempting to take justice into our own hands.

We all have need of mercy. "And ye shall also forgive one another your trespasses; for verily I say unto you, he that forgiveth not his neighbor's trespasses when he says that he repents, the same hath brought himself under condemnation" (Mosiah 26:31; Matthew 6:14–15). Letting go of resentment can bring peace. The scriptures do not qualify whom we should forgive: "I, the Lord, will forgive whom I will forgive, but of you it is required to forgive all men" (D&C 64:10).

Prayer. "As soon as we learn the true relationship in which we stand toward God (namely, God is our Father, and we are his children), then at once prayer becomes natural and instinctive on our part (Matt. 7:7–11). Many of the so-called difficulties about prayer arise from forgetting this relationship. Prayer is the act by which the will of the Father and the will of the child are brought into correspondence with each other. The object of prayer is not to change the will of God, but to secure for ourselves and for others blessings that God is already willing to grant, but that are made conditional on our asking for them. Blessings require some work or effort on our part before we can obtain them. Prayer is a form of work."[14]

Temple worship. The temple is the house of the Lord. There we can feel his peace, be renewed in spirit, and receive personal revelation.[15] Reminders of our covenants and his promises can provide needed perspective and strength.

Care for our physical bodies. Under constant stress, our bodies may remain on heightened alert and can wear down. On the other hand, when our bodies are perpetually inactive, they may lack the strength to deal with demanding situations. Our spiritual responsiveness is restricted or fostered to the degree our physical tabernacle, the body, is well maintained.[16] Adequate rest, vigorous exertion, and healthy food are all prescribed in prophetic teachings (D&C 88:124; 89). We are taught to abstain from substances that adversely impair or addict our bodies. When taken under the direction of competent physicians, medications for bipolar disorder, psychosis, obsessive-compulsive disorder, major depression, and similar conditions can help apparent chemical deficits or excesses in our nervous system.

Self-reliance. Interdependence in relationships means that we both provide and obtain needed assistance. However, assistance is not the same as problem solving. We rarely "solve" others' problems, and we usually cannot turn over our problems to others without those problems recurring in another form. As a simple example, children learning to tie their shoes probably could not do so without an adult showing them how, but in the end, they must fumble with the knots themselves until guidance is no longer necessary.

Personal growth occurs when we practice needed skills ourselves.

Therefore, although persons receiving professional counseling may greatly benefit from gaining new insights and personal growth, they still must develop new skills, which means doing things differently outside of counseling sessions. Professional counseling is most helpful not when it is used as a dumping ground for hurtful feelings (shifting responsibility to the therapist) but when it is used as a recycling center where hurts can be changed into usable tools for the future, such as motivations or principles that can be applied in real life. We are responsible to work out our own solutions. Hence, the gospel emphasizes the principle of self-reliance, turning to God and others for help but then working as if everything depended on us.[17]

Productivity balanced with wholesome recreation. As children of the Creator, we have sparks of his creative powers, such as when we beautify our surroundings or improve situations for ourselves and others. Work is part of our nature, and hard work can bring deep satisfaction. Accordingly, we can do our best efforts in the spirit of creation, not simply distancing ourselves from strained relationships, gratifying our pride, selfishly amassing riches, or avoiding dealing with other responsibilities.

Our labors will be most productive when they are balanced in proportion to our other priorities. After our relationship with God, family relationships are typically our highest priority, and so long as family members have adequate food, shelter, and safety, they will need our time and attention more than they will need additional income.

In our work, we should not "run faster than [we have] strength" (Mosiah 4:27). Balance can come through wholesome recreation. Indeed, "wholesome recreation is part of our religion, and a change of pace is necessary, and even its anticipation can lift the spirit."[18]

Conclusion

Our lives contain many challenges, many of them emotional and some ripping at the threads of sanity. However, help is available for all circumstances.

That help is as varied and comprehensive as our conditions. "In ev'ry condition . . . as thy days may demand, so thy succor shall be."[19]

Elder John K. Carmack testified: "During those chaotic moments we all seem to experience—when suffering anxiety or despair, when misunderstood and depreciated—as our days demand, our Savior can and will provide that succor or help in time of need. His succor brings us peace. Did He not say, 'In the world ye shall have tribulation,' but 'in me ye might have peace'"?[20]

Notes

1. Elder Boyd K. Packer observed: "True doctrine, understood, changes attitudes and behavior. The study of the doctrines of the gospel will improve behavior quicker than a study of behavior will improve behavior. Preoccupation with unworthy behavior can lead to unworthy behavior. That is why we stress so forcefully the study of the doctrines of the gospel" ("Little Children," *Ensign*, Nov. 1986, 17).

2. Elder John H. Groberg testified: "I know He lives. I know He loves us. I know we can feel His love here and now. I know His voice is one of perfect mildness which penetrates to our very center. I know He smiles and is filled with compassion and love. I know He is full of gentleness, kindness, mercy, and desire to help. I love Him with all my heart. I testify that when we are ready, His pure love instantly moves across time and space, reaches down, and pulls us up from the depths of any tumultuous sea of darkness, sin, sorrow, death, or despair we may find ourselves in and brings us into the light and life and love of eternity" ("The Power of God's Love," *Ensign*, Nov. 2004, 11).

3. Sister Kathleen H. Hughes, of the General Presidency of the Relief Society, said: "I have heard numerous accounts of Christ's healing power. There is so much suffering in mortality, so many causes for pain. I know people who have sent loved ones into harm's way and who daily pray for their safety in battle. I talk to parents who are frightened for their children, aware of the temptations they face. I have dear friends who are suffering from the ravaging effects of chemotherapy. I know single parents, abandoned by spouses, who are rearing children alone. I have dealt myself with the debilitating effects of depression. But I have learned from my own experience, and I learn from those I meet, that we are never left to our own resources. We are never abandoned. A wellspring of goodness, of strength, and confidence is within us, and when we listen with a feeling of trust, we are raised up. We are healed. We not only survive, but we love life. We laugh; we enjoy; we go forward with faith" ("Blessed by Living Water," *Ensign*, May 2003, 13).

4. Boyd K. Packer, "'The Touch of the Master's Hand,'" *Ensign*, May 2001, 23.

5. Elder Richard G. Scott urged: "When memory of past mistakes encroaches upon

your mind, turn your thoughts to the Redeemer and to the miracle of forgiveness with the renewal that comes through Him. Your depression and suffering will be replaced by peace, joy, and gratitude for His love" ("The Path to Peace and Joy," *Ensign*, Nov. 2000, 26).

6. Elder Boyd K. Packer taught: "We are indoctrinated that somehow we should always be instantly emotionally comfortable. When that is not so, some become anxious—and all too frequently seek relief from counseling, from analysis, and even from medication. It was meant to be that life would be a challenge. To suffer some anxiety, some depression, some disappointment, even some failure is normal. Teach our members that if they have a good, miserable day once in a while, or several in a row, to stand steady and face them. Things will straighten out. There is great purpose in our struggle in life" (*That All May Be Edified* [Salt Lake City, 1982], 94).

7. Elder Dennis E. Simmons taught: "Our God will deliver us from sickness and disease, *but if not.* . . . He will deliver us from loneliness, depression, or fear, *but if not.* . . . Our God will deliver us from threats, accusations, and insecurity, *but if not.* . . . He will deliver us from death or impairment of loved ones, *but if not, . . . we will trust in the Lord*" ("But If Not . . . ," *Ensign*, May 2004, 73).

8. Smith, *Teachings,* 343.

9. Jeffrey R. Holland, "The Grandeur of God," *Ensign*, Nov. 2003, 70.

10. President Boyd K. Packer taught: "We know that some anxiety and depression is caused by physical disorders, but much (perhaps most) of it is not pain of the body but of the spirit. Spiritual pain resulting from guilt can be replaced with peace of mind" ("The Touch of the Master's Hand," 23).

11. Richard G. Scott, "Removing Barriers to Happiness," *Ensign*, May 1998, 85.

12. Franklin D. Richards, in Conference Report, Oct. 1970, 80.

13. Richard G. Scott, "To Be Healed," *Ensign*, May 1994, 8–9; emphasis added.

14. Bible Dictionary, LDS edition of the King James Version of the Bible, 752–53.

15. President Ezra Taft Benson stated: "Do we return to the temple often to receive the personal blessings that come from regular temple worship? Prayers are answered, revelation occurs, and instruction by the Spirit takes place in the holy temples of the Lord" ("Come unto Christ and Be Perfected in Him," *Ensign*, May 1988, 84).

16. President Ezra Taft Benson taught: "The condition of the physical body can affect the spirit. That's why the Lord gave us the Word of Wisdom. He also said that we should retire to our beds early and arise early (see D&C 88:124), that we should not run faster than we have strength (see D&C 10:4), and that we should use moderation in all good things. In general, the more food we eat in its natural state and the less it is refined without additives, the healthier it will be for us. Food can affect the mind, and deficiencies in certain elements in the body can promote mental depression. A good physical examination periodically is a safeguard and may spot problems that can be remedied. Rest and

physical exercise are essential, and a walk in the fresh air can refresh the spirit" ("Do Not Despair," *Ensign,* Nov. 1974, 65).

17. Elder Gene R. Cook wrote: "Pray as if everything depends on God . . . work as if everything depends on us. A great example of this is the story of Nephi, when he went back to Jerusalem to get the brass plates. He and his brothers tried one thing after another as they sought to obtain the plates; and they 'failed' each time. But Nephi wouldn't give up. He knew it was the Lord's will that they succeed, and he wasn't going to quit until he had done all in his power to accomplish his purpose. (See 1 Nephi 3–4.)" (*Receiving Answers to Our Prayers* [Salt Lake City: Deseret Book, 1996], 153–54).

18. Ezra Taft Benson, "Do Not Despair," 65.

19. Keen, Robert. "How Firm a Foundation." *Hymns,* no. 85.

20. Carmack, "United in Love and Testimony," *Ensign,* May 2001, 77.

8

Latter-day Saint Readings and Resources

John P. Livingstone and Marleen S. Williams

Many helpful resources are available for Latter-day Saints to learn more about mental health from a Latter-day Saint perspective. Following is a partial list of such resources.

The Scriptures

The scriptures can be a powerful source of comfort and instruction. When we read them, the Spirit can help us apply them to our own situation and concerns. Often when we read with a particular problem in mind, the Holy Ghost can help us understand a passage as it relates to our own life, as well as that of other family members.

The Topical Guide can be a good place to start. Finding and reviewing scriptural topics related to problems can bring peace and inspiration. Some topics that have helpful and insightful scriptures include the following:

Accountability, Age of	Courage	Long-suffering
Adversity	Distress	Mercy, Merciful
Affliction	Endure	Overcome, Overcame
Anchor	God, Love of	Patience
Broken-hearted	God, Mercy of	Problem-Solving
Cheer	Hope	Tribulation
Comfort	Jesus Christ, Advocate	Trust in God
Compassion	Jesus Christ, Savior	Worth of Souls

Temple Attendance

President Gordon B. Hinckley taught, "There is need occasionally to leave the noise and the tumult of the world and step within the walls of a sacred house of God, there to feel His spirit in an environment of holiness and peace."[1]

The temple is a place of peace where we can leave behind the problems of this world and feel comfort. Temple attendance can also help us focus on putting mortal challenges into an eternal perspective and receive comfort and help from God. We can also receive personal inspiration and guidance in the temple. Of the blessings of temple attendance, President Ezra Taft Benson said:

"Sometimes in the peace of lovely temples, the serious problems of life find their solutions. . . . Pure knowledge flows to us there under the influence of the Spirit. . . . it is in the temples that we obtain God's greatest blessings pertaining to eternal life. Temples really are the gateways to heaven."

He added, "May we remember always, as we [visit and work in these glorious temples], that the veil may become very thin between this world and the spirit world. I know this is true."[2]

Church Magazines

Latter-day Saint magazines have published many articles related to mental illnesses. Following is a partial list of these articles. They are all available on the Internet at lds.org. They can be found by searching the Gospel Library under Magazines.

ADHD

Laurie Wilson Thornton, "The Hidden Handicap," *Ensign,* Apr. 1990, 44–48.

Alzheimer's disease

Lola B. Walters, "Death of a Personality," *Ensign,* June 1987, 62–64.

Jean Hedengren Moultrie, "Of Walkers, Wheelchairs, and Wisdom," *Ensign,* Aug. 2003, 8–11.

Lola B. Walters, "The Holy Ghost: A Living Presence by My Side," *Tambuli,* Mar. 1988, 13.

James E. Faust, "Where Do I Make My Stand?" *Ensign,* Nov. 2004, 18–21.

David F. Evans, "Lessons from the Old Testament: Obedience Is Better Than Sacrifice," *Ensign,* June 2006, 56–57.

Dianne Dibb Forbis, "Fitly Framed to Keep Out Rain," *Ensign,* Aug. 2002, 60–62.

Barbara Vance, "Taking Care of Mom and Dad," *Ensign,* Sept. 1995, 56–60.

Lola B. Walters, "Sunshine in My Soul," *Ensign,* Aug. 1991, 16–19.

Anxiety disorders

Jan Underwood Pinborough, "Mental Illness: In Search of Understanding and Hope," *Ensign,* Feb. 1989, 50–58.

Dawn and Jay Fox, "Easing the Burdens of Mental Illness," *Ensign,* Oct. 2001, 32–35.

Cecil O. Samuelson, "What Does It Mean to Be Perfect?" *New Era,* Jan. 2006, 10–13.

Allen E. Bergin, "Toward a Theory of Human Agency," *New Era,* July 1973, 33–41.

Claigh H. Jensen, "About Trauma," *Ensign,* Feb. 2008, 49.

Janele Williams, "Helping Children with Traumatic Events," *Ensign,* Feb. 2008, 46–48.

Autism spectrum disorders

Gayle M. Clegg, "Teaching Our Children to Accept Differences," *Ensign,* June 2004, 40–44.

"I Have a Question," *Ensign,* Feb. 2000, 61.

Carmen B. Pingree, " 'So Near and Yet So Far': Living with Autism," *Ensign,* Aug. 1983, 56–59.

Laurie Wilson Thornton, "The Mathematics of Multiple Disabilities," *Ensign,* Oct. 1991, 64–69.

Bipolar mood disorder

Dallin H. Oaks, "He Heals the Heavy Laden," *Ensign,* Nov. 2006, 6–9.

Name Withheld, "Light in Darkness," *Ensign,* June 1998, 16–21.

Marleen S. Williams, "Raising a Child with a Disability," *Ensign,* Oct. 2004, 12–16.

Carmen B. Pingree, "Six Myths about the Handicapped," *Ensign,* June 1988, 18–22.

Alexander B. Morrison, "Myths about Mental Illness," *Ensign,* Oct. 2005, 31–35.

Dawn and Jay Fox, "Easing the Burdens of Mental Illness," *Ensign,* Oct. 2001, 32–35.

Jan Underwood Pinborough, "Mental Illness: In Search of Understanding and Hope," *Ensign,* Feb. 1989, 50–58.

A Loving Daughter, "Looking Back . . . I Knew My Mama Loved Me," *Friend,* Aug. 1989, 42–44.

Cerebral palsy

Laurie Wilson Thornton, "The Mathematics of Multiple Disabilities," *Ensign,* Oct. 1991, 64–69.

Karen Gibson, "Mandy's Therapy," *Friend,* June 1996, 35–37.

Artel Ricks, "Deacon in Motion," *New Era,* Sept. 2003, 14–15.

Boyd K. Packer, "The Moving of the Water," *Ensign,* May 1991, 7–9.

Stephen D. Nadauld, "Faith and Good Works," *Ensign,* May 1992, 82–83.

Judy C. Olsen, "Special Victories," *New Era,* Jan. 1989, 20–25.

Floy Daun Mackay, "A Little Miracle," *New Era,* Oct. 1984, 16–19.

Depression

Dallin H. Oaks, "He Heals the Heavy Laden," *Ensign,* Nov. 2006, 6–9.

Russell M. Nelson, "Perfection Pending," *Ensign,* Nov. 1995, 86–88.

Cecil O. Samuelson, "What Does It Mean to Be Perfect?" *New Era,* Jan. 2006, 10–13.

Robert D. Hales, "We Can't Do It Alone," *Ensign,* Nov. 1975, 90–93.

Alexander B. Morrison, "Myths about Mental Illness," *Ensign,* Oct. 2005, 31–35.

David G. Weight, "Why Is My Wife (or Husband) Depressed?" *Ensign,* Mar. 1990, 27–29.

Sean E. Brotherson, "When Your Child Is Depressed," *Ensign,* Aug. 2004, 52–57.

Val D. MacMurray, "When Life Is Getting You Down," *Ensign,* June 1984, 56–60.

Steve Gilliland, "Awake My Soul!: Dealing Firmly with Depression," *Ensign,* Aug. 1978, 37.

Mollie H. Sorensen, "My Battle with Depression," *Ensign,* Feb. 1984, 12–16.

Jeffrey R. Holland, "For Times of Trouble," *New Era,* Oct. 1980, 6–15.

G. G. Vandagriff, "Escaping My Valley of Sorrow," *Ensign,* Mar. 2000, 64–67.

Dean A. Byrd, "After Divorce: Help for Latter-day Saint Men," *Ensign,* Aug. 2003, 58–63.

Disorders that begin in childhood

"Dealing with Disabilities," *Ensign,* June 1993, 66.

Hilarie Cole, "He Will Be There to Help," *Ensign,* May 1995, 95.

W. Craig Zwick, "Encircled in the Savior's Love," *Ensign,* Nov. 1995, 13–14.

"Embracing Members with Special Needs," *Ensign,* Aug. 2005, 12–15.

Andrea C. Hobart, "I Can Read!" *New Era,* Mar. 1998, 8–9.

Eating disorders

James E. Faust, "Who Do You Think You Are?" *New Era,* Mar. 2001, 4–9.

Katie May Hess, "My Battle with Anorexia," *New Era,* Apr. 2006, 42–45.

Lynn Carol Maynes, "Warning Signs," *New Era,* Apr. 2006, 44.

Diane L. Spangler, "The Body, a Sacred Gift," *Ensign,* July 2005, 14–18.

Janet Thomas, "Eating Disorders: A Deadly State of Mind," *New Era,* Feb. 1993, 36–39.

Harold A. Frost, "The Thinness Obsession," *Ensign,* Jan. 1990, 70–73.

W. Craig Zwick, "Taking the Higher Road," *Ensign,* Aug. 2002, 42–47.

Barbara Day Lockhart, "Our Divinely Based Worth," *Ensign,* June 1995, 50–54.

Susan W. Tanner, "The Sanctity of the Body," *Ensign,* Nov. 2005, 13–15.

Epilepsy

Greg Jensen, "Chickens, Junkyards, and Carnival People," *New Era,* Jan. 1989, 30–33.

Lauralee Stephenson, "Like an Angel," *New Era,* Nov. 2004, 9.

Mental retardation

Boyd K. Packer, "The Moving of the Water," *Ensign,* May 1991, 7–9.

Thomas S. Monson, "Labels," *Ensign,* Sept. 2000, 2–6.

Thomas S. Monson, "Miracles—Then and Now," *Ensign,* Nov. 1992, 68–70.

Mark G. Warner, "The Things I've Learned from You," *Ensign,* Sept. 2001, 40–41.

Marleen S. Williams, "Raising a Child with a Disability," *Ensign,* Oct. 2004, 12–16.

Elizabeth VanDenBerghe, "Helping and Being Helped by the Intellectually Impaired," *Ensign,* Oct. 1993, 26–31.

James E. Faust, "The Sanctity of Life," *Ensign,* May 1975, 27–29.

Thomas S. Monson, "Meeting Life's Challenges," *Ensign,* Nov. 1993, 68–71.

Schizophrenia

Dallin H. Oaks, "He Heals the Heavy Laden," *Ensign,* Nov. 2006, 6–9.

Alexander B. Morrison, "Myths about Mental Illness," *Ensign,* Oct. 2005, 31–35.

Marleen S. Williams, "Raising a Child with a Disability," *Ensign,* Oct. 2004, 12–16.

Dawn and Jay Fox, "Easing the Burdens of Mental Illness," *Ensign,* Oct. 2001, 32–35.

Jan Underwood Pinborough, "Mental Illness: In Search of Understanding and Hope," *Ensign,* Feb. 1989, 50–58.

Bruce R. McConkie, "The Salvation of Little Children," *Ensign,* Apr. 1977, 2–7.

A Loving Daughter, "Looking Back . . . I Knew My Mama Loved Me," *Friend,* Aug. 1989, 42–44.

Traumatic brain injury and stroke

Susan Waldrip, "Waiting Patiently on the Lord," *Ensign,* Apr. 2004, 32–35.

Sue Bergin, "Communication Disorders: Breaking through the Barriers," *Ensign,* Feb. 1991, 46–50.

Bruce Stucki, "Prayer, Faith, and Family: Stepping-Stones to Eternal Happiness," *Ensign,* May 2006, 96–98.

Sandra Ferrin Strange, "The Uses of Suffering," *Ensign,* Mar. 1987, 56–59.

Carol Ann Prince, "Steve's Victory," *New Era,* July 1987, 18–19.

Candice Cooper Crockett, "Dad's Recovery," *Ensign,* Dec. 1994, 27–29.

Internet

Several Internet sites have helpful material on mental health specifically for Latter-day Saints.

disability.lds.org: This is part of the official LDS Church Web site. It is devoted to understanding disabilities and knowing how to help. It has information on mental illness, as well as memory loss and other chronic illnesses.

lds.org: Click on "Home and Family," "Provident Living," "Social and Emotional Strength," and then "Ten Common Challenges Facing Families" you will find mental health information.

mentalhealthlibrary.info: This site is sponsored by the Mental Health Resource Foundation. It is not an official LDS site but is operated by members of the Church.

ldscounselers.net: Many LDS mental health professionals are listed in this international database. It is not sponsored by the LDS Church, but those listed are LDS.

ldsability.org: This site addresses many kinds of disabilities and has links to other resources. It is not an official LDS site but is operated by a Latter-day Saint and is sensitive to LDS values.

Books

Alexander B. Morrison. *Valley of Sorrow: A Layman's Guide to Understanding Mental Illness for Latter-day Saints.* Shadow Mountain, 2003.

Hymns

Music can have a soothing spiritual effect. It can often exceed the power of words alone to touch our emotions and bring peace to our souls. Many hymns have messages of comfort and encouragement. Elder Dallin H. Oaks expressed the power of music:

"We who have 'felt to sing the song of redeeming love' (Alma 5:26) need to keep singing that we may draw ever closer to him who has inspired sacred music and commanded that it be used to worship him. . . . Before the Savior and his Apostles left the upper room where they had the sublime experience of the Last Supper, they sang a hymn. After their hymn, the Savior led them to the Mount of Olives."[3]

Christ understood the power of hymns to sooth and comfort the soul. He used them before the painful experiences of Gethsemane and the cross to provide strength to himself and to his disciples. Hymns can touch both our mind and our heart to bring calm and comfort. Music is often used in therapy because of the powerful effect it has on emotions. Neuroimaging shows the positive effects that soothing music has on the brain.

Hymns that have messages of comfort and hope include the following from *Hymns of The Church of Jesus Christ of Latter-day Saints:*

"Be Still, My Soul," no. 124.
"Cast Thy Burden upon the Lord," no. 110.
"Does the Journey Seem Long?" no. 127.
"I Know That My Redeemer Lives," no. 136.
"My Redeemer Lives," no. 135.
"Though Deepening Trials," no. 122.
"Where Can I Turn for Peace?" no. 129.
"Count Your Blessings," no. 241.
"Abide with Me!" no. 166.
"As I Search the Holy Scriptures," no. 277.
"How Gentle God's Commands," no. 125.
"I Need Thee Every Hour," no. 98.
"Be Thou Humble," no. 130.
"I Am a Child of God," no. 301.
"I Believe in Christ," no. 134.

"I Know My Father Lives," no. 302.

"Lead Kindly Light," no. 97.

"Sweet Is the Peace the Gospel Brings," no. 14.

Notes

1. Gordon B. Hinckley, "Of Missions, Temples, and Stewardship," *Ensign,* Nov. 1995, 53.

2. Ezra Taft Benson, in Thomas S. Monson, "The Temple of the Lord," *Ensign,* May 1993, 5.

3. Dallin H. Oaks, "Worship through Music," *Ensign,* Nov. 1994, 12, 10.

Section III

Understanding Some Common Mental Disorders

9

Disorders That Begin in Childhood

Tina Taylor Dyches

Four disorders that begin in childhood include specific learning disabilities, attention-deficit/hyperactivity disorder (ADHD), mental retardation, and autism spectrum disorders. Although these disorders affect how the brain works and are generally diagnosed by medical professionals, they are usually considered to be mental disabilities (most often treated with special education services) rather than mental *illnesses* (most often treated with psychological or psychiatric services). These four disorders are discussed here, beginning with the most common.

Other common disorders that begin in childhood, including communication impairments and such severe emotional disturbance as depression, bipolar disorder, anxiety, and obsessive-compulsive disorder are discussed elsewhere (see Index).

Specific Learning Disabilities

A specific learning disability is a neurological disorder that affects the brain in receiving, processing, storing, and responding to information. It is often considered a "hidden handicap" or "invisible disability" because it is not readily apparent and is generally not detected until school age. Currently, learning disabilities are *not* diagnosed with a medical test. Rather, the diagnosis is based on observational evaluations of a student's performance on spoken or written language tasks. According to recent education law, students are not classified as having a specific learning disability unless they have demonstrated no or low response to consistent, proven, and research-based instruction.

Specific learning disabilities involve problems in the ability to listen, speak, read, write, spell, or do mathematical calculations that cause performance inconsistent with the individual's age, schooling, and level of intelligence. Most individuals with specific learning disabilities are affected in the area of reading, although some have difficulty with writing and mathematics. Specific learning disabilities have also been called learning disabilities, learning disorders, reading disorders (dyslexia), disorders of written expression (dysgraphia), and mathematics disorders (dyscalculia).

Other general symptoms of specific learning disabilities include problems with organization, such as managing time, completing assignments, and locating belongings. Some people with learning disabilities have problems in social relationships. They act inappropriately in social situations because they misinterpret tone of voice or facial expressions of others. Because many individuals with specific learning disabilities also have ADHD, they may exhibit symptoms of hyperactivity, impulsivity, or inattention. For example, these symptoms may include having trouble completing tasks or waiting turns, being restless and distractible (unable to pay attention), and failing to carry out requests. Symptoms of three learning disabilities are listed below.

Dyslexia

Poor decoding skills

Poor reading comprehension, even though all words in a passage can be decoded

Difficulty rhyming words

Inability to distinguish or separate sounds from spoken words

Poor reading fluency

Dysgraphia

Poor spelling

Inability to remember letter sequences in common words

Grammatical and punctuation errors

Excessively poor handwriting

Impaired ability to copy written work or to write from dictation

Poor organizational skills in written work

Dyscalculia

Difficulty recognizing numbers and symbols

Difficulty learning math facts

Difficulty memorizing math facts

Difficulty understanding abstract math concepts

Difficulty following mathematical steps

What Causes Specific Learning Disabilities?

No single cause of specific learning disabilities has been found. However, computerized electroencephalography (EEG) and functional magnetic resonance imaging (fMRI) have demonstrated a slowing of brain activity in the frontal and central regions of the brain in those who have been diagnosed with specific learning disabilities.

Because learning disabilities tend to run in families, heredity appears to be involved. Also, there is a relationship between learning disabilities and maternal problems during pregnancy and birth, such as drug and alcohol abuse during pregnancy, low birth weight, and lack of oxygen at birth. Evidence indicates that environmental factors may be associated with learning disabilities, including exposure to toxic substances such as lead.

Specific learning disabilities are not caused by poor instruction (particularly in reading), economic disadvantage, cultural differences, or insufficient opportunities to learn. Drug abuse has not been demonstrated to cause specific learning disabilities, but many individuals who have learning disabilities are at risk for substance abuse because of accompanying problems of low self-esteem and history of academic failure.

How Are Specific Learning Disabilities Treated?

Special education is the most common treatment for specific learning disabilities in children. While most students with learning disabilities are served primarily in regular classrooms with their peers, they still receive individualized instruction in their area of difficulty. Strategies are designed specifically for each child by a multidisciplinary team of specialists and are recorded on the student's Individualized Education Program (IEP).

Some individuals with learning disabilities receive help from professional counselors. Counseling can help children, teenagers, and adults develop a better understanding of their strengths and challenges, gain greater self-control, and develop a positive attitude.

Neurofeedback is another treatment that addresses the deficits associated with specific learning disabilities. The patient who receives this therapy is given visual and auditory feedback via a computer screen and is coached to change brain activity; thus, the patient is able to better process auditory and visual information and to stay on task for longer periods of time.

How Are Specific Learning Disabilities Experienced?

Specific learning disabilities are generally considered to be lifelong disorders. However, with the right treatment, the effects of these disabilities can be significantly reduced and managed so that those affected can lead productive and meaningful lives. However, if a specific learning disability is left undiagnosed and untreated, a cycle of failure, frustration, and self-defeating attitudes can continue into adulthood.

The Americans with Disabilities Act prohibits discrimination against people with disabilities. Under this law, citizens with learning disabilities should have access to and receive appropriate help in employment, transportation, government activities, and communication. Adults with learning disabilities who are seeking or maintaining employment may face such barriers as taking time-limited examinations; obtaining employment based on only one criterion, such as a written test; or having to function in a work setting with many distractions. Physical, environmental, and attitudinal barriers can and should be minimized. When an adult with a learning disability works cooperatively with supervisors and coworkers, effective accommodations can be implemented.

How Can You Help Yourself if You Have a Learning Disability?

Focus on your strengths and interests to get the type of support you need to either reduce or accommodate your learning disability.

Find alternative ways to access printed information if your learning disability affects reading. Ideas include listening to audio files and using text-to-speech software.

Inform your teachers, supervisors, and peers regarding your specific learning disability and the accommodations necessary for your success.

Visit a counselor to get support and reassurance and to learn how to best manage your learning disability.

Join a support group for those with specific learning disabilities, or read accounts of others who have been successful despite having learning disabilities.

Don't give up! If you are an adult and still haven't learned to read adequately, there is hope. It may take more practice and repetition for you than it would for others, but your wealth of life experience and your determination can provide you with the foundation for increased literacy.

Adults may consider enrolling in a literacy or adult education program sponsored by a church, library, public school, or community college.

How Can You Help Those with Learning Disabilities?

Avoid labeling individuals with learning disabilities. Labels such as behind, slow, lazy, different, or low achiever can result in feelings of low self-esteem and may further exacerbate their problems.

Let them know you have confidence in their abilities. Provide frequent opportunities to increase their self-esteem by matching tasks to their ability level and interests.

Model appropriate interpersonal relationships, and teach specific social skills when necessary.

If you are teaching someone with a learning disability, the following strategies may be helpful:

Don't embarrass a student by randomly calling on him to read in front of a group. Instead, prepare the person for reading assignments by giving advance notice.

Provide processing time when you ask questions. This wait time helps the individual to process the question and then process the answer.

Instead of surprising a student with random questions, arrange in advance to give a particular cue signaling that you will call on the student. This cue may be something like standing right in front of the student.

Divide instruction and practice into smaller units of information for those who have difficulty learning and remembering.

Teach organizational strategies. Don't expect the student to demonstrate organizational skills without instruction and feedback.

What Is It Like to Have a Specific Learning Disability?

"Frances J. Wright, Ed.D., of Murray, Utah, has struggled with learning disabilities throughout her life. Although she has an I.Q. of 140, Frances had difficulty learning to read as a child. She has an auditory disability that makes it difficult to process sounds fast and accurately. She also has an auditory discrimination problem that causes her to confuse similar sounds, particularly in a noisy environment. She frequently finds herself in awkward social situations because her responses—based on what she thinks she heard rather than on what is actually said—seem strange and inappropriate. 'I honestly thought I was crazy when I was a child,' she says, 'because I could think of no other explanation for my social blunders.'

"Although Frances has a doctorate in educational psychology and is a successful teacher, her learning disabilities continue to cause problems for her. She sometimes has difficulty following scriptures when they are read aloud, even if she is following along in her book. 'And you can imagine what ward members think when a family with small children sits next to me and I get up and move,' she says. 'I try to sit alone because any noise around me makes it very difficult for me to understand the speakers. I tend to be a front-row seeker because there, I can see the teacher well enough to read his lips, but it isn't always possible to sit there.'"[1]

Sadly, when problems such as these are not handled sensitively, they may contribute to an individual becoming less active in the Church. Some adults struggle with their feelings about the Church because they are unable to pray in public or read from the scriptures.

Attention-Deficit/Hyperactivity Disorder

Attention-deficit/hyperactivity disorder is an umbrella term that describes conditions characterized by strong and enduring patterns of inability to pay attention and/or hyperactive impulsivity (overactive behavior and difficulty controlling behavior) in at least two environments, such as school and home. For someone to be diagnosed with ADHD, these patterns of behavior must be excessive compared to the individual's cultural group and developmental age.

Some behavioral patterns that are often associated with ADHD may be characterized as follows:

Inattention

Failure to pay close attention to details

Frequent careless mistakes

Messy work

Difficulty sustaining attention to tasks

Appearance of being spacey or having one's mind elsewhere

Failure to follow through or complete tasks

Difficulty organizing tasks and activities

Distractibility

Forgetfulness in daily activities

Inability to keep one's mind on conversation

Hyperactivity

Being fidgety or squirmy

Engaging in excessive and inappropriate running or climbing

Experiencing difficulty engaging in quiet activities

Being constantly on the go

Talking excessively

Feeling restless continually

Impulsivity

Being impatient

Having difficulty delaying responses

Blurting out answers

Interrupting frequently

Making comments out of turn

Intruding on others

Grabbing objects from others

Many individuals with ADHD also have specific learning disabilities, which makes it even more difficult for them to be successful in school and at work. It is common for males who have ADHD to also have oppositional defiant disorder (ODD). Men so afflicted may lash out at others, become belligerent, or have extreme temper tantrums. Many adolescents and adults who have ADHD also experience anxiety and depression.

What Causes ADHD?

The exact causes of ADHD are unknown, but research shows that ADHD runs in families. This means that there is a strong possibility of a genetic component involved. If an individual has ADHD, it is common for that individual to have a close family member who also has ADHD or who has mood and anxiety disorders, learning disorders, substance-related disorders, or antisocial personality disorders.

Research has shown that individuals with ADHD have different brain activity, brain structure, and brain chemistry than those without ADHD. However, no single cause appears to apply to everyone with ADHD. Viruses, exposure to harmful chemicals such as lead, prenatal exposure to harmful drugs, genetics, problems during pregnancy or delivery, or anything else that inhibits early brain development may contribute to ADHD.

We know that ADHD is not caused by poor parenting, family problems, poor teaching, ineffective schools, or excess sugar consumption. This does not mean that people with ADHD do not *experience* difficult family or school situations but that these difficulties have not been shown to *cause* ADHD.

How Is ADHD Treated?

There are three main approaches for treating ADHD: medication, education, and therapy. No single treatment is as powerful as using a combination of treatments, such as medication along with education.

Medication. The most common medicines used to treat ADHD are stimulants (see chapter 3, "The Brain and Medical Treatment for Mental Disorders").

Education. Most students with ADHD are served by general education teachers in classes with their peers. However, some are served by special educators, and their unique educational needs are governed by Individualized Education Programs (IEPs). Many IEPs of students with ADHD include changes in the learning environment and strategies intended to reduce distraction and promote increased attention to school tasks. Suggestions include the following:

> Plan length of activities according to the student's skills, not according to age expectations.
>
> Set manageable goals for task completion.
>
> Seat the student in an area with few distractions.
>
> Provide an area in the classroom or school where the student can release extra energy.
>
> Provide visual reminders, such as a schedule for the day, task-completion lists, and written classroom rules.
>
> Provide visual instructions for tasks, such as pictures or a written list of each of the subtasks necessary for completing the larger task.
>
> Allow the student extra time to complete work.
>
> Reduce the workload by providing shortened assignments, while assuring that the student has sufficiently mastered the skill.
>
> Teach the student how to organize materials.
>
> Teach the student how to create and follow classroom routines.

Therapy. Cognitive-behavioral therapies are effective in teaching individuals with ADHD appropriate strategies to reduce ADHD symptoms. Some of these strategies include instruction in self-monitoring, clarification of rules and expectations, reinforcement of on-task behavior, and training in social skills. When people with ADHD also experience anxiety, depression, or other mental health issues, they should receive therapy or other treatments for these conditions.

While other treatments for ADHD are promoted and used, caution must be exercised when determining which treatment might be most effective for each individual. Some treatments that do not have sufficient research support include restricted diets, colored eyeglass lenses, chiropractic adjustment and bone realignment, and treatment for yeast infection.

ADHD throughout Life

Many symptoms of ADHD in young children differ from those experienced in teen years and adulthood. Whereas most young children with ADHD appear to be overly active and distractible, most adolescents and adults have learned to control much of their outward impulsive and hyperactive behavior, or they avoid situations that require sustained attention (such as a desk job) and activities that inhibit physical movement. Many adolescents and adults report feeling restless and fidgety, and they may try to do several things at once.

Because ADHD can affect school performance if not treated properly, it can also affect personal relationships, particularly in adolescence. Teenagers with ADHD may feel confined by external rules and therefore break those rules, leading to trouble in the family and in other relationships. Adolescents may also experience increased difficulty with schoolwork because organizational demands are heightened as students are expected to have independent task-completion skills.

Most adolescents and many adults still need stimulant medication to be successful in school and work. ADHD is not considered to be a condition that one grows out of, but with appropriate treatment, many of the symptoms can be reduced and a high quality of life is possible.

How Can You Help Yourself If You Have ADHD?

You can do many things to help yourself if you have ADHD. They fall into three main categories: self-awareness, attention strategies, and social support.

You must be aware of your strengths and limitations. Use your natural talents, interests, and motivations to realize goals you have set for yourself. You also have many characteristics that are associated with successful entrepreneurs:

high energy, a tendency to do many projects simultaneously, courage, capacity to be comfortable with change, ability for innovative thinking, and willingness to take risks. Learn to use these strengths. Also realize that many people don't understand what it is like to have ADHD; they may call you *lazy, spacey,* or *daydreamer.* Take the initiative to teach them what it means to have ADHD, and teach them the types of supports you need to be successful.

Some of the supports you may need include learning attention strategies such as using a study carrel or settings with minimal distractions. It often helps to share personal challenges and success stories with others who have experienced similar situations.

How Can You Help Those with ADHD?

To help a person with ADHD, learn what it means to have the disorder. Realize that these individuals are not willfully inattentive, disruptive, or impulsive. Their brains work differently, and this affects their ability to focus. Avoid calling them names or using trite and harmful phrases, such as "Earth to Johnny!" While this may seem funny to others, it isn't funny to Johnny, who doesn't want to be labeled.

Many of the educational and therapeutic supports mentioned earlier can be employed by those not in educational or therapeutic professions. Remember to have a positive attitude and communicate high expectations for the person with ADHD while adapting to his unique learning needs.

What Is It Like to Have ADHD?

"Jimmy, a bright, likable child who has ADHD, is a case in point. Sitting still for three hours of meetings is difficult for most children, but for a child with Jimmy's condition it is impossible. Once when he was six, Jimmy was having a hard time being quiet in sacrament meeting. A big man behind him leaned forward and whispered gruffly, 'If you don't sit still, I'll chop your arms off!' Jimmy tried desperately for about two minutes to sit quietly, but realizing he simply couldn't do it, he turned to his mother and sadly said, 'Just tell him to go ahead and get it over with.'"[2]

Mental Retardation

Mental retardation is a common disability that is manifested before age eighteen and that affects an individual's general abilities for learning and adaptive behavior.

The term *mental retardation* is used in most of the United States and in other countries where English is the primary language, yet terms such as *intellectual disability, cognitive disability, mental impairments,* and *general learning disability* are also used to describe the same condition. Further, labels such as *slow* or *developmentally delayed* are often used by the general public.

Today, common means of describing mental retardation include the types of support such individuals need, rather than how severely they are affected by their disability. The levels of support are described as being *intermittent, limited, extensive,* or *pervasive.* Different types of support can be applied in various circumstances. With this knowledge, providers, family, and friends are able to give individualized support based on needs, strengths, and interests of the individual.

Symptoms of mental retardation include those manifested before age 18, such as:

Significantly below average general intellectual functioning (generally meaning an IQ score of approximately 70 or below)
Substantial difficulty (in at least two areas) in adjusting to environmental demands that require conceptual, social, and practical adaptive skills in such areas as communication, self-care, and social skills

Individuals who have mental retardation will learn concepts at a slower rate than their peers who do not have mental retardation. However, this does not mean that they just need extra time to catch up; in reality, they may never learn some abstract or otherwise difficult concepts. Further, many students with mental retardation have difficulty retaining or remembering concepts they have previously learned. Parents may become frustrated when their child seems to have understood a concept or learned a skill on Friday but then needs to relearn it on Monday.

What Causes Mental Retardation?

There are many causes of mental retardation, which are generally divided into four risk factors. However, most occurrences of mental retardation are of unknown origin.

Biomedical causes of mental retardation include genetic and nutritional factors. Conditions with these causal factors include Down syndrome, phenylketonuria, fragile X syndrome, Prader-Willi syndrome, and Tay-Sachs disease.

Behavioral causes include harmful behaviors, such as infections or diseases carried by the mother (like HIV) and by the mother's substance abuse, including smoking and drug or alcohol abuse while pregnant with the child.

Social factors include poor family or interpersonal interaction, such as minimal child stimulation and adult responsiveness. (Social factors are often associated with mild intellectual deficits.)

Educational-disadvantage factors include the absence of family instruction and other educational supports that promote intellectual development and adaptive skills. (Educational factors are often associated with mild intellectual deficits.)

How Is Mental Retardation Treated?

Mental retardation is a condition that affects general learning ability, but all aspects of an individual's life may become involved. Therefore, treatments must go beyond education. Individuals with mental retardation may need support in the following activities:

Human development (fine motor, gross motor)
Education (functional academics, problem solving)

Home living (housekeeping, dressing)

Community living (transportation, shopping)

Employment (learning job skills, completing work-related tasks)

Health and safety (taking medication, maintaining good nutrition)

Behavior (making appropriate decisions, controlling anger)

Social functions (socializing with the family, making and keeping friends)

Self-protection and obtaining legal services

How Is Mental Retardation Experienced Across a Lifespan?

Mental retardation is a lifelong condition for which the needed levels and types of support differ from individual to individual. Individuals with mental retardation begin life needing pervasive support to grow physically, emotionally, socially, and intellectually, and because of their slow rate of learning, some may continue to need this same level of support throughout their lives.

Some adults with mental retardation may be unable to use the bathroom on their own, feed themselves, or communicate verbally. However, most people with mental retardation need only intermittent or limited support in some areas as they learn and grow from life's experiences. For example, a teenager with mental retardation may need extensive support to assure that she takes the proper dosage of her seizure medication at the right time, but she may need only intermittent support in completing her schoolwork.

How Can You Help Yourself If You Have Mental Retardation?

If you have some form of mental retardation, one of the most important things you can do to help yourself is to believe in yourself. Believe that you are a child of God with divine nature and potential. Believe that you have important work to do while on this earth to improve yourself. Believe that you won't be happy just waiting for your blessings to come after the Resurrection.

Find your strengths, focus on them, and use them to bless your life and the lives of others.

Like others, you must be realistic about your potential. Realize that you can't do everything, and you shouldn't be required to do everything. You have family, friends, and professionals who are willing and able to help. Make sure that your goal for independence does not interfere with your ability to be *interdependent*—helping others as they in turn help you.

Become a self-advocate. Learn of your rights and work with others to assure that these rights are respected. Learn how to recognize bullies or others who may hurt you. Don't be afraid to tell them no and to tell those you trust about times when others make you feel uncomfortable.

How Can You Help Others with Mental Retardation?

One of the most important things you can do to help those with mental retardation is to respect them. Respect is often demonstrated in how we talk about and interact with others. Using *person-first language* is one way to demonstrate respect to those with mental retardation or other disabilities. Such language highlights the human nature of the person rather than focusing on the disability. Person-first language recognizes that disability is just one aspect of the person's life, and it isn't necessarily something that the person *is* ("he is retarded") but rather something that the person *has* ("he has mental retardation").

For example, a teenage girl with Down syndrome may be offended when she is referred to as "the Down's girl," because she sees herself as a Mia Maid who loves hip-hop music, likes watching movies at her friend's house, and has a knack for making chocolate chip cookies.

You can also help individuals with mental retardation by interacting with them. Many want to be included in activities with their peers but are often ignored, neglected, and made to feel unwelcome. Usually only minor adjustments are necessary to promote full inclusion of individuals who are mildly affected by mental retardation. Work with family members and professionals to find out how to make an activity appropriate.

When teaching students with mental retardation, make your examples as *concrete* as possible. Make them real, explicit, and precise so that the concepts you are teaching can be easily understood. For example, to teach the concept of resurrection, you may use a glove to represent the human body and your hand to represent the spirit. However, some people with mental retardation may focus only on the glove and the hand, not transferring that information to the relationship of the body and the spirit. More realistic, tangible examples, such as using a puppet in the form of a human body, may be more easily understood.

Individuals with mental retardation need more *repetition* to learn concepts and skills. Be sure to provide many opportunities to learn a skill, allowing the student to practice in natural environments. This repetition should be made across many situations so the student can *generalize* the skill beyond the classroom. Generalization can occur across materials, instructional cues (a prompt or cue for a certain response), settings, persons, and time of day. Just because Juan can sit quietly in Primary class for ten minutes does not mean he can sit quietly under other circumstances. Generalization cannot be left to chance; it must be planned.

Finally, you should consider the *functionality* of the skill to be taught. Functionality refers to the usefulness of a given skill in the life of the student. A student with mental retardation might find learning to add single digits functional if this skill relates to her real-world experience. For example, if Megan needs to earn two dollars per day for two days before she can rent her favorite DVD, then learning to add 2+2 becomes motivating and functional for her.

What Is It Like to Have Mental Retardation?

"John Drake was four years old when his family noticed that he was mentally regressing for reasons they are even now not sure of. But whatever the cause of the intellectual impairment that left him unable to read or to think analytically, John, now forty-seven, leads a productive life. Congenial and able to remember details, John gets along well with others. He takes a bus to work, where he packages clothing, and lives in an apartment decorated with his own paintings. He likes to entertain friends and visitors, among them assistants who help him with shopping and goal setting.

"John needs help from members of the Church, too. Since John moved into his new place from a sheltered group home, he hasn't been to church much—possibly because he doesn't have a driver's license, and therefore needs a ride to meetings and activities. John wishes he could have a Church calling. He sings, is an Eagle Scout, and serves as a leader for others who are under state supervision in his apartment complex, which makes him think that 'people could learn something from me, too.'

"The members of Garth Wardle's ward have learned a lot from him.

"Intellectually impaired since childhood, Garth, now fifty-seven, serves as assistant to the high priests executive secretary and as his Sunday School class president. Most would agree, however, that Garth's greatest contribution to the ward has been through thirty-five years of Scouting leadership, most recently as the Blazer B leader. Because of Garth's attention to detail, concern for his Scouts, and excellent camping skills, he recently received the Silver Beaver award, one of Scouting's highest honors for adult leaders."[3]

Autism Spectrum Disorders

Autism spectrum disorders (ASD) is a term used to describe disorders that have similar characteristics but vary in their expression of symptoms. They are mainly social and communication disabilities and restricted behaviors, interests, and activities. However, the spectrum of autism can also affect intellectual abilities, sensory sensitivity, and motor skills. No two individuals with ASD are alike; their strengths and weaknesses may fall at various points along several continua.

Autism spectrum disorders are considered to be pervasive developmental disorders (PDD). This means they are persistent and all-encompassing, affect normal development, and have disabling effects in the lives of those diagnosed. Pervasive developmental disorders is an umbrella term describing five related disorders:

Autistic Disorder (known also as autism)
Asperger Disorder (Asperger syndrome)
Rett's Disorder (Rett syndrome)
Childhood Disintegrative Disorder
Pervasive Developmental Disorder—Not Otherwise Specified
(PDD—NOS; autistic-like, autistic tendencies, or atypical autism)

Pervasive Developmental Disorders

Autism

Asperger Syndrome

Rett Syndrome

Childhood
Disintegrative Disorders

PPD
Not Otherwise Specified

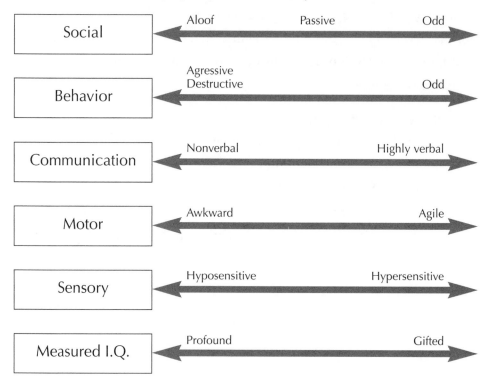

Common Symptoms of Autism Spectrum Disorders

Each of these disorders has distinct characteristics. Generally, Asperger syndrome is acknowledged as different from the others because it is not diagnosed if the child has not exhibited significant delays or disorders in language skills. Individuals with Asperger syndrome, which also affects social and behavioral skills, have normal or gifted intellectual skills, whereas intellectual disabilities often, but not always, accompany the other PDDs.

Common symptoms of Autism Spectrum Disorders include the following:

Social

Delayed development of appropriate peer relationships

Impaired spontaneous sharing (interests, achievements)

Lack of social and emotional reciprocity

Impaired nonverbal behavior (eye contact, facial expressions)

Behavioral

Inflexible, nonfunctional routines or rituals

Repetitive motor actions (hand flapping, body rocking)

Persistent preoccupation and restricted patterns of interest

Self-injurious behavior

Abnormal mood

Hyperactivity

Odd responses to sensory experiences

Communication

Delay or lack of spoken language

Conversational impairment

Repetitive language

Poor receptive language

Poor expressive language

What Causes Autism Spectrum Disorders?

The exact cause of ASD remains unknown, but there is no single specific cause. Recent clinical and biological research has demonstrated that autism is a neurological disorder that may begin before birth. The strongest evidence to date supports a genetic component. However, investigations into environmental toxins, problems with the immune system, and other biological factors are being conducted. Autism is not caused by poor parenting, failure of a mother to bond with her child, or a child's willful retreat into his own world.

How Are Autism Spectrum Disorders Treated?

The methods of treating ASD vary. Some are experimental, resulting in many different outcomes. Some treatments claim to "cure" or "recover" the child with autism, while others are targeted to reduce the effects of the disorder. There are several types of treatments; the most common include these components:

Educational

Applied behavioral analysis—breaking tasks into small, manageable parts and reinforcing success

Structured teaching—providing visual and structural support to prevent failure

Relationship development—developing a positive and nurturing relationship with the child

Social stories—using stories that describe how to engage in positive social situations

Augmentative and alternative communication—sign language, picture-based systems, computerized communication devices

Biomedical

Nutritional/dietary

Wheat/milk-free diets

Vitamin, herb, and mineral supplements

Medication

Therapies

Speech/language

Occupational

Physical

Sensory integration—visual, tactile, auditory

Relaxation techniques

Autism Spectrum Disorders Across a Lifespan

The intensity and duration of the symptoms of ASD vary across a lifespan. Depending on the severity of symptoms, toddlers may demonstrate much more extreme reactions to their environment than adolescents or adults with autism.

Adolescents with ASD experience the same challenges as those without disabilities. However, their intense reactions to normal events may worsen some of these challenges. Many adolescents with ASD develop friendships based on common intense interests, such as computer games, Japanese animation, and science fiction; and they learn to choose environments where they know they'll be accepted.

Instruction of youth with ASD is incomplete if it does not prepare them to acquire and maintain employment, manage their money, use their academic skills in everyday living, and engage in appropriate social skills, such as following directions, accepting "no" for an answer, asking for help, and disagreeing politely with others. However, most adults with autism do not live independently; they live with family, or they live in group homes or other supported living environments.

Some adults with ASD have written books or have developed Web sites to help others understand how their life experiences are both enriched and challenged by their autism. A common theme is to respect people with ASD, despite their unusual behaviors and habits, rather than try to cure or change them.

How Can You Help Yourself if You Have ASD?

Most individuals with ASD are classified as having autism. Up to 70 percent of those with autism have an accompanying intellectual disability that inhibits outward expression of self-awareness and self-advocacy. These individuals often rely on family members, school personnel, and community support for improving their quality of life. However, many individuals with high-functioning autism or Asperger syndrome have made great strides in advocacy and in sharing information with the public.

As an individual with ASD, you will benefit from increasing your self-awareness. Many adolescents and adults who have previously considered themselves odd or unconventional have received comfort in finding an ASD label, which provides an explanation for the way they are. You may be like many individuals who do not consider Asperger syndrome to be a disability but rather a mere *difference* in the way you view and experience life.

Knowing the effects ASD has on daily life will help you develop appropriate coping strategies, learning strategies, and social relationships. It is important that you provide information to your family, caregivers, education professionals, and employers regarding your interests, preferences, and goals. If a current strategy, therapy, or treatment is not working, then you have the right to stop the treatment.

Many individuals with ASD have developed social relationships with others by joining a local autism group or e-mail discussion list, entering autism-related chat rooms, going to autism retreats and conferences (held by and for those with ASD), and joining clubs (such as science fiction book clubs or chess clubs). You may engage in less structured face-to-face social relationships by interacting with others who have similar interests.

Build on your strengths and pursue your special interests. However, don't bore others with your special interests if they don't understand you or share your passion.

Finally, beware of bullies, particularly when they pretend to be your friend. They may take advantage of you. Stand up for your rights, and know what to do when you have been treated unfairly.

How Can You Help Others with ASD?

You can do many things to help persons with ASD. First, do what you can to understand what it means to have ASD. There are many books, Web sites, and other materials you can access. Realize that because of communication impairments, some individuals with ASD appear to be noncompliant or stubborn, when in reality they may not understand the directions given to them.

However, the best way to understand ASD is to be a friend of someone with ASD. You may think that he doesn't want to be friends with you, but most likely he just doesn't know how to engage in regular social relationships. He needs you to be understanding and tolerant of his differences and then to nurture and teach him appropriate social skills.

Next, you can help persons with ASD understand what is expected of them in various environments. Generally, individuals with autism spectrum disorders respond well to environments that are highly structured, visual, and predictable. For example, they need to know what is expected of them in various settings and what they need to do at certain times of the day. Visual schedules such as calendars, personal digital assistants, daily planners, and picture-based schedules facilitate the predictability of a structured setting. Also, providing a break area for individuals with ASD helps them to know they have a safe place to retreat when they are overstimulated.

What Is It Like to Have ASD?

"Hour after hour he rocks there, this beautiful little three-year-old stranger who is our son. Through the family room window the afternoon sun highlights his well-formed body and flawless features. Brothers and sisters run by, calling his name. He stares, riveted in his rhythmic rocking. Repeated attempts to hold him or share his world are stiffly rejected. . . . At night we lay him in bed, and our good night kisses are pushed away. . . . Half sleeping in the bedroom above, we hear the light switch being flicked on and off, on and off, by his tiny hand. Morning comes all too quickly, but he does not call or reach out for us. . . . We dress him and the cycle begins again. Tennyson unknowingly described our Brian when he wrote, 'He is so near and yet so far.'"[4]

Notes

1. Laurie Wilson Thornton, "The Hidden Handicap," *Ensign,* Apr. 1990, 46.

2. Thornton, "The Hidden Handicap," 46.

3. Elizabeth VanDenBerghe, "Helping and Being Helped by the Intellectually Impaired," *Ensign,* Oct. 1993, 27.

4. Carmen B. Pingree, "'So Near and Yet So Far': Living with Autism," *Ensign,* Aug. 1983, 57.

10

Asperger Syndrome

Richard A. Moody and Carol P. Moody

Kyle, age fourteen, is viewed as a clueless geek who is "out of it." He's obsessed with trains, local train schedules, and the aerodynamics of train engines. At a moment's notice, he can rattle off the arrivals and departures of all the Amtrak trains in his local area.

In preschool, few people took notice of Kyle's obsession with trains. In early childhood, other children found it easy to overlook his quirky behaviors. Those were better days—when his young peers were innocent, naïve, and accepting of him. However, as Kyle has entered the middle school years, life has become a war zone. From his perspective, the recess and lunch hours might as well be the streets of Baghdad.

Like a scene out of a *National Geographic* special, Kyle, the weak species in the animal kingdom, is targeted and preyed upon. Scores of typically developing young men quickly zero in on Kyle's overtly awkward behaviors, vulnerability, and uncoordinated movements. Kyle can no longer rely upon the protection of childhood innocence; he now has to make his way through a social minefield with few natural skills to protect him.

For Kyle, even church activities can be a battleground as fellow priesthood quorum members hone in on his weaknesses. The Scouting and Young Men programs, designed to help young men become productive, goal-oriented individuals, are implemented as intermediate steps in the journey leading to serving missions and marrying in the temple. But to Kyle, these activities and programs are confusing, unpredictable, and agitating. He views merit badge requirements, campouts, and sporting activities—intended to help young men productively channel their youthful energy and develop self-esteem—as chaotic and even humiliating.

Kyle is poorly equipped to understand sarcasm and participate in the quick, witty conversational exchanges within his quorum. Instead, he wants to talk endlessly about trains with no regard for his conversational partners' lack of interest. He especially doesn't understand the reason he should earn merit badges or the utility in attending Scout camp. Well-meaning Church leaders may view Kyle as being lazy, lacking discipline, being the product of bad parenting, or even having spiritual or character flaws. Then, if Kyle chooses not to serve a mission, some might speculate that he has a worthiness problem or that he lacks discipline.

"So, what *is* wrong with Kyle?" This is the resounding question of his peers, teachers, and ecclesiastical leaders. The answer is that Kyle has Asperger syndrome. At first glance, he may appear fairly normal. But upon closer contact, it becomes apparent that he has difficulty with natural conversation, has an intense fascination for a particular area of interest, and is a bit clumsy and awkward. To Kyle, the social world is confusing, unpredictable, and illogical. Most typical individuals understand social interactions and expectations automatically, quickly, and naturally. Kyle, however, lacks social understanding— the mortar of our existence as social beings.

Unfortunately, many individuals like Kyle go undiagnosed and deal with severe social impairments with little support. Because the world is largely social, navigating those waters can be uncertain and overwhelming. Of those who are left undiagnosed, teachers, church leaders, and even parents may have the same expectations for the individual with Asperger syndrome as they do for typically developing siblings or peers.

What Is Asperger Syndrome?

Children diagnosed with Asperger syndrome demonstrate similarities to children with high-functioning autism (HFA), a milder form of autism (see chapter 9, "Disorders That Begin in Childhood," and chapter 18, "Cognitive Disorders"). Children with HFA meet the autistic spectrum disorder criteria but have comparatively normal thinking, learning (meaning they have normal intelligence—IQ's above 70), and language skills (they speak close to the level of other typical children their age).[1]

Those with Asperger syndrome may behave similarly to those with autism, but they do not typically share the same difficulties with communication. This means that individuals with Asperger syndrome may have similar types of problems with back and forth social interactions and with restrictive and repetitive behaviors, but they don't exhibit the same problems with language production—grammar, vocabulary, and pronunciation. In fact, a diagnosis of Asperger's requires that a child's language develop on time by having a few words by age two and by producing simple phrases ("more milk" or "go bye-bye") by age three. Some children with Asperger syndrome may even seem remarkably advanced in their speech development and sound like little adults by age three.

Child Development

A developing child who has Asperger syndrome can appear just fine, reaching most developmental milestones right on schedule. The child may even possess a happy, even temperament. As the child becomes verbal, he may develop a large vocabulary and yet have difficulty with using language. The child may demonstrate pronoun reversal and refer to himself as "he" or "you" instead of as "me" or "I."

Such children may also display *echolalia,* a condition in which they repeat the content of speech they hear or recite scripts from a favorite movie word for word, over and over again. These children may lack the natural give and take of conversation. Instead, they may bombard people with questions or respond inappropriately to the questions or comments of others.

As a child with Asperger syndrome develops play skills, he may engage in parallel play alongside other children, which is appropriate until about age three. Between the ages of three and four, most children move into more socially complex play. For the child with Asperger syndrome, interest in, and ability to engage in, interactive play can be limited or even absent. As the child's peers engage in more complex social play, the child with Asperger's may spend more time alone and withdraw into his own little world. The child may give the impression that he is not interested in play interactions, but he likely may not know how to join in the play or understand the rules associated with interactive play.

Because of adequate and even seemingly advanced language development and normal intelligence, the child's parents may not have cause to worry until their child enters school. Kindergarten is typically when social awkwardness and restricted interests seem more obvious when compared to other typically developing children. This is also a time when the quirky behavior can interfere with normal functioning and age-appropriate social expectations.

Social Behaviors

Children with Asperger's are usually perceived as quite unusual because of their peculiar social behavior. They have limited use of gestures and facial expressions, their movements are clumsy and stiff, and they may have a restricted range of motion. Also, they may have a strange gaze as if they were daydreaming, appearing not to be listening when spoken to. When they speak, even if excited about something, they may show little voice inflection or ability to modulate their volume. Typical behaviors demonstrate a lack of social awareness as in giggling when someone is in distress and having a tantrum over a seemingly insignificant change in routine.[2]

The child with Asperger's may prefer being and playing on his own.

When peers want to be included, the child can become extremely agitated and may ignore them altogether. If there is interactive play, the child may come across as being selfish, insisting on playing by his own rules and following his own routines. The child has little or no room for flexibility, and he may be unsophisticated in discerning that rules apply to everyone involved. When he is disciplined for a particular behavior and then witnesses someone else getting away with the same behavior, he may become furious and passionately protest the inconsistency. An insistence on sameness and rigidity colors most of the child's social interpretations and interactions.

At recess or lunchtime, the child is often found on his own in a secluded area. He may prefer to interact with older adults who are more predictable and calm:

Knowing the classroom rules and consequences, Ryan intentionally acts out or misbehaves in class so that his teacher will make him stay inside during recess. This avoidant behavior allows him to get out of facing the unpredictability and, at times, hostility awaiting him during recess. The stigma of being in trouble with the teacher is much more tolerable than the dicey world of the playground.

Children with Asperger's also demonstrate narrowed areas of interest in unusual topics:

Eight-year-old Brandon developed a keen interest in The Beatles after watching a documentary about them on television. For his birthday and Christmas, Brandon would ask for Beatles books, movies, and compact discs; he couldn't get enough. He could name all the song titles and the correct order of songs on each album. He knew birthdates, marriage dates, and all concert dates and venues. When interacting with peers, he would ask if they had ever heard of The Beatles. Regardless of how they answered, he would then proceed to bombard them with everything he knew about them. Needless to say, this didn't bode well for his social life.

Typical peer pressure to give heed to the latest fashion, music, or gadget trends tends not to show up on the radar of those with Asperger's. They usually have no interest or desire to conform to peer pressure. This typically contributes to their being left out by peers:

Jenny, age sixteen, was just a year younger than her brother, Eric, who had Asperger's. Jenny was appalled by the way he wore his pants cinched up several inches above his waist. She felt a strong need to try to protect him from ridicule by pleading with him to dress and wear his clothing in a more contemporary manner. He said he didn't like the feel of having his pants hanging down. Besides, Eric added, he couldn't care less about what anyone thought about how he dressed.

Sensory Problems

Some individuals with Asperger syndrome are overly sensitive and easily overwhelmed by everyday sounds, tastes, odors, and touch. Sudden, unpredictable sounds can be extremely agitating to some people with Asperger's. It can be torture for them to hear a baby suddenly scream or to be in the same room with someone laughing loudly. Often they exhibit an extreme startled reaction or irritation to normal sights, sounds, or smells.

One boy, for example, adamantly refused to hold his mother's hand when crossing the street because he didn't want to get the scent of her lotion on his hands. Another child refused to go into a local grocery store because of the smells and unpredictable sounds he might experience.

Strong preferences to wearing particular clothing can become an issue. A child may insist that tags be removed from shirts so that they don't rub against his skin. Clothing may feel too tight or too loose, or socks may be worn inside out because of discomfort with stitching.

Learning Styles

Children with Asperger's can be puzzling for teachers. They can appear gifted and talented because they have an excellent memory and can recite minute details that often go unnoticed by others. They can become proficient in naming facts and dates and in remembering names even if they are insignificant to the overall theme or topic.

Typically, children with Asperger's can perform satisfactorily in school until around the third grade, when learning becomes more difficult, abstract, and socially interactive. It is difficult for these children to learn concepts and then apply them across different situations, particularly if they need to work cooperatively in groups, catch on to subtle reasoning, or understand exceptions to rules.

These children tend to be literal in how they interpret the social world. Idioms are very much part of American culture. It is quite easy for most people to automatically pick up on phrases like, "Has the cat got your tongue?" "Keep your eye on the ball," or "If looks could kill, I'd be dead." But these phrases can become quite confusing for those with Asperger's because they take them quite literally. They might ask, "Why would a person pull out his eye and place it on a ball?"

Learning styles differ because of how individuals with Asperger syndrome process language and socially related information. They need more time, more concrete examples, and more opportunities to practice how concepts can be generalized to different situations. They especially need help to take another's perspective. Understanding that another's feelings and thoughts are different from their own is particularly difficult.

Working with Those Who Have Asperger's

Through greater understanding and implementation of effective strategies, people who work with affected individuals can help them have more successful social experiences. Some parents find it useful to prepare a short fact sheet about their child to give to adults who teach or interact with their child. This information gives helpers tips on how to be accepting and supportive.

Professional helpers. Parents can enlist the help of involved professionals, such as speech therapists and occupational therapists, to help design intervention plans for use at school, home, and church. Speech therapists, for example, can offer ideas to help improve the individual's understanding and usage of language and conversational skills. Therapists can also provide a social skills group to practice interactions.

Occupational therapists (OT's) can help with ideas for improved sensory regulation. For example, an OT can help structure a typical day to include time-outs from overly stimulating activities, or the OT can suggest earplugs for loud events, such as football games or school assemblies. Psychiatrists and psychologists can assist with accompanying mood or anxiety disorders.

Teachers using the LDS Church curriculum. Working with individuals with Asperger syndrome requires knowledge of the disorder, as well as a recognition of specific strengths and weaknesses. Acknowledgment of individual talents, such as memorization skills and orientation for details, can help individuals feel appreciated and a part of the group.

Additionally, explaining abstract gospel principles, such as *service* or *testimony,* using real-life, concrete examples helps make learning easier. Even acting out scripture stories can help with understanding the perspectives of prophets and other leaders of the Church. Creativity and working with family members is key to making an experience at church rewarding. Finding another person similar in age to be a "church buddy" is also helpful. With the family's permission, a sensitive discussion about the individual's need for social understanding and help will be beneficial to all involved. Specific mention of a label or diagnosis need not be included, depending on the age of the affected individual and the wishes of the family.

Decoding the social world. Children with Asperger's lack a natural understanding of social interactions. What most people know without being taught about socializing is confusing and haphazard to affected individuals. Those with Asperger's need more time working on cognitive thinking skills and social routines to decode their world.

Children with Asperger's can easily read a book but not a face; they are tuned into facts but not feelings. Consequently, they need to be taught the how and why of social relationships. Helping them understand the social world involves teaching them problem-solving and perspective-taking skills; how to decode jokes, sarcasm, and idioms; and how to make related comments without asking a series of questions. In essence, they need to learn to read nonverbal cues while maintaining a back-and-forth conversation.[3] As one might guess, such decoding and dissecting of the social world involves a long-term, sometimes lifelong, process of acquiring and effectively using skills. It can be a marathon of learning information and behaviors, getting feedback and guidance, and ultimately, having positive experiences.

One example of a particularly helpful technique often used with children with Asperger's is writing social stories.[4] Social stories help children to make sense of social interactions and to see how their behavior can affect others. Following is an example of a social story about using self-control.

I Can Use Self-Control

When I feel frustrated, I can do the following:

Stop and count to ten

Think about how my body feels

Think of my choices: walk away, take a deep breath, talk to someone, write about what I feel

Act out my best choices (other people like it when I use self-control)

The preceding story can help a child with Asperger syndrome understand the concept of self-control and what it means to himself and to others.

Children with Asperger's need continual support with reading nonverbal communication, such as body language and understanding emotional expression. Helping children in this area involves providing numerous opportunities to practice with a skilled adult or supportive peer. One technique that is useful is watching movie clips that portray a variety of emotions of people in social interactions. A skilled adult can pause the clips and discuss the emotions being expressed and the accompanying nonverbal cues.

For their growth and improvement, children with Asperger's need multiple opportunities to practice understanding emotional expression. Helping those with Asperger's recognize the emotional expression of others can help them interpret the feelings of others. This skill helps them know that other people can think and feel differently from what they think and feel. Eventually, they can better read emotions and learn words to communicate their own emotions and the feelings of others. Then they can also role-play with others in a supportive social skills group or supportive family setting.

Social and peer support. Techniques that help affected individuals more closely understand and examine social interactions can also help them know what to say and when to say it in social situations. They need to learn to work in groups and be part of teams. Essential to this process is identifying supportive and empathetic people and peers who can help affected individuals with social interactions. Such supportive individuals can help them understand typical social interactions and even rehearse with them what is appropriate to do in each setting.

Working with supportive peers and other helpful people can also guide those with Asperger's to know how and when to ask for help, how to start and end a conversation, and how to recognize what conversational content is appropriate and what is not. Also, a leader or mentor to help individuals develop job skills and leisure-time skills is essential to long-term success. Overall, interacting with empathetic leaders and friends helps them feel successful while getting valuable feedback and information about their social behavior.

Discovering their strengths. Most important, individuals with Asperger syndrome need to see themselves as uniquely important and competent contributors to society. Significant others and church leaders need to emphasize an individual's personal strengths and abilities. Individuals with Asperger's can realize that they are different but also that they have great individual worth. Realizing real strengths and interests while being participating members of the LDS Church is key to maintaining involvement and enjoying rewarding interactions. Those with Asperger syndrome can realize a truly happy and fulfilling life.

Notes

1. American Psychiatric Association, *Diagnostic and Statistical Manual of Mental Disorders.*

2. Attwood, *Asperger's Syndrome: A Guide for Parents and Professionals,* 30–32.

3. Klin and Volkmar, "Treatment and Intervention Guidelines," in *Asperger Syndrome,* 340.

4. C. A. Gray, "Social Stories: Improving Responses of Students with Autism with Accurate Social Information," *Focus on Autistic Behavior,* 8 (1993): 1–10.

11

Anxiety Disorders

Marleen S. Williams, W. Dean Belnap, and John P. Livingstone

Anxiety is a part of normal life. You have likely experienced feelings of anxiety in stressful situations, such as speaking or performing in public, taking a test, or doing an important assignment. We all know the experience of feeling weak in the knees, jittery, or like there are butterflies in our stomach. These are normal feelings of anxiety that everyone has from time to time.

In some circumstances, anxiety is helpful. For example, if you have to walk alone some evening down a dark, unfamiliar street, feeling a little afraid can help you to be alert, prepared, and ready to respond should you encounter something that seems threatening. Your body experiences anxiety as a means of self-protection and to keep you alert.

Normal anxiety responses include a surge in heart rate and blood pressure, as well as increased breathing, sweating, and overall metabolism. These are healthy responses to threatening situations. But if you feel extremely worried or afraid much of the time, or if you repeatedly feel panicky, consider seeking medical advice.

How Does Normal Anxiety Differ from an Anxiety Disorder?

People who experience anxiety disorders have symptoms that are so severe that they interfere with their normal daily activities. Unlike the normally brief, relatively mild anxiety responses described above, feelings of fear and panic become chronic, relentless, and overwhelming. Anxiety disorders interfere with the quality and enjoyment of life. They may be so severe that a person cannot leave the house, work effectively, or enjoy relationships with others.

Anxiety disorders are the most common category of mental disorders. Approximately nineteen million American adults and millions of children suffer from an anxiety disorder. Most anxiety disorders start in early childhood, but they tend to last well into the later years. Many people may have a biological tendency toward an anxiety disorder, but it may lie dormant until triggered by an unusually stressful event. Older adults can become more susceptible to anxiety that is caused by illness or a medication. Common symptoms of anxiety disorders may include the following:

Overwhelming feelings of fear
Uncontrollable and intense thoughts and worries that occur again and again
Painful, intrusive memories
Recurring nightmares
Physical symptoms, such as feeling sick to your stomach, startling easily, feeling tense, feeling short of breath, experiencing a fast heartbeat
Difficulty relaxing or sleeping

Related Disorders

Panic attack is a sudden wave of intense apprehension, fearfulness, or terror with physical symptoms, such as shortness of breath, fast heartbeat, chest pain, dizziness, sweating, nausea, abdominal distress, chills, hot flashes, or other unpleasant sensations.

Whenever Larry felt overwhelmed by too many demands on his time, his heart began beating quickly, and he felt as if he could not breathe. Sometimes his heart would beat so loudly in his head that he felt as if he were going crazy. He could feel his hands shake, and he feared he was having a heart attack. He visited his family doctor, who ruled out a heart condition but recognized that Larry was experiencing panic attacks.

Agoraphobia is an intense fear of experiencing incapacitating or extremely embarrassing panic symptoms or other physical problems. Individuals with agoraphobia are often afraid to leave the house or go out in public places.

Larry became so worried about having another panic attack when in a public place that he became fearful of leaving home. He was afraid that his panic would be so intense that he would lose control and be embarrassed if others knew about his attacks. His fear made it difficult for him to attend meetings and other public assignments.

Phobia is intense anxiety caused by exposure to a feared object or situation.

Suzy was afraid of worms. She would get very upset whenever she came near one. Her fear became so great that whenever it rained and worms came up and covered the sidewalks, she would not go to school.

Obsessive-compulsive disorder is characterized by recurrent, unwanted, distressing thoughts that a person cannot control. A person with this disorder uses behaviors or rituals to reduce anxiety provoked by the thoughts. The symptoms are chronic and recurring. They cause significant distress or interfere with normal activity. They often are related to ideas and subjects that the person may find offensive and objectionable. The rituals may be either behaviors or thoughts used to try to get rid of unwanted thoughts. Common rituals include washing, checking, putting things in order, repeating comforting words over and over, counting, and other mental activities. If unable to perform the ritual, the person will experience increased anxiety. Obsessive-compulsive disorder can occur in children. It may be triggered by stressful events, a high fever, or a head injury.

Jared was a careful young man who took good care of his health. When he left home to attend college, he began to worry constantly about getting sick. He feared that his new surroundings were not clean enough, and he could not stop thinking about germs. If he touched a doorknob or other object that was frequently touched by others, he had to wash his hands immediately in order to stop worrying. This ritual of constant washing interfered with his ability to attend class and participate in normal social activities. He had a strong desire to serve an LDS mission but was very afraid he would be called to serve somewhere that might not be "clean enough."

Sister Smith worried constantly about not being good enough. She frequently feared that she would accidentally or unknowingly commit sins, even though she tried hard to live a good life. Each week she would stop her bishop to confess something that she believed she had neglected or not done right during the week. Each week, he reassured her that she was striving to keep the commandments and that her offenses were normal, human errors. She could not rid herself of constant, nagging thoughts that she was a sinful person, and she worked harder to be perfect.

Post-traumatic stress disorder and acute stress disorder are characterized by chronic symptoms that develop following a traumatic event that threatens a person's life, safety, or well-being. These symptoms include reexperiencing the event through intrusive memories or dreams, feeling as if the event is recurring, experiencing intense distress when events or cues remind the person of the trauma, avoiding or withdrawing from normal activities that may remind the person of the trauma, having difficulty feeling normal emotions, and feeling chronically irritable or wound up and having trouble falling asleep.

Brother Wilson recently returned from military service in Iraq. He was proud of having served his country, but he began to struggle with psychological symptoms after he returned. He had witnessed multiple bombings in which members of his company had been killed. He had barely escaped death and had frequently feared for his life while in Iraq. He thought when he returned home, it would all be over. Instead, he has constant nightmares of being on a dangerous mission. He wakes up dripping with sweat and with his heart pounding. Whenever he hears a loud, unexpected noise, he becomes so startled that one time he actually fell to the floor and covered his head. He feels agitated and anxious whenever he watches news reports of Iraq on television. He had been an emotionally expressive person before going to Iraq, but his wife has noticed that he seldom expresses tender emotions any more. He seems to be emotionally numb except for periodic outbursts of anger.

Sister Mano lived in a place where frequent earthquakes occurred. She had felt several minor tremors, but they had never frightened her until a powerful earthquake shook her town without warning. Several of her friends were killed, and her home was destroyed. She had barely left her home when the earthquake hit. She felt fortunate to be alive and at first felt relief. After a few weeks, however, she began to have nightmares about the earthquake. She found it difficult to relax enough to fall asleep. She felt anxious when indoors and carefully watched for any sign of movement in the buildings she entered. When she took a streetcar, the rumbling noise and motion frightened her even though she knew she was safe. Sometimes it was as if she could actually see it all happening again. She started to avoid riding streetcars.

Social phobia is a strong fear of social situations, such as participating in conversations, attending social events, speaking in public, and dating. This fear is especially intense if the person is afraid he will not perform well or will be embarrassed. This fear leads to avoiding these situations.

Brent was an active seventeen-year-old priest in his ward. He was terrified of speaking in public. He worried constantly that he would not say something right or that others would laugh at him if he made a mistake. He wanted to participate in speaking assignments with the other youth in his ward. He would become so frightened, however, that if asked to speak in sacrament meeting, he would feel physically sick the day of the meeting. He also found it difficult to speak with girls his age. He had never been on a date because he was too afraid to ask anyone. His fear also kept him from giving spoken reports in school. He would rather fail the assignment than speak in front of a class.

Generalized anxiety disorder is excessive anxiety and chronic worry about a variety of things. Anxiety may be experienced with physical symptoms, such as muscle tension, dizziness, restlessness, excessive fatigue, concentration problems, and sleeping difficulties.

Rick described himself as a "worrier." He had been this way since childhood. He tried not to worry, but there was always something that made him upset and over-concerned. His body felt so tense that at times his muscles hurt. His constant worrying made it difficult to concentrate on work or other responsibilities that took mental energy. It would irritate him that his parents did not share his worries and fears.

Anxiety can be caused by medical conditions, medications, or drug use.

Elder Johnson grew up in a desert community. When he began serving as a missionary in a place with many trees, he began to be troubled with allergies. He found an over-the-counter medication at the drug store that seemed to stop the sneezing and watery eyes. He noticed, however, that he started feeling anxious and wound up. Often he felt so nervous that he could hardly sit still. His mission president recommended that he visit the local doctor who cared for the missionaries. The doctor recognized the symptoms as a side effect of the allergy medication and prescribed a medication that helped the allergies but had fewer side effects.

What Causes Anxiety Disorders?

Your body's anxiety response originates in the brain, but like most mental disorders, biology, genes, behavior, upbringing, psychology, and learned coping skills can all interact and influence the length and severity of anxiety disorders. Scientists have discovered certain abnormalities in the brains of chronic anxiety sufferers. Neuroimaging has helped identify the structures and circuits that are active when anxiety strikes. Chemicals in the brain called neurotransmitters (such as norepinephrine and serotonin) also play a role in anxiety. This is why medications that target these chemicals can help in reducing symptoms of anxiety.

The nervous system throughout the body is able to trigger feelings of fight or flight. These interactions create responses that are experienced as anxiety. Correcting biochemical imbalances helps the brain to function more normally and reduces the risk of severe anxiety.

Anxiety disorders have been found to run in families, suggesting a genetic basis for more intense responses in certain people. This genetic tendency can be managed by learning coping strategies for the body's responses.

Constant stress or traumatic events can actually create changes in the brain that lead to anxiety disorders. When people, especially children, are constantly overwhelmed by excessive fear or threat, the brain trains itself to react differently. Chronic or highly stressful events in childhood make it difficult for the developing brain to learn to respond normally. Such experiences can include abuse or neglect, emotional deprivation, and separation from people with whom children have an important attachment. The Savior's warning concerning our obligation to protect children (Matthew 18:5–6) is a reminder of the importance of caring for the emotional safety of children.

Chronic emotional trauma, as well as addictions, can cause an increase in hormones in the brain. They can create an open faucet that floods the body with excessive hormones. This can keep the body in a constant state of alert. Intense childhood events, such as being attacked by a dog, can also lead to fears and phobias in adulthood.

Personality traits also play a role in the development of anxiety disorders. Some traits, such as shyness, are inherited. Children who are shy and inhibited are more likely to develop anxiety disorders. People who are overly critical of themselves or sensitive to criticism and rejection are also more vulnerable.

Patterns of running away or using avoidance as a main way of coping with fears can also contribute to anxiety disorders.

Medical illnesses have also been shown to create changes in the brain that lead to intense anxiety responses. Some medical conditions that affect other body organs and systems can initiate the onset of anxiety disorders. Some prescription medications, as well as over-the-counter medications (including caffeine), also cause anxiety reactions. Exposure to such chemicals as paint fumes, some insecticides, and many illegal drugs can cause anxiety disorders. It is important to see a medical doctor to rule out these sources if they are suspected as being the cause of an anxiety disorder.

Anxiety can also be learned by a process called classical conditioning or by observational learning. Classical conditioning occurs when an otherwise nonfrightening event or object is repeatedly paired with a frightening event or object. For example, if a child is teased or humiliated whenever he speaks in public, he may learn to experience intense anxiety whenever asked to speak in a meeting. When the child becomes an adult, giving a talk in public may trigger intense anxiety even though he is now in a supportive and caring environment.

Observational learning is acquired when a person observes the reactions of others. For example, if a child observes his father getting tense and afraid whenever he sees a dog, the child may also learn to fear dogs and develop a phobia.

Psychological factors, such as how a person interprets events and conditions, can also contribute to anxiety. Negative beliefs about one's own worth, skills, and ability to manage the demands of life can create excessive stress that triggers anxiety. Feeling helpless or being in situations where the person feels unable to predict, control, or obtain results can also contribute to anxiety.

How Are Anxiety Disorders Treated?

If you think you may have an anxiety disorder, see a physician for a physical exam. This exam can rule out physical illnesses with symptoms similar to anxiety, such as an ulcer, overactive thyroid, or asthma. It is also helpful to tell your doctor if you take any medicines or substances, such as caffeine, diet pills, or decongestants.

There are three primary modes of treatment: medication, cognitive-behavioral therapy, and exposure therapy. Interpersonal and skill-training therapies may also be useful if the source of anxiety is related to problems in these areas.

Medications can, in many cases, reduce or eliminate anxiety symptoms (see chapter 3, "The Brain and Medical Treatment for Mental Disorders").

Several types of therapy, especially cognitive-behavioral therapy, also help control anxiety by teaching people to adopt more positive thoughts and behavioral patterns.

Exposure therapy teaches people how to relax the body. They are then gradually exposed either to real-life situations or mental imagery of things they fear. They learn through gradual exposure to overcome phobias and unreasonable fears.

Anxiety management focuses on teaching relaxation techniques, such as deep breathing and muscle relaxation to help control anxiety. Cognitive restructuring teaches people how to recognize the thought processes that lead to anxiety and replace them with new thoughts and expectations. Group skill-training therapy can also be of significant help in building confidence in social situations.

How Can You Help Yourself?

Suggested ways to help yourself include learning relaxation strategies, such as the following:

Relax muscles by choosing a specific muscle, holding it tight for a few seconds, and then relaxing it. Work through all of the major muscle groups in the body until you feel more relaxed.

Breathing deeply and slowly restores the oxygen-carbon dioxide ratio in your body and reduces anxiety. Try to focus your thinking on your breathing. To practice deep breathing, place your hands just above your navel so that your fingers touch each other. Breathe slowly and deeply to make your fingertips part. Hold your breath for a second or two and then breathe out slowly.

Exercise regularly. Research shows that yoga is especially helpful in calming anxiety.

Get sufficient sleep. Try to have regular hours for sleeping and waking so your body stays in a pattern.

Avoid self-medication with drugs, alcohol, tobacco, caffeine, or over-the-counter substances. You may think it helps temporarily, but self-medication can actually intensify the problem later. Many substances act as stimulants in your body and can make the anxiety worse.

Try to understand the things that have made you anxious in the past. You can recognize *triggers* for your anxiety and try to manage those events and thoughts that are upsetting you. Most people who experience anxiety try to cope by avoiding events, activities, and things they fear. However, running away usually makes the anxiety worse. Learning to confront fears safely and calmly is more effective than avoidance. Developing skills to manage triggers is a more lasting way of reducing anxiety.

Do relaxing activities before you try to sleep. Engage in pleasant thoughts and activities on a regular basis. Soothing music can also help to calm the brain.

Learn to ride out panic attacks by slow deep breathing and relaxing. Panic attacks usually reach a peak and then taper off and stop. Getting upset about having them usually prolongs them and makes them worse.

What is it Like to Have an Anxiety Disorder?

"Libby Salk was sitting in a restaurant with family and friends when, without warning, she felt a dull pain in her head. Suddenly, she became dizzy, and her heart began racing. 'I felt sure I was going to pass out,' she recalls, 'and thought I must be having a heart attack or some kind of seizure.' When she stood up, explaining that she thought she needed to go to a hospital, her legs almost gave way and her arms grew numb. Terrified, she wondered if she was going to die.

"Libby was not in any danger of dying; she was experiencing her first panic attack. The attacks recurred over the next several months as Libby went to doctor after doctor, looking for an explanation for her problem. She became frightened of being in a place where she could not get help if she had another attack. Sitting in church or in a crowded theater became extremely stressful.

"Even when she was not having a full-blown attack, Libby felt more and more anxious, sometimes even disoriented. She had trouble concentrating at work and found herself forgetting common words and familiar names. Over the next two years, she experienced a variety of physical complaints—from severe headaches to difficulty in swallowing. Occasionally, her heart would suddenly start racing in the middle of the night, waking her from a sound sleep.

"'One particularly bad night, I called a dear friend from my ward,' recalls Libby. 'I couldn't explain what was wrong with me, but she sat with me through a long night when the feelings of fear and impending doom were almost more than I could bear.'

"After several months of praying and searching for help, Libby was amazed to learn that a new member of the bishopric of her ward was a doctor specializing in the relationship between the mind and body. 'I described my problem to him and asked for help,' recalls Libby. 'That day he gave me a priesthood blessing that completely relieved my symptoms for several hours. This was a great comfort and gave me hope as I then followed the treatment that brought more permanent relief.'"[1]

Note

1. Jan Underwood Pinborough, "Mental Illness: In Search of Understanding and Hope," *Ensign*, Feb. 1989, 56.

12

Mood Disorders

Marleen S. Williams, W. Dean Belnap, and John P. Livingstone

We all experience many kinds of emotions. Normal human emotions may include joy and sadness, confidence and discouragement, hope and helplessness, and pleasure and emotional pain. Emotions are a divine gift that helps us understand our mortal experiences. We can experience the Holy Ghost in our heart through how we feel (D&C 8:2). Emotions have other important functions:

They can be messages that help us stop and evaluate what is happening.

They can teach us about others and ourselves.

They can warn us of danger.

They can help us in making important decisions.

They can enrich our lives as we experience joy, love, and other pleasant feelings.

They can prepare us to take action, when necessary.

They can help us to repent and change.

Emotions usually occur in response to either events in our lives or to personal, internal thoughts, memories, and experiences. These emotional responses tend to come and go and change as thoughts and events change in our lives. We all experience ups and downs in life as we encounter both pleasant and difficult experiences.

What Are Mood Disorders?

Sometimes painful or difficult emotions may feel *stuck*. When emotions persist, it becomes difficult to change, or snap out of, an emotional state. We call these persistent emotions *moods*. When these emotional states become so lasting and intense that they interfere with normal activities and relationships, they may be a sign of a mood disorder.

To understand mood disorders, you need to know they are not just the normal reactions to difficulties that we all experience in life. Mood disorders are more than sad emotions. They are whole body illnesses that influence many changes in the body. They can make it difficult to change your mood by willpower alone. Mood disorders are related to changes in brain functioning and include problems in normal body processes beyond just emotions.

There are two main categories of mood disorders—unipolar and bipolar. Unipolar disorders have symptoms that are consistent with depression. Bipolar disorders have symptoms of mania or may alternate between mania and depression. Common symptoms of depression may include the following:

Persistent sad, anxious, or *empty* mood

Feelings of worthlessness or excessive and inappropriate guilt

Feelings of hopelessness or constant pessimism

Inability to feel enjoyment and pleasure in activities, hobbies, or
    relationships that once were enjoyable

Decreased energy, fatigue, or feeling slowed down

Decreased sex drive

Difficulty concentrating, remembering things, or making decisions

Restlessness or irritability

Insomnia, waking up too early in the morning, oversleeping, or
chronic difficulty waking up

Changes in appetite (wanting to eat all of the time or not wanting
to eat at all) or unwanted weight loss or gain

Persistent physical symptoms that do not respond to treatment,
such as headaches, digestive problems, or chronic pain

Persistent thoughts of death or suicide; suicide attempts

Common symptoms of mania include the following:

Abnormal or excessively high or euphoric feelings

Extreme irritability or distractibility

Decreased need for sleep

Marked increase in energy or activity

Rapid or pressured speech

Racing thoughts or feeling that you cannot slow down your mind

Trouble concentrating and being easily distracted

Periods of poor judgment, risk taking, or bizarre behavior

Exaggerated belief in one's own abilities or characteristics

Increased sex drive

Little or no insight into behavior changes

Unipolar Depression

"Oh that my grief were thoroughly weighed, and my calamity laid in the
balances together! For now it would be heavier than the sand of the sea" (Job
6:2–3).

These are the words of faithful, righteous Job. He had experienced painful
losses and difficult events in his life. He felt intense emotional pain.

Adversity, sorrow, and pain are a necessary part of mortality (2 Nephi
2:23). We all have some grief, disappointment, sadness, hurt feelings, and

other unpleasant emotions. These feelings actually help us develop wisdom, compassion, and spiritual resources for coping. Even the Savior was described as "a man of sorrows, and acquainted with grief" (Isaiah 53:3). Difficult experiences come and go in our lives. Spiritual and emotional strength are usually sufficient to endure, progress, and grow.

It is important to understand how these normal emotions differ from clinical depression. Clinical depression is more than mere sadness, a bout of the blues, or a troubled heart. Clinical depression is an actual illness that affects our thinking, concentrating, eating, sleeping, and other daily activities. People with clinical depression cannot just snap out of it. All depression, regardless of the cause, involves changes in brain chemistry. It is not simply a character flaw. Without treatment, depression can last for months or even years. Some biological forms of depressions are so severe that they may persist even with treatment. Most people receive some improvement with treatment, however.

What Are the Symptoms of Unipolar Depression?

Here are some common changes that occur with depression:

Changes in thinking. You may have difficulty thinking clearly and making decisions. Ongoing, negative thoughts are also characteristic of depression. You may experience poor self-esteem, self-criticism, and excessive, unrealistic guilt. Sometimes thoughts of death, suicide, or other self-harm arise.

Changes in functioning. Depression disrupts body functions, such as energy, appetite, sleeping, and sex. Chronic tiredness, even after sleep, is common. You may feel very tired, slowed down, restless, or agitated. You may either lose your appetite or eat too much. You may struggle to fall asleep, awaken often, or want too much sleep. Sexual desire may disappear, or normal sexual functioning may be difficult.

Changes in emotions. You may feel sad for no reason. Depression can also numb your emotions. It can be difficult to feel the Spirit even though you are living a worthy life. In extreme depression, you have feelings of both hopelessness and helplessness.

Changes in behavior. You may feel apathetic. Activities and hobbies that were once fun are no longer enjoyable. You may withdraw from social activities or close friends and relatives. Crying or anger comes easily. You may neglect grooming and hygiene. With severe depression, you may find it difficult to even get out of bed.

If you experience many of these symptoms for longer than two weeks, you may be depressed. This should be confirmed by a medical doctor or mental health care professional.

Types of Depression

Depression can occur in different forms. These are mainly determined by the length and intensity of your symptoms and the cause of your depression.

Major depression. You must have at least five of the symptoms of depression (including either depressed mood or loss of interest or pleasure) listed above under the symptoms of unipolar depression. The symptoms must last at least two weeks. You may have only one episode of major depression, or it can be a recurring problem over your lifetime. About 50 percent of people who have one episode of major depression (and receive no treatment) have another episode later. Those who have a second episode have a 70 percent chance of having another episode. Those who have a third episode have a 90 percent chance of continued depression. Continuing episodes tend to get worse. Treatment can reduce the chance of recurrence.

Sister Jones started feeling very sad and frequently cried over things that normally did not upset her. She was tired all of the time. She tried getting more sleep but still felt very tired. She put on ten pounds in a month and could not control her eating because food seemed to soothe her sadness. She used to enjoy gardening and going for walks, but recently nothing sounded fun. Making even little decisions, such as which flowers to plant in her garden or how much money to spend, overwhelmed her. She felt like she could not trust herself to make right decisions. She had a habit of berating herself for mistakes, but now it seemed like she could do nothing right.

Dysthymia. Symptoms are less severe but more chronic. You may have fewer symptoms, but they last for at least two years. People with dysthymia can also have an episode of major depression.

Sam felt like he had been depressed most of his life, but it was not so bad that he could not work. He had finished a college degree and held a good job. He attended church regularly and fulfilled callings and assignments when asked. But other parts of his life seemed sad and meaningless all of the time. He had tried several hobbies but could not get excited about anything. He mostly stayed home alone and stared at the television after work.

Adjustment disorder, with depression. This type of depression is often called *reactive depression*. It usually occurs after a difficult trauma, significant loss, or other challenging adjustment. The symptoms are less severe than for major depression, but you may still develop symptoms following a difficult life crisis that meet criteria for major depression.

Brother and Sister Richards moved to a new city. Sister Richards had grown up in a small town, where she knew everyone. This was the first time she had ever been separated from family and lifelong friends. She was naturally shy and felt overwhelmed by the big city. Her husband's new job kept him frequently away from home. She missed the familiarity of her hometown, family, and friends. She would often cry and feel depressed. She started having trouble sleeping at night and worried about adjusting to her new community. She tried to get out, meet new friends, and find enjoyable activities, but her lack of energy and tiredness made it difficult.

Postpartum depression. Changes in your body because of events like the menstrual cycle, pregnancy, the postpartum period (after having a baby), infertility, and menopause can all contribute to changes in mood (see chapter

14, "Women and Depression," and chapter 15, "Women's Mental Health in the Reproductive Cycle"). Postpartum blues are common in up to 80 percent of new mothers. Postpartum depression, however, is much more severe and less common. It occurs in about 10 to 20 percent of new mothers. It can begin any time after delivery and can last up to a year. The symptoms are similar to major depression but may also include specific fears, such as excessive worry about the baby's health or frequent, unwanted thoughts and fears of harming the baby.

In rare cases, a woman may experience a postpartum psychosis following the birth of her baby (see chapter 16, "Schizophrenia and Other Psychotic Disorders"). It usually comes on suddenly and severely. It is important that new mothers who have postpartum depression or postpartum psychosis get treatment quickly. If you have had postpartum psychosis, you are likely to suffer from it again with your next pregnancies. Postpartum depression and postpartum psychosis are related to hormone fluctuations following childbirth. Stress and worry related to being a mother can increase the risk.

Mary had looked forward to being a mother, and she loved her first baby very much. Shortly after giving birth, she began to feel exhausted and overwhelmed, and she cried frequently. She thought it was just the baby blues, but she continued to feel even more depressed as time went on. After three months she could hardly get up to care for the baby. She would lie awake all night and worry that the baby might stop breathing or choke in the night. She was afraid to pick up the baby when her husband was not at home and doubted her own ability to be a good mother. She felt paralyzed to even provide daily care.

Seasonal Affective Disorder (SAD). Some people are especially vulnerable to depression in the winter months. As daylight hours become shorter, the symptoms of depression become worse. The onset of SAD is related to the lack of sunlight. You may feel like you just want to hibernate over the winter. You may crave sweet and starchy foods and tend to gain weight and feel heavy and fatigued. Oversleeping and having difficulty waking in the morning are common. The symptoms usually go away in the spring. SAD may be mild or disabling. It is much more common in northern geographic regions. Changes in mood tend to come and go at about the same time every year. They are usually not related to stressful events that may occur seasonally, such as not being employed in the winter.

Jenny grew up in a warm, sunny climate. After high school, she decided to attend a university that was much farther north than her hometown. At first, she loved college life, made new friends, and did well in her classes. As the weather began to turn cold and the days became shorter, she noticed that she felt tired and apathetic. By January, she struggled even to get out of bed to attend classes. When she tried to study for her classes, she had difficulty reading and comprehending the textbook.

She had never had this kind of trouble before and wondered what was happening to her mind. She felt hungry most of the time and began eating doughnuts and pastries. This upset her because she put on weight. She withdrew from her friends and slept so much that her grades started to drop. As spring approached, she started to feel better. She thought the depression was just a temporary adjustment to college. The second year, however, the problem returned in the winter months.

Depression Caused by Illness

Some diseases can cause changes in the body's chemistry that lead to depression. These diseases include multiple sclerosis, stroke, hypothyroidism (insufficient thyroid production), adrenal gland tumors, heart disease, and brain tumors. It is emotionally difficult to have a chronic illness, but sometimes it is difficult to determine if the disease is the only cause of the depression.

Brother Thompson was a happy, active man. Recently, however, he has noticed many symptoms of depression. He could not understand why he felt so sad, tired, and uninterested in life. His life was going well and he had much to bring him happiness. He had been putting on weight, but this did not greatly affect his self-image. He decided to get a physical examination from his family physician. When he told the doctor his symptoms, the doctor ordered several medical tests. The tests showed that Brother Thompson had an underactive thyroid, for which the doctor prescribed medication. After a while on the medication, Brother Thompson started feeling good again.

Depression Caused by Substance Use

Many substances can cause depression. Illegal drugs, alcohol, prescription, and over-the-counter medications and toxic substances have all been linked to depression. It is important to read the side-effect information for medications to see if they can cause depression. Alcohol is a depressant, as are many illegal drugs, and they can create a chemical depression. Many people who become addicted to alcohol and drugs start using them to try to self-medicate a mental problem. Some people may use pornography and masturbation in an attempt to soothe themselves. If you are struggling with any addictive problem, see a mental health care professional to determine if you have clinical depression.

Rachel had occasional problems with allergies. Her eyes would itch, and she sneezed a lot. She bought some over-the-counter medication for allergies, which stopped the symptoms. After a few days on the medication, she began to feel depressed and tired. She read the label on the allergy medication. It listed depression as a common side effect. She remembered that she frequently had side effects from medications, so she consulted her doctor about one that would be better for her.

What Causes Unipolar Depression?

Changes in body functioning are part of depression, but becoming clinically depressed is usually the result of an interaction of inherited, biological, social, and psychological factors. Stressful events can also trigger an episode. The factors vary from person to person.

Genetic (inherited) vulnerability. Inherited biology contributes to about half of all cases. This kind of depression runs in families. Family studies show that if you are the child of parents who have depression, you are two to four times more likely to develop the illness than children whose parents have not had depression. Children whose parents have depression also tend to develop depression at an early age. There is higher risk even when such children are adopted into families without depression. This suggests that depression is related more to heredity than to environment.

Biology. Why is depression sometimes called a *chemical imbalance?* Modern neuroimaging technology allows researchers to study what happens in the brain during depression. Nerve cells communicate with each other through electrical and chemical processes (see chapter 2, "A Look at Your Brain," and chapter 18, "Cognitive Disorders"). Three neurotransmitters play a strong role in depression: serotonin, norepinephrine, and dopamine.

Research suggests that the chemical problems in depression can work two ways. Brain chemistry affects behavior, but behavior also affects brain chemistry. This is why both medication and psychotherapy are often the most useful treatment.

Stress. Stress can also trigger depression even when no genetic factor exists. Excessive or chronic stress drains the body's chemical resources. You can compare this to leaving the lights on in your car. You may have a good car, and you may be a good driver, but if you leave the lights on without running the engine, the car's battery runs down and the car will not start. When a person faces a threat, it activates the hypothalamus in the brain. The hypothalamus serves as the command center for the nervous and hormonal systems of the body. It releases chemicals that travel to the pituitary gland, which in turn stimulates hormonal glands throughout the body.

This process results in excessive amounts of a chemical called *cortisol* being released into the body. When this happens, you experience stress. Ultimately, the price paid for chronic stress can be depression. High levels of cortisol also contribute to weight gain and other health problems. A growing body of research suggests that stress experienced early in life can lead to a higher risk for depression later in life. Extreme stress early in childhood may affect the brain cells in a way that leads to chronic overproduction of cortisol, which contributes to depression.

The Lord tells us not to "run faster or labor more than you have strength" (D&C 10:4). He has also counseled us to "retire to thy bed early" (D&C 88:124) and to be "temperate in all things" (1 Corinthians 9:25). It is important that we pay attention to the signals from our bodies. Signals such as hunger, fatigue, pain, and stress all tell us that we need to take care of our bodies. Managing stress sometimes requires that we make careful choices about what we can and cannot do. Making choices helps us learn to use our agency. When we prayerfully line up our priorities, we discover the things that matter most. When we let go of things that matter least, we protect our health.

Perfectionism. Perfectionist thinking can contribute to depression. If you expect everything always to be perfect, you will constantly feel inadequate. There is a difference between a healthy quest for striving, growth, and progression and the unhealthy counterfeit called perfectionism.

Some people misunderstand the Savior's teaching to "be ye therefore perfect" (Matthew 5:48). This command was to enter into a covenant *process* that begins with baptism and involves repentance, change, and growth. This process of perfection is dependent on the Atonement, which makes change and growth possible. President Joseph Fielding Smith talked about this process when he said:

"Salvation does not come all at once; we are commanded to be perfect even as our Father in heaven is perfect. It will take us ages to accomplish this end, for there will be greater progress beyond the grave, and it will be there that the faithful will overcome all things, and receive all things, even the fulness of the Father's glory."[1]

The Prophet Joseph Smith described the path to perfection as a journey:

"When you climb up a ladder, you must begin at the bottom, and ascend step by step, until you arrive at the top; and so it is with the principles of the gospel—you must begin with the first and go on until you learn all the principles of exaltation. But it will be a great while after you have passed through the veil before you will have learned them. It is not all to be comprehended in this world; it will be a great work to learn our salvation and exaltation even beyond the grave."[2]

When you feel overwhelmed by your weaknesses, focusing on becoming perfected through Christ's atonement gives hope. The false substitute of perfectionism, however, causes you to rely only on yourself. This leaves you constantly feeling inadequate and without hope. You cannot compare yourself to others. We are all given different assignments, challenges, and mortal experiences. Having a correct understanding of this principle can strengthen you when you struggle with limitations in energy and ability that clinical depression can create.

Learn to recognize the difference between perfectionism and a healthy spiritual quest for perfection. Understanding the difference can improve your mental health.

Healthy Quest for Perfection through Christ	Perfectionism
Setting obtainable, realistic goals	Setting unrealistic goals
Self-worth is inherent	Self-worth is based on achievement
Rejoicing in growth and progression	Never feeling satisfied or good enough
Doing your best without comparing yourself with others	Comparing yourself with others or having to be the best in all you do
Recognizing that mistakes are part of the learning process; learn from mistakes and keep trying	Intense fear of failure; mistakes result in feeling shame and humiliation
Finding joy in the process of growth	Feeling driven by fear or duty
Confidence to try even when the task is hard	Afraid to try unless you can do something perfectly
Able to keep life balanced and let go of less important things when necessary	Having to do it all; constantly feeling overwhelmed
Faith in the Atonement; trust in a process of repentance, change, and growth	Reliance only on one's own ability; trying to be perfect without God's help

Cognitive distortions. Chronic negative thought patterns can also keep you feeling depressed. Cognitive distortions are often part of depression. *Cognitive* means *thoughts.* When thinking is distorted, thoughts often lead to painful emotions.

Mary's friend usually calls her every week. Two weeks went by, and her friend did not call. Mary began thinking, "I know she must not like me anymore. She probably thinks our friendship is a waste of time. I guess I just don't have any friends, and no one will ever really like me." Mary begins to feel depressed whenever she thinks these thoughts.

Mary is using *mind reading* and is *overgeneralizing*. These thought distortions ignore other possible reasons that her friend has not called and assume that no one likes Mary because one friend has disappointed her. There are many kinds of cognitive distortions. They all ignore important parts of the truth. Below are some examples of other cognitive distortions:

Labeling: "I am a bad wife because I am not a good cook." (Labeling yourself because of a weakness or lack of skill is an extreme form of overgeneralizing.)

Emotional Reasoning: "I feel really bad, so I must be a bad person." (Accepting a feeling as proof of a fact can cause pain and hurt feelings even when you have done nothing wrong.)

Fortune Telling: "I did not prepare my lesson well. Now the bishop will never give me another calling." (Do not jump to conclusions without considering other possibilities.)

Magnifying Negatives: "I ate another dough-

nut. Now I will be fat for the rest of my life, and no one will ever like me." (Dwelling on a negative event gives it too much importance and too much influence on your emotions.)

Discounting Positives: "Everyone said I gave a good talk, but they are only being nice." (You ignore positive events so that their importance and influence is lost.)

Catastrophizing: "I only earned a C on my exam. This is the most horrible thing that could ever happen. I don't think I can stand it. It is so unfair that I can't go on. I cannot imagine anything worse that could happen in life." (You exaggerate events to be excessively awful or unbearable.)

Learning how to change cognitive distortions to healthy thinking patterns can help change your mood and reduce depression.

Problems in relationships. Painful and difficult relationships can contribute to depression. Women are more likely to define their worth or value based on relationships with others. If you see your success or failure in life as being dependent on the success of your relationships, you may increase your risk for depression. It is important to realize that others have moral agency to make their own choices.

Relationships that have constant conflict also contribute to depression. Constantly living in a battlefield with troubled relationships creates stress that can lead to depression. Loss of important relationships through death, divorce, or other long separations can also contribute to depression. Children are especially vulnerable when they lose their parents.

Abuse. Physical, sexual, and emotional abuse all have painful emotional consequences. Even so-called milder forms of abuse, such as verbal abuse, affect how you feel about yourself. Often people do not realize how powerful verbal abuse can be. "Sticks and stones may break our bones," but words can break our hearts. Feelings of isolation and helplessness related to abuse contribute to depression.

Neglecting the emotional and physical needs of children can contribute to depression and can affect the development of the brain, leading to chronic struggles with depression.

Children and adolescents may experience bullying at school. This can have the same effect as abuse. Children often do not know how to stop the bullying and can feel helpless and humiliated. Recognizing abuse and getting help to stop it are critical for good mental health. It is especially important that adults protect little children from abuse and neglect. Chronic exposure to abuse can lead to problems with self-esteem, trust, and the ability to form relationships, and it can even cause changes in the brain.

Emotional conflict between behavior and values. When we know the difference between moral and sinful behavior, sin creates emotional conflict. Having integrity means that we are who we say we are, we do what we say we will do, and we do not do what we say we will not do. When we lose our integrity, we lose our self-respect. This can lead to feelings of low self-worth and depression.

If a person lives a double life by keeping secrets about sinful behavior, he creates mental distress. "A double minded man is unstable in all his ways" (James 1:8). It has also been said, "Our secrets keep us sick." Spiritual sickness can come from pretending to keep commandments but secretly continuing sins. Repentance provides a way to feel whole and at one with both God and self. "Draw nigh to God, and he will draw nigh to you. Cleanse your hands, ye sinners; and purify your hearts, ye double minded" (James 4:8).

We can feel more whole through understanding that repentance is a loving gift to us. It can give us access to the healing power of the Atonement. Spiritual well-being can reduce emotional conflicts that can contribute to depression. Having the gift of the Holy Ghost can also strengthen us to be able to change behaviors that lead to emotional conflicts.

How Is Depression Treated?

If you think you or a loved one may have clinical depression, see a medical doctor or mental health professional. They can make an evaluation to determine if you are suffering from normal sadness or serious depression. A physical exam can also rule out medical problems that may be causing the symptoms. Be sure to tell the doctor about any medications, over-the counter drugs, or herbal supplements you are taking. These can contribute to depression, and they can interact harmfully with each other and with antidepressant medication.

Depression usually responds to treatment. A small percentage of people seem to have treatment-resistant depression, but most people see improvement. Getting treatment can reduce the risk of having another episode of depression. The most common treatments are medication, psychotherapy, or a combination of the two. Mild cases of depression may respond quickly to psychotherapy. Not all people with depression need medication. People who have what are called *melancholic symptoms* usually do need medication. These symptoms include a loss of the ability to feel pleasure or enjoyment, depression that is worse in the morning, waking up early and not being able to go back to sleep, feeling as if the body is slowed down, significant weight loss, and excessive or inappropriate guilt.

Antidepressant medication usually takes several weeks to reach full effectiveness. It is important to take the medication long enough for it to work (see chapter 3, "The Brain and Medical Treatment for Mental Disorders").

You may have heard of some alternative over-the-counter treatments for depression. St. John's wort, SAM-e, 5-HTP (tryptophan), and Omega-3 fatty acids have all been advertised as alternatives to antidepressant medication. Research shows effectiveness in some cases, and these supplements may eventually become part of standard treatment. Such supplements, however, have not all been studied sufficiently to establish safe and effective doses. Some can even be dangerous when not properly used. It is not clear how they interact with other medications and medical problems. It is wise to be cautious in using any herbal or over-the-counter treatments. Be sure to talk with your doctor about these supplements rather than ignorantly self-medicating.

Psychotherapy helps depression in several ways. Having a safe place to talk about problems can help you gain insights into them. Getting support from a caring person helps you feel less hopeless and alone. When you are depressed, it is hard to think clearly, and you may miss possible solutions to your problems. A therapist can help you think through problems more carefully and see more options for solving problems. Psychotherapy can also help you learn coping skills. This increases your ability to tolerate stress.

Cognitive therapy works to uncover your thought distortions. It helps you think in ways that are more useful. It can also help you generate positive goals.

Behavioral therapy focuses on changing behaviors that contribute to depression. For example, it can be helpful to learn how to set limits if you tend to do too much. Learning how to set priorities can also help you do the most important things first. This can reduce stress that leads to depression.

Interpersonal therapy looks at problems in personal relationships. This can be helpful if your depression is related to a loss of an important relationship or role, lack of social skills, or difficulty in relationships. It explores ways of solving those problems rather than repeating old patterns.

Phototherapy is effective with seasonal affective disorder. It involves exposure to bright lights that are similar to early morning sunlight and many times brighter than normal light bulbs. Desktop light boxes and special light bulbs are sold by companies that specialize in light treatment. Phototherapy helps your body to regulate a brain substance called *melatonin*.

Electroconvulsive therapy (ECT) may be used in severe and chronic cases of depression. This treatment has improved over the years. It can be a highly effective treatment for severe, resistant depression when other treatments have failed.

Research shows the effectiveness of all of these forms of therapy. Many counselors adapt therapy to your unique concerns. Your mental health care team may also use more than one form of therapy.

Teenagers and Depression

Adolescence can be an unsettling time, when many changes occur in the bodies and lives of teenagers. They need support and direction to understand all these emotional and physical changes. Teens often feel stressed out and moody. Sometimes, however, these moods may be a symptom of clinical depression. The brain changes and grows during the teenage years and into young adulthood. Many biological mental illnesses show their first symptoms in adolescence. Depression among teens is increasing at an alarming rate. It is important to recognize depression. Teenagers may act out their distress rather than talking about it. Many teenagers who commit suicide are depressed but may not recognize that they have a treatable problem. Some symptoms to look for in adolescent depression include the following:

Losing interest in school and allowing grades to drop

Withdrawing from friends and activities

Feeling an increase in anger and hostility

Trying alcohol, drugs, or sexual promiscuity (these are often misguided attempts to feel better when a teenager is depressed)

Being overly sensitive to criticism and rejection

Having difficulty concentrating or experiencing unusual forgetfulness and frequent accidents

Undergoing changes in eating and sleeping patterns; sleeping all day

Experiencing a lack of energy or motivation to do anything; chronic boredom

Feeling restless and agitated

Acting out by getting in trouble with the authorities

Experiencing chronic physical complaints that cannot be medically explained

Having suicidal thoughts or actions. Suicide in adolescents has tripled since 1960. It is the third-leading cause of death in teenagers. Young people may view a temporary problem as a permanent condition. They do not have enough mature experience in solving problems and may see no other way out of their distress. It is important to take suicidal threats seriously (see chapter 6, "Perspectives on Suicide and Mental Illness")

Sometimes adolescents act out depression when they cannot talk about their feelings. Youth may self-medicate depression with drugs, alcohol, or sex, including pornography. Interestingly, however, recent studies have found that teenage sexual involvement and drug use more frequently precede the onset of depression. In two large studies involving more than thirty-two thousand adolescents, research found that sexual activity and drug use increased the risk for depression. Teens who abstained from sex, alcohol, and drugs had a much lower incidence of depression. Girls who experimented with sex were more than twice as likely to develop depression as those who did not. Those who used drugs were more than three times more likely to develop depression. Boys involved sexually were one and a half times more likely to become depressed and were three to four times more likely to become depressed if they used drugs.[3]

Observance of gospel standards related to the Word of Wisdom and chastity can help to reduce the risk for depression in adolescents. Although young people may be biologically sexually mature, they lack important skills for maintaining interpersonal relationships, solving problems, and managing emotions. They may feel that they are adults sexually, but their brains still need the growth and *wiring* that develops in the late teens and early twenties. Important changes occur in the frontal lobe of the brain at this time that make it easier to control impulses, make wise decisions, and solve problems. Following Church counsel concerning chastity, not dating before age sixteen, and keeping dating standards can help teenagers to avoid situations that could contribute to depression.

Treatment for depression in teenagers is similar to treatment for adults. Both medication and psychotherapy are helpful. It may be beneficial to seek a counselor who has expertise in working with adolescents. Parents are key sources of information for mental health care providers because teenagers may not be able to put their feelings into words or may lack insight into their own behavior.

How Can You Talk to Depressed Teenagers?

Some suggestions for talking to depressed teenagers include the following:

Tell them you care and are worried about them.
Remind them that as sons or daughters of God; they are of great worth.

Talk honestly and openly about how you feel about them and their problems.

Do not try to make them feel guilty about their depression.

Consider whether *your* expectations are too high or the goals *you* have set for them are too difficult for them to reach.

Be supportive and show you want to help. Provide information about depression.

Encourage them to use their own agency to make choices that will help them feel better.

Be ready to listen when they are ready to talk. Try not to take it personally if they have trouble talking about feelings or are angry.

Depression and the Elderly

Depression is common in older adults. Estimates are that 15 to 25 percent of the elderly are depressed. The number increases if they have a chronic illness or are in a nursing home. Depression in the elderly is more common than dementia. Elderly people face challenges that make them vulnerable to depression. They experience many losses—loss of work, physical abilities, health, and social status can all contribute to depression. Deaths of friends and loved ones are difficult experiences. The elderly may feel that their life is meaningless if they cannot be involved with family or activities. Many medications prescribed for the elderly can have the side effect of chemical depression. Medical illnesses in later life can also cause depression.

If you are elderly and depressed, try to keep your mind and body as active as possible. Finding meaning and purpose in the activities available at your stage of life can reduce your risk for depression. Be around other people who are supportive and pleasant.

Family members may not realize when an elderly person is depressed. Many of the symptoms of depression in elderly people can look similar to dementia. Family members and other supporters need to watch for subtle changes that may be signs of depression. A complete physical examination can help determine the causes of the changes. Some of the highest risks for suicide occur in the elderly, especially in men. It is helpful to keep elderly people involved in enjoyable relationships and activities.

How Can You Help Yourself?

Some suggestions include the following:

Remember that God loves you. He knows of your suffering and cares. Even his Son experienced suffering in mortality.

Do not make major life decisions, such as getting married, divorced, or changing jobs without talking with others who know you well and can be objective. Seek wise counsel from your bishop if the decisions could affect your spiritual well-being.

Get regular aerobic exercise (exercise that increases your breathing and heart rate). This helps to energize the body and reduces tiredness caused by depression. Set reasonable goals for exercising, and try to make it fun.

Break tasks into smaller goals. Learn to set priorities, and do not take on more than is wise.

Try to engage in activities that you enjoy and that lift your spirits. Start a new hobby or do something that helps you feel confident and competent.

Do not blame yourself for being depressed. This will only make you more depressed.

Recognize and change negative thinking. Some excellent self-help books are *Feeling Good: the New Mood Therapy* and *The Feeling Good Handbook,* both written by Dr. David D. Burns.

Try to be with people you enjoy. Make relationships a priority. Do not become isolated.

Do not set difficult goals for yourself or take on excessive responsibilities. Give yourself time to get better.

Be patient with yourself. Do not compare yourself with others.

Take good care of your body. Try to eat healthfully, get adequate sleep, and do relaxing activities every day. Exercise boosts endorphins in your body. These are feel-good chemicals in your brain.

Seek professional help. This can help you to both understand your depression and to recover faster.

How Can You Help Others?

Learn more about depression. Sometimes well-meaning but uninformed people do more harm than good. Do not give answers or solutions that blame the person. Support the person in finding spiritual meaning in the experience. This can be more helpful than trying to suggest a meaning yourself. Alma taught that one of the promises we make at baptism is to "bear one another's burdens, . . . mourn with those that mourn; . . . comfort those that stand in need of comfort, and to stand as witnesses of God at all times and in all things" (Mosiah 18:8–9). Showing love and empathy to the person with depression can be a way of witnessing that God also loves the person. Some of the least helpful things you can say include the following:

"Just stop whining and feeling sorry for yourself."

"There are people who are worse off than you."

"You could change the way you feel if you would just try hard enough."

"If you had more faith, you would have overcome this depression."

"Just throw out your medication and pull yourself together."

"Everybody has sad days. I've been sad before, and I just got out and forgot my problems."

"You must need this trial for your progression or you would not be having this problem."

"Just figure out what you are doing wrong and the depression will go away."

Some helpful things to say to a person experiencing depression are the following:

"I care."

"You are important to me."

"It will pass. I will still be here and so will you. We can ride it out together."

"I am sorry you are in so much pain."

"I listen to you talk about it, and I can't imagine what it must be like for you. I can see that it is hard and that it hurts."

"Even if I cannot fully understand what you are feeling, I offer my compassion."

"I know God loves you. Even if we cannot understand all of the reasons for affliction in mortality, I know he is a loving God."

"I will remember you in my prayers."

"Is there something I can do to help?"

"All I know to do is to give you a hug and a shoulder to cry on."

"You are not alone."

"I love you."

What Is It Like to Have Depression?

"Nancy works overtime at trying to make other people happy, including her husband and children, but in recent weeks she has felt discouraged. Activities she used to accomplish on a daily basis now seem overwhelming. Just looking at a sink of dishes gives her a sense of exhaustion and despair. She lacks the affection she used to feel for her husband and loved ones, and spends more and more time hiding in her bedroom. 'I'm not worthy of anyone's love,' she thinks, 'not even of Heavenly Father's.' "[4]

Bipolar Mood Disorder

Bipolar mood disorder (manic-depressive illness) is a lifelong illness of the brain that afflicts about 1 percent of all people. This means that between two and three million people in the United States have some form of bipolar disorder. It causes more intense moods than people normally experience. You may have also heard it called *manic-depression.*

Bipolar mood disorder is characterized by extreme mood swings that go beyond the ups and downs of normal moods. It is treatable and manageable, but two-thirds of those with bipolar mood disorder are not properly diagnosed and treated; in fact, it may be hard to diagnose. If people seek treatment only when depressed, health care professionals may miss the highs of the disorder. People rarely seek treatment during these high episodes unless forced to do so by others. They may have no insight into their own behavior and often enjoy the manic phase. Without treatment, the impact of the illness can be devastating not only to individuals but also to those who love and care for them.

People with untreated bipolar mood disorder are much more likely to abuse drugs and alcohol and are more vulnerable to addictions and divorce. The risk for suicide is also much higher. Many people with this disorder may not recognize that their emotional struggles are related to a treatable mental illness. They may attempt to calm their extreme moods with dangerous or ineffective solutions. With proper treatment, people with bipolar disorder usually can live happy, normal, productive lives.

Symptoms frequently start in young adults between ages seventeen and twenty-five, but they can start at any time in life. Younger children and adolescents can also have bipolar mood disorder.

If you or a loved one show symptoms that suggest bipolar mood disorder, it is important to have an evaluation by a mental health care professional.

Symptoms of Bipolar Mood Disorder

Bipolar mood disorder is different from the lows of unipolar depression in that you experience extreme high moods. These high moods are called manic episodes. People with bipolar disorders may also cycle into the low of depression. The depressive episodes are similar to those described in the chapter on depression.

It is important to seek treatment if you experience at least three of the following symptoms for more than a week because you could be experiencing a manic episode:

Intense increase in physical and mental energy. You feel revved up and full of more energy than usual. You may take on more activities than is normal or reasonable.

Heightened mood, optimism, and self-confidence. You feel like you could take on the world. You may feel euphoric and boundlessly happy for reasons that make little sense to others.

Excessive irritability or aggressive behavior. Rather than feeling extremely happy, you may feel extremely agitated, irritable, and easily angered over things that normally do not bother you. Some people may become dangerous and threatening when manic. It may be necessary to call police and involuntarily hospitalize a person for his own protection and the protection of others (see chapter 19, "Mental Health and the Law").

Decreased need for sleep without feeling tired. You feel like you do not need sleep. When you miss normal sleep, you still do not feel tired.

Grandiose delusions, inflated self-esteem, or intense feelings of self-importance. You may feel powerful, as if nothing can stop you.

You may also believe you have special powers or gifts that others do not recognize. You may have unrealistic beliefs about your abilities and think you can do more than is reasonable. In severe manic episodes, these beliefs may be psychotic, such as believing you are destined to take over the world, have superhuman abilities, or are a famous person.

Rapid speech, racing thoughts, and flight of ideas. You feel pressure to keep talking or talk very fast. You cannot focus your thoughts but experience thoughts racing through your mind, jumping from one idea to another. You have difficulty concentrating. Speech may become loud, rambling, rapid, difficult to interrupt, and may include excessive humor, jokes, rhymes, and plays on words.

Impulsiveness and poor judgment. Others may tell you that you are acting differently and not thinking clearly before you act. You may not recognize that what you are doing is not wise, even when others tell you.

Reckless behavior, such as spending sprees, impulsive business decisions, erratic driving, excessive or inappropriate sexual behavior. You may engage in more activities that you feel are fun or pleasurable but can have painful consequences.

In severe manic episodes, you may have delusions and hallucinations (see chapter 16, "Schizophrenia and Other Psychotic Disorders").

Some of these symptoms can also be related to other mental disorders, such as attention-deficit/hyperactivity disorder and schizophrenia. Some drugs and medications can also cause symptoms of a manic episode. It is important that manic episodes are recognized and accurately diagnosed. An episode can escalate, creating such poor judgment that the person can be a danger to himself or others.

Bipolar disorder is a chronic condition with recurring episodes. Much like diabetes, it generally requires ongoing treatment. If left untreated, it tends to get worse, and its symptoms become more intense. About half of all people with bipolar disorder attempt suicide. The episodes of mood swings may last days or months. With proper treatment, the illness can usually be controlled. Like diabetics, most people with bipolar disorder can lead happy, productive lives if they stay in treatment.

Types of Bipolar Mood Disorder

The patterns of episodes vary greatly throughout a person's life and from person to person. Some people may have only occasional episodes of mild mania, called *hypomania*, and repeated episodes of depression. Others may have only mania with no depression. Symptoms of both mania and depression can occur together in what is called a *mixed state* or *mixed mania*. People with mixed mania may feel sad and hopeless and have trouble sleeping while still feeling energized and agitated. Often a manic episode will follow a period of depression.

Rapid cycling is a rare form of bipolar disorder in which sufferers cycle rapidly between mania and depression. The cycles last only a few hours or a few days. It is more common in women. Antidepressants can trigger rapid cycling when they are taken without a mood-stabilizing medication. Rapid cycling bipolar disorder often has symptoms that may look similar to borderline personality disorder. This diagnosis is biologically and psychologically different from bipolar disorder and can have different treatment strategies. Some of the different forms of bipolar disorder are the following:

Bipolar I. You have had at least one manic episode. The manic episodes last at least one week. Many people have several episodes of depression before the first manic episode. Some, however, may have only manic episodes. Those who have a severe manic episode need to be hospitalized until their mood is stable.

Elder Thompson first struggled with depression in high school, but it lifted after a few months. At first, he thought it was related to some personal struggles he was experiencing at the time. When he served as a missionary, however, the depression returned. He talked with a counselor provided by his mission president, and he started feeling better after a few months. When he returned from his mission, he continued his education at a university. He again began to experience a depressive episode. He tried many of the strategies he had learned in counseling and tried to wait out the depression. He began to feel his mood lift, but this time he started feeling more and more energy.

Although normally quiet and reserved, he began socializing constantly. He felt like he could talk constantly at parties and ward activities. He was so confident about his skills and abilities that he starting asking out nearly every single woman in his stake regardless of whether she had shown interest in him. He became angry and irritable if they turned him down. He started spending more money on clothes and electronic toys than he could afford. His credit card debt began to mount, but he could not see that this was a problem. He also stayed up at night writing what he believed would become the next best-selling novel. This seemed more fun than doing his homework.

He showed part of the manuscript to his English teacher. She told him it was not publishable. He became angry and told her off. He believed that she was jealous of his great talent. He sent a letter to the newspaper, saying he was going to be the next great American writer and inviting them to interview him. His parents finally convinced him to see a psychiatrist who recognized the manic symptoms. After the doctor prescribed a mood-stabilizing medication, he began to return to normal, reasonable behavior.

Bipolar II. You experience one or more episodes of depression and at least one hypomanic episode, but you never have a full manic episode. (A person who has hypomanic episodes, however, may still have a full manic episode later. The diagnosis then changes to Bipolar I.) Hypomanic episodes last at least four days and have symptoms similar to manic episodes, but they are much less severe and disabling. People often enjoy hypomanic episodes. They are less likely to cause serious problems than full manic episodes, but good judgment can still be impaired.

Sally struggled with bouts of depression, which interfered with her ability to perform well on her job. She would frequently call in sick when she was depressed. Normally, she enjoyed her job and could keep up with her work. She did not like to go out with friends or have fun when she was depressed. She cried a lot when depressed and frequently blamed herself for not being stronger. Sometimes she felt so down that she wished she were dead. When she was not depressed, she enjoyed going to movies and out to dinner with her close friends. She noticed, however, that occasionally she would experience times when she had bursts of energy. She could work much faster at her job and still come home and have energy to clean her apartment and then go out with friends. When she felt these energetic moods, she liked to go to parties. She could tell jokes and be the life of the party. She dressed more dramatically when in these moods. After the party, she would frequently make out with someone she had just met. It seemed so fun when she was in a great mood. Afterward, when her mood returned to normal, she felt bad and could not understand why she had acted in a way that went against her personal values.

Cyclothymia. You experience numerous, chronic mood swings. These episodes are more severe than the normal ups and downs of daily living but are not as severe as full manic or depressive moods. These mood swings last for at least two years (one year for children or adolescents), and you are never without mood swings for more than two months. Most people enjoy the hypomanic episodes and do not see them as a problem. The depressive episodes, however, are distressing enough to make you unhappy. They are severe enough to create problems in your life.

Jenny loved being a full-time mother to her three children. Normally she was able to cope with the demands of caring for the children, keeping up with household tasks, and serving in the Church. Sometimes, however, she noticed that she would sink into despair for no apparent reason. She would have episodes during which she would cry about things that normally did not bother her. She was more tired than usual and could not keep up with her work. She felt worthless when she had these episodes and would berate herself for being a bad mother. She normally loved to cook, but it did not seem fun when she was in what she called a "dark mood." These dark moods usually lifted after a few days.

At other times, she felt full of energy. She would start many new projects around the house. She liked these moods because they were so much fun. When she felt energetic, she usually bought supplies for her projects that exceeded her budget. She felt bad about this later and wished she could control her spending. She also noticed that she could not finish all of the projects she had started. She had thought that finishing them was reasonable when she felt up. When she felt energetic, she also liked to call friends and talk for hours on the phone. Sometimes this annoyed her friends. When she felt up, she would commit to serving on more committees, helping friends with projects, or signing up for service projects that later overwhelmed her. She wondered why she could not control these ups and downs and just will them to go away.

What Causes Bipolar Mood Disorder?

While we do not completely understand what causes bipolar disorders, research has unlocked many of the mysteries of this illness. A family history of a mood disorder is the most common risk factor. About two-thirds of people with a mood disorder can identify a close family member with a mood disorder. Genetic studies show that the chance of developing the disorder is about 30 percent for people with a brother, sister, or parent with the disorder. If both parents have the disorder, the risk rises 50 to 75 percent. If a person has an identical twin with the disorder, the risk is 70 percent.

These statistics are also true if a child has a bipolar disorder in her genetic (birth) family but is adopted into a family with no history of a disorder. This suggests that genetics, rather than parenting, are the source of the problem. Researchers have been searching for specific genes—the building blocks of DNA inside the cells of our bodies. DNA is passed from parents to their children. Research has yielded some results in finding genes linked to bipolar disorder with certain groups of people. It is most likely that several different genes work in combination to create vulnerability to bipolar disorder. This helps to explain why not everyone in a family develops the disorder, though it can still show up in later generations.

Genetic vulnerability, however, does not make it inevitable that a person will develop the disease. These risk statistics also tell us that genetics are not the only things that cause the illness. Other factors in a person's life can contribute to the genetic vulnerability being expressed. Stress and ability to cope influence whether a person will become ill. The illness often begins during a stressful experience in the person's life because stress can turn on the genetic vulnerability. We can conclude that biology is the basis of the disorder, but other events and problems can set it in motion.

A person's personality also makes a difference in how symptoms are expressed. If you have a biological vulnerability to bipolar disorder, it is important to take extra care to protect your health. Keeping on a regular wake-sleep cycle is especially important. Sleep deprivation can trigger mania. For some individuals, however, the biology is so powerful that they can develop the illness without the presence of highly stressful events.

Antidepressant use can also trigger a manic episode if you have a biological vulnerability. It is important to tell your doctor before you take any medication if you have a family history of bipolar disorder. In rare cases, hypothyroidism (insufficient thyroid production) has also been shown to trigger the onset of bipolar disorder. Hormonal changes, especially those associated with childbearing, menstruation, and menopause can trigger mood disorders, including mania.

Substance abuse is linked with bipolar disorder. Substance abuse can create changes in the brain's chemistry that turn on the illness in a person who is vulnerable. Many people with bipolar mood disorder try to self-medicate with drugs and alcohol. This only makes the illness worse. Keeping the Word of Wisdom is truly wise for those who have a family history of bipolar disorder.

Neuroimaging studies show that the prefrontal cortex of many people with bipolar disorder is less active than normal. In some people, there is actually a lack of nerve tissue in the frontal and prefrontal cortex of the brain (see diagrams in chapter 2, "A Look at Your Brain)." Normally, brain processes help us feel joy, excitement, and other intense pleasurable feelings. In people with bipolar disorder, however, the emotional experience can be so intense that it feels overwhelming. If the prefrontal cortex is also not working properly, it may be overwhelmed by the emotional centers of the brain.

It is hard for people with bipolar disorder to think through decisions related to intense emotions. For them, information is not relayed from one part of their brain to the other. A medical test called computerized electroencephalography, commonly known as an EEG, shows that electrical activity in the brain is greatly increased during manic episodes. It is as if the brain were on hyperdrive. This eventually leads to depression and fatigue of the nervous system.

Abnormalities in neurotransmitters, or brain chemicals, are also found in the brains of bipolar patients. There is a significant increase in dopamine and acetylcholine in the limbic system (emotional center), as well as in the basal ganglia. This is associated with a decrease of serotonin in the frontal and prefrontal part of the brain (see diagrams in chapter 2, "A Look at Your Brain").

It is often difficult to determine how much of a person's problems are under his control and how much is related to the brain's inability to function and process information correctly. We do not always know when the person no longer has the ability to correctly understand and make choices. We may not be able to tell where the limits of accountability exist, but we can still trust that an all-knowing God can. When we struggle to understand the complex issue of accountability in people with brain diseases and disabilities, it can be comforting to know that these afflictions of the flesh will be taken into account in the Final Judgment. We can trust that a loving God will ensure that all judgments are just.

Children with attention-deficit/hyperactivity disorder often struggle with being distractible, restless, and impulsive. Some of these children learn to manage their behavior and seem to grow out of it. Others struggle all of their lives with these challenges. Still others, however, develop the more severe symptoms of bipolar mood disorder as they get older. It can be challenging for parents who have tried behavior management programs, discipline, love, and acceptance to discover that their child still struggles to manage his behavior.

If you have done all you can to be a good parent, it is important that you do not blame yourself for your child's illness. Caring, responsible parents still have children who develop diabetes, heart problems, cancer, and other illnesses. You did not *cause* your child's bipolar disorder any more than you *caused* your child to develop other illnesses.

How Is Bipolar Mood Disorder Treated?

It is important to recognize that bipolar mood disorder is a real illness. You can learn to manage it if you learn about it and get good treatment. It is also important that your family and other important people in your life understand the illness. Studies show that an ill person copes much better when the family understands the illness and can recognize behaviors and problems that are part of the illness.

Medication is an important part of treating bipolar illnesses. Many people do not like to take medication. They may believe that they should be strong and disciplined enough to change their mood swings. They may try to just learn how to be happy. If you respond well to medication and begin to feel better, you may think you are *cured*. Often people stop taking their medication when they begin feeling well. They do not recognize that it is the medication that is helping them feel better. When they stop the medication, the symptoms return. This can make it harder to get the symptoms under control when they have the next episode. Untreated bipolar disorder tends to get worse. If you had another illness, such as diabetes, you would not blame yourself or tell yourself that if you were a better person, you would not need any medication (see chapter 3, "The Brain and Medical Treatment for Mental Disorders"). Medication is an important part of treatment, but it is also important to get help with other psychological, social, and behavioral problems that might make the illness worse.

Psychotherapy can help you to learn coping skills, change thoughts and habits that make your illness worse, and improve your relationships with others.

Education about your mental illness can teach you how to recognize the symptoms of the onset of an episode. This can help you adjust your life so that you are safe and can take care of yourself.

Family therapy also helps other family members to understand what you are experiencing and how they can help.

Social rhythm therapy can help you learn how to keep your daily routines regular and how to adapt your lifestyle to mood swings. It is helpful to have other people who know you well help you to recognize changes that may evidence the onset of a new episode. They may recognize changes in your behavior that signal the beginning of a depressive or manic episode before you do.

What about hospitalization? Sometimes it is necessary to hospitalize those who experience a severe depression or manic episode. The symptoms may be so severe that they cannot take care of themselves. Hospitalization is also a protection if they are suicidal or their judgment is so impaired that they may harm themselves or someone else. People often resist going to the hospital, but sometimes it is necessary to admit them involuntarily (see chapter 19, "Mental Health and the Law"). Sometimes it is also necessary to adjust medication while they can be observed in a safe, controlled environment. As difficult as it is to be hospitalized, it can save lives and allow people to be stabilized.

Residential psychiatric treatment centers and day-treatment centers are also good options for treatment. These are less intensive than a hospital. They can help you get help when it is hard to help yourself. These settings can help you learn skills for managing your illness. They can also provide a transition to help you get back into regular activities after a serious episode. It often takes time to recover even after you are stable enough to leave the hospital.

Learn Your Legal Rights

In the United States, government law supports and protects people with disabilities. People with bipolar mood disorders can have serious impairments that qualify for accommodations in many settings. Children, adolescents, and young adults in schools and universities can get extra support in overcoming some of the problems they face in getting an education. Disability laws in the United States require written Individual Educational Plans (IEPs) for children and adolescents in public schools. Bipolar mood disorder is considered a qualifying disability. Many children and adolescents with bipolar disorder have difficulty learning through certain classroom methods. A school psychologist can help your child's teacher learn how to make accommodations that help your child.

It is also helpful to know your legal rights related to employment, questions about your illness, and qualifications for government assistance. Some people become so disabled by their illness that they are unable to work. If you have questions, contact a community mental health clinic, the National Alliance on Mental Illness (NAMI), or a lawyer who is familiar with mental health and disability laws. (See also chapter 19, "Mental Health and the Law.")

How Can You Help Yourself?

Some suggestions for helping yourself cope with bipolar illness include the following:

Learn as much as you can about bipolar illnesses. This can help you recognize what is happening with your body and how to take care of yourself.

Maintain good health habits. This will not cure the disorder, but it can help you feel better. Get enough sleep and exercise, and eat healthy foods. Avoid caffeine, sugar, and salty foods.

Keep a regular schedule. Avoid shift work, if possible.

Keep a log of your mood swings. This can help you to recognize your body's pattern, as well as what may trigger mood changes.

Avoid using alcohol, illegal drugs, or other substances that are known to interact with the illness. Do not try to alter your moods with addictive substances or activities like pornography. You may think you feel better at the time, but these addictive activities will only make you feel worse in the end. They can block your road to recovery (see chapter 1, "What Is Mental Illness?" section "Dual Diagnosis").

Find a mental health care counselor with whom you can have a good relationship. Look for someone who understands bipolar mood disorder and has had experience in treating people with bipolar disorders. A counselor who knows you well can help you recognize mood changes and learn how to cope. Be a partner with your doctor in sharing information, asking questions, and being honest in reporting concerns, medication side effects, and stressors you are experiencing.

Do exercises that help you relax. Learn relaxation strategies (see chapter 11, "Anxiety Disorders").

Participate regularly in wholesome recreational, creative, and social activities. Listen to uplifting, soothing music.

Avoid intense stress. Learn how to set appropriate limits.

If you travel through time zones, allow extra time for your body to adjust to the change.

Develop friendships with caring, supportive people with whom you can talk or attend a bipolar or manic-depressive support group.

If you struggle with suicidal thoughts, have a close, supportive person you can contact, and establish a plan for safety.

Every day give yourself credit for coping with a difficult illness. Bipolar mood disorder is an illness, not a character flaw. Remember that you are not your illness. The illness may require you to change your life and some of your plans, but you can still find meaning and purpose in life.

Remember God loves you and understands your challenges. Seek spiritual help in finding comfort and learning how to cope. Remember that you are not required to "run faster or labor more than you have strength" (D&C 10:4).

How Can You Help Others?

Some suggestions for helping others cope with bipolar illness include the following:

Learn as much as you can about the illness. This can help you know the difference between symptoms and interpersonal and behavior problems. Learn to recognize the difference between the *person* and the person's illness. The National Alliance on Mental Illness (NAMI) offers family education classes. Reliable information is also available on NAMI's Internet site (nami.org), as well on the site for the National Institute of Mental Health (nimh.nih.gov).

Create a low-stress, comfortable environment. Keep sensory stimulation, such as noise, at a low level. Keep life predictable.

Boost confidence through positive comments about the person's successes and abilities.

Recognize that it takes time to recover from an episode of mania or depression. The person may not be able to resume normal activities immediately.

Take care of your own emotional and spiritual well-being. Living with a loved one's mood swings can be difficult. Seek strength through prayer and spiritual resources. Seek professional counseling or an appropriate support group, if necessary, to learn more about how to cope.

Develop plans for how to respond in an emergency or during a relapse. If the person has extreme mood swings and cannot think realistically, you may have to deal with dangerous situations. Be aware of how to quickly access emergency help (see chapter 19, "Mental Health and the Law").

Set rules when the person is in a stable mood. Discuss such safeguards as withholding credit cards, car keys, access to a checking account, or anything else that could be used to harm the person or others, provided these have contributed to serious problems in the past.

Pay attention to talk of suicide. Prevent access to anything that could be used for self-harm, such as weapons, large amounts of medication, or other items. Learn to recognize signs and symptoms that may accompany suicidal feelings (see chapter 19, "Mental Health and the Law").

Show care and respect by maintaining as normal a relationship as possible. If children or adolescents are affected, help them to understand that the person has a medical illness that requires continuous love and attention. Help them to understand that it is not a result of something the person has done wrong.

Remember that the person is a child of God. Try to keep an eternal perspective rather than focusing only on the illness.

What is it Like to Have a Mood Disorder?

"As a young man serving a mission, I didn't realize that the wide swings in my enthusiasm and energy were anything out of the ordinary. Now I realize that my actions resulted from my first major episode of an affective disorder [mood disorder] named bipolar, frequently called manic depression.

"During the manic phase of the disorder, I felt absolutely wonderful, as if I could accomplish anything. My energy level soared and my mind seemed so clear that I felt in total control of my life and my future. Getting along with people and making friends was easy, even though I sometimes became frustrated with others because I thought they weren't working 'up to speed.' I demanded perfection in everything I did, and my seemingly heightened abilities made me feel like I could do it all without help from anyone.

"After a few months, I cycled into the depression phase of the disorder. My energy and enthusiasm waned as I realized that my goals were unreachable. Feeling sad and hopeless, I lost interest in nearly everything, including food and sleep. I couldn't concentrate, and I even thought about suicide. I felt totally worthless and isolated from family, friends, and Heavenly Father. Eventually things would come back to normal until the cycle started over again."[5]

Notes

1. Smith, *Doctrines of Salvation,* 2:18.

2. Smith, *History of the Church,* 6:306–7.

3. Hallfors, et al, "Which Comes First in Adolescents—Sex and Drugs or Depression?" *American Journal of Preventive Medicine* 29 (2000): 163–70.

4. David G. Weight, "Why is My Wife (or Husband) Depressed?" *Ensign,* Mar. 1990, 27.

5. "Light in Darkness," *Ensign,* June 1998, 18.

13

Men, Masculinity, and Depression

A. Dean Byrd

The shortest sentence in the holy scriptures is one of the most permission-giving scriptures for men. The scriptures do not record that the Master shed a few tears, nor do they record that the Savior cried. Rather, they tell us, "Jesus wept" (John 11:35). Weeping carries with it a powerful emotional response associated with loss, grief, trauma, and profound sadness.

The picture of a man, even the most perfect man, weeping conjures an uncomfortable image that does not fit well in our society. Indeed, such images make us uncomfortable because men are not supposed to cry, much less weep. Men are supposed to find other outlets for their pain, frustration, depression, and other problems.

Men may feel that it is weak and unmanly to admit feelings of depression. Yet mental illness, especially depression, is no respecter of persons. Often labeled the common cold of mental illness, depression can strike anyone regardless of age, ethnic background, and socioeconomic status.

Help-Seeking Behaviors

Research supports the popular notion that men are reluctant to seek help when they experience problems. Men are far less likely than women to seek assistance for life's struggles, such as depression, substance abuse, and physical disabilities.

The reasons behind these differences between men and women in help-seeking behaviors have been explored, but no consistent causes have been found. Some researchers have speculated that women recognize difficulties more readily. Others suggest that societal expectations of men preclude help-seeking behaviors because of the stereotypical notion of such behaviors being incompatible with masculinity. That is, men are socialized to believe that seeking help from others and recognizing and admitting difficulties conflict with societal messages that men receive about the importance of toughness, particularly physical and emotional toughness.

Other researchers have suggested that men fear emotional struggles like depression because such struggles are perceived to be a part of who they are, thus affecting their sense of self-worth. For example, depression may be perceived as an attack on a man's ego in such a way as to interfere with his ability to provide for his family, a family that may depend less on a man with such manifest weakness.

Still, other researchers have suggested that male help-seeking behaviors may be associated with fears of losing control or power. "Seeking help," they say, "may show a sign of weakness."

Men are socialized for independence, self-reliance, and control, all of which are wonderful virtues but when carried to the extreme become vices. Despite social norms, at times in a man's life, it is appropriate to seek help in dealing with overwhelming challenges. Such appropriate seeking of help is a sign of strength, not weakness; a sign of responsibility, not loss of control.

Regardless of the reasons men have for not seeking help with life's challenges, research is clear that they seek help significantly less often than women and that the lack of such help-seeking behavior may have consequences in both a man's life and in the lives of those he loves.

Consequences of Depression

Though men are significantly underrepresented in mental health clinics (women are more than twice as likely to seek assistance for mental health problems), they are more likely to suffer from alcoholism, drug abuse, and dependencies, as well as from a number of severe personality disorders. Researchers are beginning to discover that these mental health problems and physical health problems may be secondary to an underlying depression.

The most compelling data on sex differences is related to suicide: men commit suicide at a rate at least three times—and maybe even up to eight times—more frequently than women, depending on the age grouping. Women, however, make more suicide attempts. Often periods of depression precede suicidal thoughts and acts.

"You are pushed to the point of considering suicide, because living becomes very painful," one source observed. "You are looking for a way out, you are looking for a way to eliminate this terrible psychic pain. And I remember, I never really tried to commit suicide, but I came awful close because I use to play matador with buses. You know, I would walk out into the traffic of New York City, with no reference to traffic lights, red or green, almost hoping that I would get knocked down."[1]

Research is beginning to demonstrate that because men are less likely to talk about feelings of depression, they seek other outlets to make themselves feel better, such as alcohol, drugs, long hours at the office, or involvement in activities outside the home. Though such activities may provide some temporary relief, in the long term they make matters worse. These activities worsen not only marital and family problems, but they also contribute to the worsening of the depression. When there is marital or family discord, therapists report, men often struggle with talking about their feelings, tending instead to seek quick, simplistic solutions that are often not available or workable. Researchers have demonstrated that trouble in marriage is the most common single problem connected with depression.

Men who experience depression often feel less positive about their bodies. There may not be significant differences in terms of frequency of sexual relationships between the sexes, but men who are depressed feel less satisfied with intimate relationships. Depression keeps men from full participation and enjoyment of life's activities, including those that protect marriage and family relationships.

Masked Depression in Men

Many men may not exhibit the classical symptoms of depression; rather, the symptoms may be masked and manifested through behaviors that may even seen incompatible with depression, such as alcohol abuse, reckless behavior, anger, interpersonal conflicts, obsessive-compulsive traits, and physical complaints.

"When I was feeling depressed, I was very reckless with my life," one man observed. "I didn't care about how I drove, I didn't care about walking across the street carefully, and I didn't care about the dangerous parts of the city. I wouldn't be affected by any kinds of warnings on travel or places to go. I didn't care. I didn't care whether I lived or died, and so I was going to do whatever I wanted whenever I wanted. And when you take those kinds of chances, you have a greater likelihood of dying."[2]

Men are less likely than women to show signs of depression following a traumatic loss. But in studies comparing the grief response of widows and widowers, men were significantly more depressed than their female counterparts after two to four years. Also, bereaved men were more likely to be diagnosed with an alcohol problem than with depression. In addition, bereaved men were more likely to be diagnosed with a serious physical illness, commit suicide, and die prematurely than bereaved women.

Recent research suggests that depression in men may make them more vulnerable to committing acts of interpersonal violence. For some men, acting out aggression may be one of the few acceptable forms of emotional release. Aggressive behavior in activities like sports is not only acceptable but also encouraged. Like the emotional release in sports, aggression in interpersonal relationships may offer an emotional expression, however inappropriate, for sadness, grief, or depression. In my own clinical work, as well as in the clinical work of colleagues, I am finding *more and more frequently* that men who are violent toward family members are masking an underlying depression. While this research is still in its infancy, there is clear evidence that *violence masks depression* in the case of some men. Similarly, reports from research on men and mood-altering drugs *also show a masking of depression*. Mood-altering drugs may help to calm feelings of impotence, anger, and self-reproach brought on by trauma or loss, and they allow men to regain an illusion of control and power in their emotional lives. Addiction in particular may act as a means to cope with depression and reduce anxiety, though it often leads to a more severe episode of depression when one is not engaged in the addictive behavior.

In reality, masking may be socially acceptable, even encouraged as a way for men to disguise their feelings of loss, sadness, and depression. With little social tolerance for strong emotional expression of trauma, loss, and grief, men may express their feelings by turning to addictive behaviors and expressions of control and anger usually found in domestic violence.

Hope and Help

Depressive disorders can make men feel exhausted, worthless, helpless, and hopeless. Negative thoughts and feelings can make men feel like giving up, perhaps even consider thoughts of suicide. Such negative views are themselves symptoms of depression and often fade when treatment begins to take effect. And treatment is the good news. Of all the mental illnesses, depression has perhaps received the most attention and, as a result, better treatments have been developed. However, treatment for depression in men lags behind treatment for depression in women. As the different responses to depression between men and women are becoming more apparent, gender-specific treatments are becoming more available. For example, though women seem to be helped simply by talking about their feelings of depression, men seem to be less helped by a focus on feelings, at least in the beginning of treatment. Men, rather, seem better helped by a process called *action empathy,* in which they are able to do something with their thoughts and feelings. A more solution-focused approach, rather than just a listening approach, seems more helpful to men.

For men who experience the symptoms of depression, the first step is to always have a physical examination. We know that certain medications and certain medical conditions—including thyroid problems, viral infections, and low testosterone levels—can cause depressive symptoms. Once medical clearance has been received, a referral to a mental health professional with expertise in helping men with depression should follow. Treatment will depend upon the clinical assessment completed by the mental health professional, but often for moderate to severe depression, some combination of medication and psychotherapy seems to have better outcomes. For milder forms of depressive disorders, psychotherapy alone seems to be sufficient.

Men can do much for themselves that will enhance the effectiveness of treatment. First and foremost, it is important to acknowledge that seeking help is a sign of strength, not weakness. It is an acknowledgment of care for self and for loved ones. The following guidelines can enhance the benefits of therapy if implemented wisely:

Engage in mild exercise. The key word is *mild*. This may involve running or walking for twenty minutes three times a week. Such activity in the company of a spouse or friend can be helpful both physically and emotionally, particularly if discussions while exercising are focused away from challenges.

Set realistic goals. The key word is *realistic*. Recall some activities that you used to do that brought you some measure of joy or pleasure, and begin doing some of those things again. It might be a hobby or something as simple as going to a sporting activity or concert. Such structure in your life will often help you have things to look forward to.

In this way, one man said, "Pretty soon you start having good thoughts about yourself and that you're are not worthless and you kind of turn your head over your shoulder and look back at that, that rutted, muddy, dirt road that you just traveled and now you're on some smooth asphalt and go, 'Wow, what a trip. Still got a ways to go, but I wouldn't want to go down that road again.'"[3]

Break large tasks into manageable steps. The key descriptor is *manageable*. More or larger is not always better. Unrealistic expectations may hinder the healing process. For, example, if the house needs to be painted, it might be better to paint one room at a time and even ask someone to assist you. The double benefit is that you will receive help in completing the task and have someone to talk with. The first is a measurable task and the latter, an immeasurable benefit.

Highlight improvements, even small ones. The key descriptor is *even small ones*. Small steps added together become powerful forces for good, even in the life of one person. Expect your mood to gradually improve and note (in a journal) ways in which things are better. This will serve as *evidence* that the depression is lifting. It is good to expect miracles, especially little ones!

"You start to have these little thoughts: 'Wait, maybe I can get through this. Maybe these things that are happening to me aren't so bad.' And you start thinking to yourself, 'Maybe I can deal with things for now.' And it's just little tiny thoughts until you realize that it's gone and you let go, 'Oh, my God, thank you, I don't feel sad anymore.' And then when it was finally gone, when I felt happy, I was back to the usual things that I was doing in my life. You get so happy because you think to yourself, 'I never thought it would leave.'"[4]

Practice allowing others to help. The key is *practice*. If you are not used to asking for help (and most men are not), it will take some getting use to. Asking for help may seem awkward in the beginning but will become more comfortable with practice.

Develop a Gospel Storehouse of Resources

Gospel resources are very important, because the gospel of Jesus Christ is a gospel of hope. Our Father in Heaven loves us despite our depression, but he does not leave us that way. He wants us to become like his Son, and he has prepared a way for that to happen. The Master knows our names, but more important, he knows our hearts. He does not even require that we knock on the door of spiritual resources in our lives, only that we listen to his knock and open the door when we hear (see Revelation 3:20). He wants us not just to know of his love but also to feel of his love. This can only happen if we have our minds on things that are higher than our challenges and if we become open to the promptings of the Spirit.

The Atonement is not just for the consequences of sin in our lives, but it is also the balm of Gilead for our shortcomings, our imperfections and strivings, and even for our depression. His love can lead us, guide us, and walk beside us to provide both comfort and sustenance. His love can lead us out of the valley of depression, allowing us to discover more about ourselves and more about him than we ever thought possible. We can learn to recognize his love and to recognize the knock on the door of our lives—a knock that will open up vast spiritual resources.

Consider implementing the following resources as a part of your life:

Have a daily conversation with the Master. He will understand perfectly. He has not experienced depression vicariously but personally. Remember, this is not a complaint session but rather a sharing time. A conversation has two parts: talking and listening; make it fifty-fifty.

Recognize your need for God, and look for his hand in your life. When you trust, you let go of control. Let go and let God. God is a stranger to us unless our eyes are turned to his influence.

Be willing to be made willing. Just as children may rebel against the greater wisdom of their parents, individuals (men, in particular) cherish their independence and control instead of submitting to God's influence. Yielding to his influence in our lives allows us to feel his love. It is his love that sustains us in difficult times and allows feelings of joy and peace in times of calm.

There are stormy times in our lives when we plead for the Master to intervene and calm the troubled waters. Sometimes he does; other times he allows the storms to rage, and he calms us. Either way, we can come to know and feel his love.

"I could feel the tears within me, undiscovered and untouched in their inland sea," one author wrote. "Those tears had been with me always. I thought that at birth, American men are allowed just as many tears as American women. But because we are forbidden to shed them, we die long before women do, with our hearts exploding or our blood pressure rising or our livers eaten away by alcohol because that lake of grief inside us has no outlet. We men die because our faces were not watered enough."[5]

Notes

1. National Institute of Mental Health, *Men and Depression.*
2. Ibid., Bill Maruyama, lawyer.
3. Ibid., Paul McCathern, U.S. Air Force, retired.
4. Ibid., Shawn Colten, national diving champion.
5. Conroy, *Beach Music,* 179.

14

Women and Depression

Christine S. Packard and Wendy Ulrich

From adolescence on, women are about twice as likely to experience depressive disorders as men; this holds true across a variety of cultures and countries. Apparently something makes women more vulnerable to depression, but researchers vary in their opinions as to which *something* is most responsible. Current theories suggest that our physiology, thoughts, experiences, and relationships may all play roles in depression. As we compare what we know about causes of depression with what we know about women's lives and bodies, we begin to see possible reasons for women being more vulnerable to depression.

Church Affiliation

Most studies of the relationship between church activity and mental health find that religious people are generally happier and better adjusted than others. People who are active in the LDS Church follow this pattern. One study found that LDS women reported fewer symptoms of depression and were more likely to rate themselves "very happy" than the average American woman. In this study, LDS women also reported higher satisfaction with their marriages and their lives in general. Another study found no difference between LDS women and non-LDS women in the amount of depressive symptoms reported. Research to date suggests that religious participation is at least neutral and perhaps generally good for mental health.

However, one study found that Utahns use more antidepressant medication than people in other states. The reasons for this finding are not clear. Church members, who are better educated on average, may simply be more knowledgeable about depression and its treatment. They may also be more likely to seek medical help rather than using alcohol or illegal drugs to self-medicate.

The study did not assess the religion or gender of those taking antidepressants. The high use could therefore theoretically be attributed to non-LDS men. Alternatively, high standards in the LDS Church may be misinterpreted by some and lead to unhealthy perfectionism, which can contribute to depression (see chapter 12, "Mood Disorders"). Some research, however, shows that LDS women are not more perfectionist than other women. More research is needed to better understand why Utahns are prescribed more antidepressants than others.

Physiology

Women's physiology is responsible for some of their increased risk for depression. Looking at health problems related to depression can help us understand why. Hormone fluctuations, low energy, and poor health habits all affect our mood, outlook, and emotional health. Good nutrition, adequate sleep, appropriate exercise, and good medical care aid in healthy hormone production. This can minimize the negative physical and emotional effects of hormonal fluctuations. These healthy habits can also help improve women's overall health, which in turn can improve their emotional state.

Hormones. Neurotransmitters are substances that allow cells to communicate information within our brains. Hormones affect how these neurotransmitters work. Changes in hormones during the monthly menstrual cycle, pregnancy, childbirth, breastfeeding, and menopause can change the amount of neurotransmitter available in the brain (see chapter 15, "Women's Mental

Health in the Reproductive Cycle"). Hormones also fluctuate more when women are stressed, tired, hungry, or sick.

Low energy. Prolonged low energy can lead to depression, and women have many reasons for having low energy. Symptoms of tiredness, low energy, and depression should be reported to medical professionals, who can evaluate what might be causing the fatigue. For example, the thyroid gland helps maintain energy level and balance metabolism. Women are prone to thyroid problems, perhaps because of the interplay between the reproductive and thyroid hormones. Depression often accompanies hypothyroidism (insufficient thyroid production).

Anemia (low iron) as a result of heavy menstrual flow, pregnancy, poor nutrition, or other problems can result in deep weariness and a sense of being bone tired. Chronic tiredness can also result from simply not getting adequate sleep. We may stay up late too often to pick up the house or fold the laundry, hoping to avoid dealing with today's leftovers tomorrow. Babies and young children can leave parents chronically sleep deprived. Age, excess weight, and other physical conditions can trouble us in the night with acid reflux, apnea (breathing problems during sleep), or waking to use the bathroom. Whatever the cause, lack of adequate sleep and the tiredness that results from it can lead to depression.

A surprising cause of chronic low energy and fatigue is dehydration. If we do not drink enough water, our body can become dehydrated. In our busy lives, we often don't take time to drink enough water in the course of a day. Caffeinated soft drinks we pick up for quick energy actually sap hydration from our bodies.

Nutrition. Women who give low priority to maintaining their physical health often feel compressed and burdened by the demands of family and work. Skipping or putting off meals until we are overly hungry can cause us to reach for empty carbohydrates in an effort to stave off hunger. A full schedule of children's activities, church callings, or work responsibilities often interferes with nutritious food preparation and the time needed to relax, enjoy, and fully digest a healthy meal.

Exercise. Regular aerobic exercise is a key ingredient in preventing and treating depression. Exercise is not only good for our muscles, but it also helps balance hormones and stabilize mood. Poor eating habits, coupled with a lack of exercise, can result in weight gain, poor self-esteem, and health problems.

Medical care. Many women see a doctor only when pregnant, menopausal, or needing a yearly gynecologic exam. Women may think they are too busy, that it is too expensive, or that it is selfish to attend to their health. Good physical health, however, is necessary for good mental health.

Thinking

Cognitive-behavioral therapy (CBT) has been repeatedly shown to have the best track record of any form of *talk therapy* for treating depression. CBT looks carefully at how people talk to themselves inside their own heads. What we tell ourselves our circumstances mean may have a bigger influence on our mood than the circumstances themselves. In general, depressed people begin to feel better as:

> They work toward realistic goals
>
> They develop patterns and routines for day-to-day living
>
> They set realistic standards for themselves and are not overloaded with shame and guilt associated with unrealistic self-expectations
>
> They can see choices and behavior in shades of gray rather than black-and-white
>
> They avoid excessive worry about faults and problems

Goals. Having too few goals gives us little to strive for and no structure and purpose in our life. Pursuing too many goals leaves us feeling overloaded. Both can lead to depression. LDS women are encouraged to pursue meaningful goals related to spirituality, service to others, and family life. As long as we do not overload ourselves with too many goals, this should be a plus for our mental health. If we worry too much about how others see us or what others want from us, we may give up what we really want for the sake of harmony with others. Staying connected to our real interests and passions helps prevent depression.

Routines. Routines are often more challenging for stay-at-home moms than for women who work outside the home. Full-time homemakers may have to adapt more to the schedules of children, a working spouse, and community activities, leaving them less able to control their own routines. Women who are home with young children can feel that it is hardly worth it to make plans that are so easily disrupted. Yet routines and plans help both moms and children, even if they have to be more flexible than they would sometimes like.

Perfectionism and excessive guilt. Perfectionism and guilt are high-risk factors for depression. Women are often the carriers of family traditions and social values. This can build self-esteem and self-image around being socially appropriate, refined, or concerned about others. Women may develop an overly harsh and punishing conscience, however, in an effort to keep these high standards and maintain self-esteem. While high moral standards help both societies and individuals, excessive shame or guilt can lead to depression rather than constructive change. Basing our self-esteem on what others think of us can pressure us to set unrealistic goals. Excessive shame promotes hiding our true feelings or difficulties for fear of others' judgments or disappointment, leaving us feeling isolated and unworthy—both factors in depression.

Scaled thinking. Seeing things in black-and-white terms instead of on a scale with many shades of gray promotes depression. If we believe that our lessons are a disaster, our children are failures, we look awful, and we have no friends, it is almost a given that we will feel discouraged, ashamed, and depressed. Depression is a less likely outcome if, instead, we can see that some of our lessons are below our personal average, that our children have many wonderful qualities, that our looks today are a six on a ten-point scale, and that we may not have as many friends as some people, but we have more than others. While this seems obvious, the onset of depressive symptoms can often be traced to simple events to which we react with black-and-white, all-or-nothing thinking that we don't even recognize as such.

Women may be more prone to all-or-nothing assessments. Homemakers get less feedback on their performance than people who work for a supervisor or a paying customer. They have fewer ways of knowing how they are doing. Many of the issues that are important to women (raising healthy children, having a clean home, serving others, being spiritual) have less clear standards than sports or jobs, so they don't know what constitutes success. Asking themselves on a scale of one to ten how clean the house is or how spiritual their day was or how happy their children are can help.

Rumination. *Rumination* is when we get stuck rerunning the same worries over and over again. Women tend to be more verbal than men and to see friendships as more meaningful if they can talk deeply about emotions and relationships. In contrast, men are more likely to value friendships based on mutual interests and activities. While deep thinking can lead to important self-discovery and change, it can also cause us to focus too much attention on problems to the exclusion of creativity, pleasure, light-hearted interaction, and fun. We need people we can be honest and thoughtful with, but we also need time to just play and work together with friends.

Emotions

What we think and understand in our heads is often different from what we feel in our hearts, and sometimes that difference causes us emotional problems. The motivations that drive us often come from our gut feelings rather than from our intellect. Clarity of thinking is impeded by depression, and when efforts to change our thoughts don't result in a decrease in depression, it may be time to look a little deeper.

As women, we have a tendency to focus on problems and on our own sense of ourselves. Simply telling ourselves that we are thinking and behaving irrationally isn't always enough to change our feelings or behaviors. We may not recognize that our quick irritability or anger in close relationships may be secondary to painful, primary feelings, such as sadness, fear, loneliness, or shame. Likewise, feelings of depression or sadness may mask deeper feelings of resentment, frustration, or powerlessness.

Painful feelings associated with believing that we are unworthy of being cared for, unlovable, or too difficult to be in a relationship with can be extremely challenging to experience and tolerate. We often distance ourselves from those feelings by expressing anger, irritability, or hopelessness. We can make some efforts to address the basic emotions that are driving the beliefs. Journal writing is particularly effective in clarifying some of the primary feelings driving unhelpful or distorted beliefs. Allowing ourselves the blank canvas of an empty sheet of paper and permitting ourselves to write anything that comes to mind may open us to fuller understanding of what we feel and believe, as well as to the inspiration of the Spirit.

Working with images or objects also sometimes allows us to move from intellectual awareness of our difficulties to tangible, workable solutions, or to at least manageable steps to take to move forward. Drawing, contemplating analogies and metaphors, reading or writing stories, or working with a therapist using miniatures and a sand tray can allow us to give form to the troubling images in our hearts and heads so that we can begin to imagine constructive alternatives. Playing with ideas, objects, and images in tangible ways helps us change perspectives and gives us the opportunity to feel new feelings and eventually to think different thoughts.

Women tend to believe that some feelings, particularly anger, are unacceptable to express. Because they may believe anger is frightening, inappropriate, or ineffective, sometimes women turn their anger on themselves by blaming themselves or overthinking instead of calmly sharing frustrations and problem-solving with others. Men are more likely to take an externalizing approach to life, distracting themselves with other interests when things feel difficult, or expressing anger openly.

While pondering can be helpful if it allows us to focus prayerfully upon healthy and spiritual options, often the ruminating and obsessing sinks us deeper into feelings of pain, fear, or hopelessness. If our fear of anger can be reduced, perhaps we can understand anger as a symptom that something is wrong about which we feel powerless. Then it becomes possible to address the feeling of powerlessness, acknowledge it for what it is, understand why we feel it, and make choices that will allow us to move forward—rather than ruminate in the rut of depression and helplessness.

Acknowledging the reality of our feelings and emotions, accepting that they exist, and realizing that they can be explored without unleashing them on others, allow us to look at them more objectively. A listening friend, inspired priesthood leader, or skilled therapist can often help us dissect a mass of emotion, gain perspective, and address issues effectively.

Emotions can feel scary, painful, and difficult to acknowledge honestly. However, because women spend so much time in the world of emotion, they often have the skills to tolerate their feelings long enough to work at understanding them more fully and expressing them more responsibly. When Nephi felt overwhelmed by his emotions and confusion, he went "into the mountain oft, and I did pray oft unto the Lord; wherefore the Lord showed unto me great things" (1 Nephi 18:3). It is interesting that the Spirit often speaks in the language of emotion and feeling. Heavenly Father has given us feelings to greatly enlarge our experiences in this life. When we seek his help to understand our feelings and express them appropriately, he can show us great things.

Roles

While increased choices for women can give them a greater sense of personal power, control, and resulting self-esteem, choices can also complicate women's lives with conflicting demands and expectations. Women who work may feel guilty for neglecting family, for having inadequate homemaking skills, or for being criticized by women who stay home. Women who give up careers to devote full time to raising children may feel less skilled or important than their working sisters, or they may wonder if their sacrifice was worth it if their children struggle anyway. For many women, the demands of multiple roles have increased without a corresponding increase in resources of time, energy, and ability. Whenever women feel that the demands on them exceed their resources or that they cannot do everything right no matter how hard they try, depression is more likely.

Women in the Church also face the perception held by some in the world that the Church oppresses women. Even if we do not feel oppressed, we may wonder why men hold positions we cannot or why they seem to have more influence and opportunity. Role differences can actually simplify our lives and allow us to focus on our half of the tennis court without having to cover it all, but we may wonder how a masculine God really feels about his feminine daughters. While most women find a peaceful resolution to these questions through studying the gospel, talking with others, having positive experiences with men and women in the Church, and enjoying personal spiritual experiences, some feel devalued and disempowered in ways that contribute to depression.

Such concerns may be complicated by a history of physical, emotional, or sexual abuse. Women who have been harmed by men are understandably more likely to distrust men's motives, fear their power, and resent their authority. Such women may more easily confuse the loving nature of God with the unloving nature of their abuser. Adults abused as children are more likely to struggle with mental health challenges as adults, have difficulties trusting authority figures, wrestle with internal images of a punishing or threatening God, and battle feelings of powerlessness and low self-esteem. Because women are more likely than men to be victims of abuse, they are more likely to grapple with these factors, all of which contribute to depression.

Making peace with our role choices and our personal history is important. We do not welcome symptoms of depression, but such symptoms may require us to reconsider the conclusions we came to as children or the choices we make as adults that may distort our self-perceptions, skew our view of reality, and limit our options. As we come to deepen our trust in God's love, goodness, integrity, and plan for us, we can find a more enduring peace. As we come to see our own options and strengths more clearly, we can also see more clearly the eternal importance of the unique roles we fill and the strengths we contribute to the world. We can prayerfully discover our own personal missions, form healthy relationships with men and women, and find satisfaction as our roles and opportunities evolve over a lifetime.

Relationships

Women are *relational* beings. From the beginning of time, women have spent much of their time and energy in creating, sustaining, and facilitating relationships. They are the source of women's deepest joy, and when relationships are disrupted or painful, they are the source of women's deepest sorrow and despair. Much of women's sense of worth and value comes from their perceived sense of success or failure in relationships. They may wrongly believe that problems in relationships are related to their own worth and forget that others also have agency to make choices.

Young women learn to look forward to and value their eventual temple marriage and family life. Lessons focused on chastity, marriage, and motherhood create an expectation and belief that if a young woman keeps the commandments, makes good choices, and safeguards her virtue, a handsome returned missionary will come into her life and sweep her off to the temple to begin their own romantic eternity. Sometimes that works out exactly as hoped, but increasingly in today's world, those expectations are not fulfilled. Many lovely and righteous LDS women become confused, devastated, and depressed when they have worked and prepared their entire lives for a marriage that doesn't materialize. Too many of these young women see their single status as evidence of some personal failure or inadequacy. When what they have dreamed of, prepared for, and held out as the best and only option for life doesn't work out, depression often results. It becomes easy to lose sight of God's eternal plan for their happiness, which extends beyond mortality.

Other young women *do* find their handsome returned missionary and enter the temple with him, only to learn within a few years that he struggles with pornography, same-sex attraction, infidelity, an unmanageable temper, or an unwillingness to acknowledge anyone's needs but his own. Other women who have given much energy and emotional focus to children may be devastated when, despite good parenting, their children develop serious problems.

Because our relationships hold so much importance for us, when we struggle in them, we struggle to hold on to a secure sense of ourselves. We may question our worth and value, as well as our importance to Heavenly Father and our family members. We may begin to wonder about promises in our patriarchal blessings, and we perhaps lose confidence in the counsel of priesthood leaders who may seem not to fully understand.

Elder Dallin H. Oaks has counseled: "Healing blessings come in many ways, each suited to our individual needs, as known to Him who loves us best. Sometimes a 'healing' cures our illness or lifts our burden. But sometimes we are 'healed' by being given strength or understanding or patience to bear the burdens placed upon us."[1]

Because the pain of depression is often relational in nature, it is important to remember that the healing is also relational. Healing is the essence of our relationship with Jesus Christ. Our Savior desires to heal us from every affliction *if* we will come unto him. No pain or sorrow is beyond the reach of his redeeming power. His Spirit will guide and direct us in Christlike paths as we struggle with difficult relationships, and his grace will be sufficient in our days of loneliness and relational discouragement.

In a complex world, we can find in the gospel of Jesus Christ a sure foundation for self-worth despite defects, hope despite history, and love despite relational challenges. We have every reason to trust in God's goodness and in his will and power to save us and those we love. Just as important, we have every reason to expect that he understands the full depths of sorrow, disappointment, and suffering that permeate our mortal experience. Depression is not cause for shame; nor is it cause for despair. It may be the experience that can eventually lift us to greater light and knowledge of God.

Notes

1. Dallin H. Oaks, "He Heals the Heavy Laden," *Ensign,* Nov. 2006, 7–8.

15

Women's Mental Health in the Reproductive Cycle

Grant Belnap and Carol Belnap

Women are more likely to experience problems with mental and emotional health during their childbearing years than at any other time. Events in a woman's reproductive life include the menstrual cycle, the postpartum period of pregnancy, and the transition to menopause, known as perimenopause. These times can be associated with specific disorders that affect a woman's mood and ability to function. These disorders often require professional attention and medical treatment in order for women to improve.

Premenstrual Dysphoric Disorder (PMDD)

Most women experience mild, temporary, physical and emotional changes around the time of their menstrual periods. These signs begin a few days before menstruation and stop shortly after the start of menstrual flow. Premenstrual syndrome (PMS) occurs when the symptoms before a period become distressing and interfere somewhat with daily life and relationships. Some women experience so many severe and disabling changes in mood and functioning before menses that they have premenstrual dysphoric disorder (PMDD).

A woman with PMDD usually has multiple symptoms that recur each month. She has significant feelings of depression, anxiety, or irritability in the days before her period. She often feels hopeless, on edge, or moody. With PMDD, a woman may have no interest in her usual activities. She may have trouble concentrating. She may feel out of control or overwhelmed.

The physical symptoms of the disorder include extreme fatigue or a lack of energy. A woman with PMDD may have difficulty sleeping or may sleep too much. Food cravings or a change in appetite may occur, along with bloating (retaining water) and temporary weight gain. Breast tenderness, joint or muscle pain, and headaches are also common.

The symptoms of PMDD are more disruptive than the symptoms of PMS. They interfere markedly with a woman's usual responsibilities, such as work and school. The disorder causes significant problems with friends and family. It disrupts recreational activities. Yet a woman with premenstrual dysphoric disorder finds that her mood, lifestyle, and capabilities return to normal the rest of the month. This on-off pattern of emotional and behavioral changes occurs during most of her menstrual cycles.

Causes

The cause of premenstrual dysphoric disorder is not completely understood, although it clearly has a biological basis. Research suggests that the syndrome is found in families and is partly inherited. In PMDD, fluctuating hormone levels in the menstrual cycle are thought to affect the brain chemicals that regulate mood.

PMDD can start at any age after menstruation begins, and it can continue from month to month until menopause. Many women report that their symptoms worsen as they get older, after they give birth, or after they have a tubal ligation. Stress seems to intensify the disorder. PMDD typically does not occur during pregnancy or in the first few months of breast-feeding. PMDD can affect women who do not have periods but who still have cycling hormone levels, such as after a hysterectomy.

Keeping a daily chart of symptoms through two menstrual cycles helps detect the presence of premenstrual dysphoric disorder. Women whose symptoms continue throughout the month probably do not have PMDD. They may have another psychiatric disorder or medical condition that intensifies before a menstrual period. Other women who experience symptoms that come and go unrelated to menstruation may have other cyclic conditions, such as bipolar disorder. However, women with PMDD often have a history of a previous mood disorder, such as major depression.

Treatment

Several options are available to women who experience mild to moderate forms of PMS, although no one treatment seems to work for everyone. These approaches include changes in diet and lifestyle and self-management of symptoms and stress. Women with PMDD also benefit from self-care, but they usually require prescription medication and help from a mental health professional to treat the disorder. You can do several things to help yourself:

Modify your diet, which can help minimize premenstrual problems. Evidence suggests that reducing intake of alcohol, tobacco, caffeine, sodium, and sugar while increasing complex carbohydrates (whole grains, fruits, and vegetables), calcium, and vitamin B6 can be beneficial to brain function.

Eat smaller, more frequent meals.

Avoid sweets.

Ask your doctor for a mild diuretic if bloating makes you uncomfortable. Be sure to drink enough water, however.

Engage in regular aerobic exercise, which can improve both physical and mental health.

Get enough sleep, which can also ease symptoms.

Try bright-light therapy during the premenstrual phase, which may lessen the severity of the disorder (see "phototherapy" in chapter 12, "Mood Disorders").

Try support groups, counseling, stress-management training, and journal writing, which are also useful in learning to cope with the cyclic nature of the symptoms.

Antidepressants are considered the most effective medications for women with PMDD. Two antidepressants, sertraline (Zoloft) and fluoxetine (Prozac or Sarafem), are approved by the Food and Drug Administration for the treatment of premenstrual dysphoric disorder. In many cases, antidepressants can be taken in relatively low doses for part of the month before a period with few side effects. Some women with PMDD may need larger doses throughout the entire month. Hormone therapy, oral contraceptives, or surgery may be used to stop ovulation to control symptoms in severe cases of PMDD.

Postpartum Mood Disorders

Many new mothers experience mild and temporary depression within two weeks of delivery called the *baby blues*. Mood swings, tearfulness, sadness, anxiety, and irritability are common. Women with postpartum blues sometimes have difficulty sleeping even when their babies are asleep. The symptoms of the blues are usually mild and go away in several days by themselves.

Postpartum depression is more severe and affects about 10 percent of women after childbirth. It usually begins three to four weeks after delivery but can develop as late as six to twelve months later. Symptoms may include sadness, anxiety, fatigue, lack of motivation, inability to enjoy activities, problems with sleep and appetite, and feelings of guilt and worthlessness. Postpartum depression interferes with a mother's ability to care for herself and her baby. A woman with postpartum depression may be overly preoccupied with the baby, or she may show a lack of concern for her infant. She may worry about harming herself or her child, or she may worry that something is wrong with her newborn.

Postpartum psychosis is a severe and rare form of postpartum depression. It usually begins in the first few weeks after the baby's birth. The new mother experiences symptoms that may include rapid mood swings, trouble sleeping, forgetting to eat, restlessness, and feeling frantic. The mother may have delusions and hallucinations. For example, she may think the baby is possessed or that she herself is evil, and she may hear voices commanding her to hurt the baby or herself.

Causes

Several factors may contribute to postpartum depression. Rapid changes in hormone levels following birth trigger changes in brain chemicals that affect mood and emotions. The various physical, emotional, and financial demands surrounding childbirth and newborn care can have a negative impact on a mother's mental health. Relationship problems with a spouse or social isolation from not being able to be out and around other people can worsen depression.

If a woman has postpartum depression, there is a 50 percent chance that she will have the disorder with her next pregnancy. Her risk of postpartum depression increases with each pregnancy-related episode. Women who have premenstrual dysphoric disorder, episodes of major depression, bipolar disorder, or a family history of these mood disorders are at increased risk for postpartum depression. Women with postpartum depression are also more likely to have future depressive episodes not associated with pregnancy.

Similarly, in the case of postpartum psychosis, a previous history of postpartum psychosis is the highest risk factor for future episodes. Many women who have had an episode of postpartum psychosis will show signs of the illness in the last trimester of the next pregnancy. Other risk factors include a history of postpartum depression or bipolar disorder, or a family history of bipolar disorder.

Treatment

Untreated postpartum mood disorders can have an adverse effect on newborns. The illness makes it difficult for the mother to bond with or properly care for her baby. Studies show that children of mothers with long-standing postpartum depression may have problems with their health, behavior, and language development.

Help and support from family and friends improve the baby blues. Rest, exercise, and good nutrition also benefit health and mood. To treat postpartum depression, psychotherapy and antidepressant medications may be required as well. Interpersonal therapy that addresses a woman's relationship issues and cognitive-behavioral therapy that employs a problem-solving approach to symptoms are effective when combined with antidepressant medication for this type of depression. Many antidepressants are considered safe to take during pregnancy and breastfeeding. Studies show that while antidepressants are present in breast milk, the effect on the developing infant is minimal. Depressive symptoms respond to medication in about three to four weeks.

In postpartum psychosis, providing a safe environment for mother and child is the primary concern. A small percentage of women with the disorder attempt suicide or try to harm their infants. Twenty-four-hour supervision is frequently required, and hospitalization is often necessary to ensure the mother gets adequate sleep, rest, nutrition, and appropriate help in caring for her baby. Getting help at home, having someone carefully watch the mother's symptoms, and educating the family are more effective than traditional psychotherapy in the early stages of postpartum psychosis. Once psychotic symptoms have been addressed, support groups and individual counseling may be helpful.

Because women with postpartum psychosis are likely to have bipolar illness rather than major depression, mood stabilizers (such as lithium and antipsychotic medications) are often used instead of antidepressants. Some of these medications should not be taken while breastfeeding. A mother with a postpartum disorder who breastfeeds should consult with her healthcare provider to choose a medication that poses the least risk to her newborn.

Another option in the treatment of *severe* postpartum mood disorders is electroconvulsive therapy (ECT). This medical procedure improves profound or complicated depression by using an electrical impulse to produce chemical changes in the brain (see chapter 12, "Mood Disorders").

Perimenopause and Depression

Perimenopause, on average, occurs between the ages of forty-seven and fifty-two. It signals the end of the reproductive years. Menstrual periods lighten and become less frequent until menstruation ceases completely at menopause. During perimenopause, symptoms such as hot flushes, night sweats, insomnia, and minor mood changes may occur. Some women develop depressive episodes during perimenopause that have all the features of major depression.

Some women become depressed for the first time in their lives during the transition to menopause. However, the women most likely to have a depressive episode during perimenopause are those who have a history of major depression. Women who had episodes of postpartum depression or premenstrual dysphoric disorder are also at risk for depression during perimenopause. Evidence suggests that women with recurrent major depression may actually reach menopause earlier than other women.

Causes

Depression may occur for several reasons during perimenopause. During this time in the reproductive cycle, a decrease in estrogen (a female hormone) levels may affect chemicals in the brain that control mood. The physical symptoms of hot flushes and insomnia may cause such distress for some women that they lead directly to depression. For women who are already at risk for mood disorders, stress related to midlife—including changes in health, relationships, and circumstances—may trigger the biological events that occur in depression.

Treatment

Hormone-replacement therapy (HRT) in pill form or with skin patch has been shown to improve the mood of women in perimenopause who may feel blue, slightly anxious, or mildly irritable but who do not have major depression. Studies indicate that women with major depression during perimenopause are treated most effectively by a combination of HRT and antidepressant medication. Interpersonal therapy or cognitive-behavioral therapy in combination with medical treatment can be helpful in dealing with stressful midlife changes that may be associated with depression in perimenopause. Regular exercise, relaxation techniques, and meaningful, productive work and social activities are also helpful when combined with the other treatments mentioned above.[1]

Note

1. Information in this chapter comes from the American Psychiatric Association, the Massachusetts General Hospital Center for Women's Health, the National Women's Health Information Center, and *Women's Mental Health,* ed. Susan G. Kornstein and Anita H. Clayton.

16

Schizophrenia and Other Psychotic Disorders

Marleen S. Williams, W. Dean Belnap, and John P. Livingstone

For many people, the words *schizophrenia* and *psychotic* may bring frightening images of madness and asylums. False media portrayals and dramatic public cases have left many people with a poor understanding of what these words really mean. Schizophrenia is the most severe but often least understood mental illness. For many years, it was falsely believed that poor parenting caused it, and families were often blamed for the illness of their loved one. This caused added burden and sorrow to those who were already suffering because of the severe changes in their loved one's thinking and behavior.

Modern science has helped us to have a better understanding of this strange and severe illness. There is now strong agreement among experts that schizophrenia has biological origins related to an imbalance in the chemicals that affect the brain's ability to process thoughts and emotions. There is also strong evidence from neuroimaging that the brain of a person with schizophrenia may actually shrink and undergo structural changes because of the disease. Whether the patient receives support and can reduce stress, however, may make a difference in how the illness expresses itself and how well the person functions. Rather than blaming families, research has shown that families can be strong partners in helping a family member cope with the illness. Family education about the illness is an important part of treatment.

Schizophrenia often has devastating consequences both to the patient and to those who care for him. The illness can severely affect the person's ability to work, manage relationships, care for personal daily needs, and see reality accurately. Many people who are homeless and unable to care for themselves suffer from schizophrenia. They can be easily victimized because they cannot accurately perceive danger. Many spend their lives in and out of hospitals, homeless shelters, and jails. Many never receive any treatment because others do not realize that they have a serious illness. They attribute the bizarre behavior to other causes and assume that the person could change by just trying hard enough.

Historically, people with schizophrenia have been treated cruelly. They were often beaten, chained in prisons, subject to exorcism, or set adrift on the ocean in a small boat named *Ship of Fools*. Modern understanding of the illness has eliminated many of the abuses of the past, but the suffering of those with this illness and those who love them is still severe.

Schizophrenia afflicts about one percent of people worldwide. It is found in all countries, cultures, races, religions, and social classes. This means more than two million Americans live with this illness. Many of them and their families suffer silently because of fear that others will not understand the illness and judge them unfairly. Myths and social stigma about severe mental illness keep many people from getting the support, understanding, and treatment they need.

Common Myths about Schizophrenia and Psychoses

Schizophrenia is a split personality. Many people confuse schizophrenia with dissociative identity disorder (DID), often known as multiple personality. This is a different mental illness with different causes and symptoms. People with schizophrenia do not alternate between good and bad personalities. The *split* in schizophrenia is a split from the ability to accurately understand reality.

All people with psychotic illnesses are dangerous and should be locked up. Some are dangerous, but most are not. The small numbers that commit violent or dangerous acts receive a lot of media attention, so people are more aware of them. Most people with psychotic illnesses, however, are not dangerous and are unlikely to harm others. Most people who commit violent and dangerous acts are not psychotic. They are fully aware of what they are doing. They may make wrong choices, but they are capable of choosing. Schizophrenia, however, makes it difficult for a person to always have the ability to make informed choices.

Schizophrenia should be *cured* only by spiritual intervention. Some people believe that schizophrenia should be *cured* by spiritual intervention, such as priesthood blessings and casting out devils rather than through medication and psychological treatment. Certainly, faith and spiritual strength can help a person who experiences any serious, long-term illness. It is also true that many people have been healed from disease and infirmities through the power of the priesthood. Blessings can be a strong comfort and support to anyone experiencing a serious illness. However, God does not release everyone from all painful mortal experiences. Righteous individuals are still subject to disease.

We would not withhold appropriate medical treatment or medication from someone with cancer, heart disease, or defects and dysfunctions of any other organ of the body. It is a mistake to withhold or discourage proper medical and psychological treatment from anyone who suffers from schizophrenia.

Families cause schizophrenia. It was once believed that problems in family interactions caused schizophrenia. There is now overwhelming scientific evidence showing that defects in the brain's ability to processes information and emotions are the basis for schizophrenic illnesses. Having a family member with a psychotic illness creates tremendous stress for other family members. The illness can contribute to problems within the family. Abuse or other serious family problems can also create added stress that makes the symptoms of the illness worse. However, these are not the basic cause of schizophrenia. It occurs in families that are loving, caring, and functional. Schizophrenia also occurs in families that are functional or dysfunctional—just as with other diseases. Research does show, however, that strengthening family relationships can help provide support for the family member who has schizophrenia.

Sin causes schizophrenia. Sin can create stress, unhappiness, and emotional conflict. These may make the symptoms of the illness more severe, but sin does not *cause* schizophrenia. Many people commit serious sins and never develop schizophrenia. Many people who do develop schizophrenia lead righteous lives, hold temple recommends, and enjoy full activity in the Church. Serious impairment in the brain's ability to think clearly, interpret reality, and make wise decisions, however, may impair the ability to always tell the difference between right and wrong. Little children under the age of eight can develop schizophrenia, as well as other psychotic illnesses. This is further evidence that it is not caused by sin or demonic possession. Little children are "alive in Christ" (Moroni 8:22) and can neither sin nor come under Satan's power (Moroni 8:10–24).

Religion causes schizophrenia. Sometimes people wrongly assume that strong religious beliefs cause schizophrenia. The content of hallucinations and delusions may be related to religion, but religion does not *cause* those hallucinations and delusions. Hallucinations and delusions are usually about people, beliefs, and concerns that are important to the sufferer. Therefore, a Latter-day Saint may have delusions about LDS concerns, a farmer may have delusions related to farming, a scientist may have delusions concerning science, and a politician may have delusions related to political concerns. These activities and concerns did not cause their schizophrenia. A person's interests, associations, and beliefs often become the focus of the delusions when the person becomes ill.

Symptoms of Psychotic Disorders

The experience of psychosis is so vastly different from most people's experience that it may be difficult to accurately understand and have compassion for those who struggle with it. We must be able to put ourselves in another's place in order to sympathize with the other's experience. Because most people have never experienced psychosis, this is harder to do than with most other illnesses. Knowing what it is like for the person can help others to both recognize it and respond with more empathy and concern.

Schizophrenia is a psychotic disorder of perception. What is *real* to other people is often not real to a person with schizophrenia. Perhaps you can understand what this is like. Think of a time when it was dark and you may have thought you saw someone in your backyard. Your brain may have misperceived something moving in the breeze, and it looked like a person in the shadows. You may have been startled or frightened.

On closer examination, you realize that you only temporarily misperceived what your eyes saw. Your brain had temporarily misinterpreted the sensory information as being a person in your backyard. Your brain, however, was able to correct that misperception, and you were no longer afraid. The brain of a person with a psychosis creates and often cannot correct distortions and the fears that come with them.

A variation of schizophrenia is schizoaffective disorder. People with this disorder have symptoms of both schizophrenia and a mood disorder (see chapter 12, "Mood Disorders"). Schizophreniform disorder and brief psychotic disorder have symptoms that are similar to schizophrenia, but they do not last as long. People with these disorders tend to recover. Schizophrenia, on the other hand, is a lifelong illness that usually progresses and becomes worse with age. Two-thirds of those who develop a psychosis do not recover. Their symptoms often progress to a more severe and chronic mental illness.

Delusional disorders are much less severe than schizophrenia. A delusional person is less impaired and does not show other symptoms except delusions. The delusions in delusional disorder are also less bizarre and tend to be about things that *could* be true but are not true. The person is usually able to work and perform normal daily activities. Behavior may be normal in every way except for the delusion. We do not know what causes delusional disorders, but they appear to be different than schizophrenia. The delusions appear to be related to psychological functioning and less severe brain abnormalities than to the biological problems found in schizophrenia. Common types of delusions are:

Believing that another person, usually of higher social status, is in love with the individual.

Believing that the person has enormous power, knowledge, gifts, identity, or worth that is not supported by reality. The person may also believe he or she has a special relationship with a powerful or famous person or with family or friends.

Being extremely jealous; believing that one's partner is unfaithful when this is not true.

Believing that others are persecuting the person and seeking to cause him harm when this is not true.

Believing that the person has a serious disease or physical defect, which is not true or verified by medical tests.

Delusions are much more rigid than the misunderstandings and false ideas that many people experience. Delusional individuals usually cannot accept any evidence to the contrary. Even when confronted with proof that these things are not true, they hold on to their mistaken belief. They may also suspect that others who try to convince them of the error in their thinking are trying to deceive them. Some common problems people with schizophrenia experience include the following:

Changes in how they experience sensory information (sound, sight, touch, smell, taste). The five senses may be either enhanced or diminished. Noise, color, smells, and other sensations flood the person with confusion and intensity. Colors and textures may look distorted, making focusing difficult because everything is so distracting. As a result, the person may feel overwhelmed. The opposite can also occur. The person may have the senses blunted and seem unaware of normal sensory experiences. It may be difficult to sort out and correctly interpret information coming through the five senses.

When Steve first began to be ill, he enjoyed the brilliance of colors. They seemed brighter and more luminous. He soon found, however, that background noises bothered him more and made it hard to concentrate. He began to feel irritable if he tried to read and there was any noise. He could not stay focused on his reading because even quiet noises seemed so much more intense. If he went to a busy or crowded place, he felt overwhelmed by all the lights, noise, people, and confusion. He started to withdraw from social activities and stay home alone. This felt less confusing and chaotic.

Delusions and hallucinations. Because the brain is not processing information correctly, the sufferer may see or hear things that are not real. Hearing voices is a common hallucination, but hallucinations can occur in any of the five senses. Delusions are strong, fixed ideas that are not based in reality. Mild delusions may only misrepresent real events, but more serious delusions may become bizarre and completely disconnected from reality. When a person experiences visual hallucinations, it is especially important that he have full psychiatric and neurological evaluations. Visual hallucinations can be related to brain damage or disease. People who have brain damage from alcohol and illegal drug use can experience hallucinations that can be either auditory or visual.

As Steve's illness progressed, he began to hear whispering noises when no one was around. At first, he thought someone was playing tricks on him, and he accused neighbors of hiding a tape recorder in his room. He soon began to hear audible voices. Because he could see no one there, he began to believe that someone had implanted a transmitter into his brain. He believed he was receiving messages transmitted from a satellite in outer space. He started believing that aliens were using him to take over the planet.

An altered sense of oneself. People with schizophrenia may have difficulty differentiating *their* body from *other* people and objects. They may experience parts of their body as being different in size or shape from reality. They may not recognize parts of their body as being part of themselves.

One of the changes Cathy noticed at the onset of her illness was feeling that her arms were heavy, large, and hard to move. Sometimes she would look in the mirror and believe that her face looked sunken and hollow—her eyes set deep into her head. She began to wonder whose face she was really seeing. She thought that perhaps she was really seeing someone else. No one else noticed any changes in her appearance.

Difficulty sorting out sensory information and responding to the environment.

As Cathy's illness progressed, it became harder to interpret and respond to daily events and tasks. For example, when she got in the shower, she became so focused on the sound of the water that sometimes she could not think of what to do next. She would stand in the shower unaware that the water was turning cold. She could not even remember the next step in taking a shower. Sometimes Cathy's husband would have to turn off the water, take her by the hand, and talk her through the steps of drying off and getting dressed.

Changes in emotions. In the early stages of the illness, the person may experience rapidly changing emotions. The symptoms may sometimes be confused with bipolar mood disorder because of intense and rapidly changing emotions. The person may also feel depressed and frightened as he or she starts to lose control of the ability to think clearly. As the disease progresses, however, the person loses the ability to feel emotions and may feel nothing at all—neither happiness nor sadness. Others may assume that the person is being insensitive or purposefully denying emotions, but the ill person does *not* choose to stop feeling. The changes in the brain as the disease progresses create apathy, lack of motivation, and loss of normal emotional responses.

Cathy's emotional indifference to her husband troubled him. She never seemed to experience or express loving feelings toward him. When he asked her if she still loved him, she replied that she knew she still loved him, but she could not 'feel' emotions that had once been there. She appreciated all that he did to help her cope with the illness but did not feel emotions as she had done before the illness. When something that normally would have been sad or joyous happened, she responded with little emotion.

Loss of insight. One of the most prominent symptoms of schizophrenia is that the person may not recognize the illness. About 40 percent of people with schizophrenia have no insight into their own illness. When we injure or develop disease in most parts of our body, our brain can comprehend that we are ill. We may feel pain or other symptoms of disease. When the brain is the organ of the body that is ill, however, it may be impaired in understanding its own illness.

Steve's family and friends began to notice changes in his behavior. As the symptoms became more strange and noticeable, they confronted him about his behavior. He insisted that nothing was wrong. He could see nothing different in himself. He concluded that others were plotting against him, and he became even more withdrawn and secretive. He refused to get any treatment, insisting that others were making this all up in order to take control of his life. His family felt helpless and frightened because they could not force him into treatment.

The illness affects the inner mental experience of the person. Because this cannot be directly observed, mental health professionals must make the diagnosis based on observable symptoms. It is helpful to get a report from family members or others close to the person. The ill person may not be aware of inaccurate perceptions and may deny that there is a problem. The person may even convince others that the delusions are real.

It may be difficult to diagnose schizophrenia correctly in the early stages. Symptoms may look similar to other problems in the beginning stages of the disease.

Clinical Symptoms

Schizophrenia usually becomes apparent in the late teens to early adult life. Schizophrenia can start in childhood, however. It also tends to be more severe in men than in women. Estrogen seems to provide some protection against schizophrenia to women. Symptoms used to diagnose schizophrenia, and which must be present for at least six months, include the following:

A slow deterioration, called *prodromal* symptoms, usually precedes the first psychotic episode in schizophrenia. The person may gradually lose interest in life, withdraw from others, or show personality changes before becoming psychotic.

Deterioration in the person's ability to work, interact socially, and care for self. Changes in grooming, hygiene, and other self-care become apparent. These symptoms tend to become more severe and apparent when the person is under stress.

Symptoms of schizophrenia are not caused by another medical condition, disease, or injury. It is important to have a thorough medical examination to rule out the possibility of a brain tumor or other disease. Some illegal drugs, such as amphetamines, can also cause symptoms that look like schizophrenia.

Other symptoms are categorized as positive, negative, or cognitive. The meaning of the words *positive* and *negative* are different from how we normally use them. *Positive* refers to things that are added to the person's personality that are not normally there. *Negative* means things that are lost from the normal personality. Negative symptoms may be harder to recognize. Acquaintances may think the person is just being lazy or unmotivated. They may not recognize that these problems are part of the illness. These negative symptoms are hard to treat and are less likely to be helped by medication. The positive symptoms are more dramatic, but the negative symptoms are the main reasons that people with schizophrenia have trouble holding a job, establishing relationships, and managing everyday situations.

Positive Symptoms

Hallucinations. Hallucinations occur when the brain creates or misperceives things that aren't real. Hallucinations can be visual, auditory, or related to taste, smell, or touch. About 70 percent of people with schizophrenia have auditory hallucinations. They may hear voices talking to them or talking to each other. Sufferers often think the voices are real, but some are aware that they are not. A person talking or laughing when no one is around is an indication that the person may be experiencing hallucinations.

Delusions. Delusions are strong, fixated, false beliefs. Delusions that people are persecuting you or want to harm you are called *paranoid delusions.* Examples are the belief that family members are trying to poison your food or that the government is secretly trying to harm you.

Delusions of reference come from the belief that everyday things are personally directed at you. Examples of delusions of reference are the belief that a newspaper article is really a message personally intended for you, seeing the number 666 on an address and believing it is a message from Satan that you are evil, or hearing people talk at a restaurant and believing that they are talking about you.

Delusions of control come from the belief that others are controlling your thoughts or actions. An example would be the belief that someone has implanted an electrical transmitter in your body that controls your actions or believing that other people are making you think certain thoughts against your will. *Thought insertion* and *thought projection* are common delusions. When these occur, you believe either that other people can put thoughts into your mind or that they can cause the thoughts of other people. *Thought broadcasting* is the delusion that other people can *hear* your thoughts or magically know what you are thinking.

Grandiose delusions are false beliefs that you possess special talents, abilities, or remarkable skills. For example, believing that you are a great world leader who is secretly in hiding, believing that you are an unrecognized artistic genius when evidence suggests otherwise, or believing that you have a special gift to hear other people's thoughts would be grandiose delusions.

Disorganized speech. This kind of speech is often incoherent. People may use words that make no sense to others, use words in unusual ways, or make nonsensical rhymes. "The tea in the bee ran around my sandwich and made my head feel like a *cloptik*" is an example of such speech. People with this symptom may also say little at all.

Negative Symptoms

Little expression. This may manifest itself as little emotion in facial expression or voice. The person does not respond normally to happy, humorous, or sad events. The voice may be flat and without expression even when the person talks about emotional topics.

Apathy, lack of interest, difficulty engaging in conversations and activities. The person may appear to be "not there" and have trouble responding to surroundings. He may not be able to organize his life and start activities and tasks that need to be done. The person loses his ability to perform on the job and in school and to take care of everyday tasks. The person may sit motionless or in strange postures or positions for long periods, staring blankly into space. The person seems to withdraw from the world and lack the ability to engage in life. It is often difficult to tell if the person is really losing interest in life or just giving up because life has become so confusing.

Anhedonia. This is the loss of the ability to feel enjoyment or pleasure. The person loses the ability to enjoy activities that were once pleasant. She feels nothing when doing activities that once brought her pleasure, such as going to a movie, seeing a beautiful landscape, or playing with children.

Cognitive Symptoms

Cognitive symptoms may not be easily recognized but do interfere with the person's ability to lead a normal life. Cognitive symptoms are related to being unable to think clearly and to being unable to mentally process information (see chapter 18, "Cognitive Disorders"). They include the following:

Difficulty understanding and interpreting information

Difficulty paying attention

Memory problems, particularly the ability to keep information in the mind and use it.

Not all people with schizophrenia have all of these symptoms. A small percentage has only negative symptoms. If you see these symptoms, however, it could mean the person has schizophrenia. It is important that someone who is trained and experienced in working with schizophrenia make the diagnosis. Other problems, such as substance abuse, attention-deficit/hyperactivity disorder, and personality disorders can sometimes make an accurate diagnosis difficult.

What Causes Schizophrenia?

The causes of schizophrenia are complex and involve an interaction of multiple problems. The exact cause may differ for different people. We call the symptoms *schizophrenia,* but there are probably many different paths to those symptoms.

Biological. The symptoms of schizophrenia are related to both chemical imbalance and structural problems in the brain. The chemical imbalance is usually due to an inadequate number of functioning brain cells. Neuroimaging, neurological testing, and other scientific studies show differences in the brains of people with schizophrenia and those without. The limbic system in the brain is also affected by schizophrenia. This is the reward center of the brain. It helps us recognize what is rewarding and enjoyable. Some of the negative symptoms are related to the malfunctioning of the brain's ability to recognize activities that are rewarding.

Neuropsychological tests show difficulty in thinking and paying attention, shifting from one activity to another, and interpreting sensory information. Neuroimaging tests also show problems in the prefrontal cortex of persons with schizophrenia. A brain-imaging technique called positron emission tomography (PET) scan shows that the prefrontal cortex does not work the same way it does in people without schizophrenia. Researchers have found a reduction in the number of neurons, or brain cells, in the prefrontal cortexes of people with schizophrenia. The prefrontal cortex helps in planning, decision making, making moral decisions, and understanding social interactions, all of which are difficult for people with schizophrenia (see illustrations in chapter 2, "A Look at Your Brain"). Neuroimaging also shows shrinkage of the brain in many people with schizophrenia.

Other biological theories include risk factors, such as a slow-acting virus. Children whose mothers had influenza while pregnant have a higher incidence of the illness. This is also true for babies born in the winter months. Medical complications during birth have also been associated with schizophrenia. Use of many illegal drugs is associated with the onset of schizophrenia. It is not clear whether they actually cause it, but their effects may mimic many of the symptoms. They may also bring about the first episode by turning on the biological predisposition in a person who already has a biological tendency. Some adolescents who start using drugs may actually be trying to self-medicate some of the beginning symptoms of schizophrenia.

The initial symptoms can be confusing to sufferers, who may not realize that they are developing a serious mental illness. People with schizophrenia are more vulnerable to addictions. They may try to soothe the distress of the illness with illegal drugs, alcohol, or pornography. About 80 percent of people with schizophrenia become addicted to cigarettes. Nicotine may temporarily reduce the symptoms of schizophrenia, but as neuroimagery shows, smoking causes a marked reduction in frontal and prefrontal lobe brain functioning. This is the part of the brain that is used for making decisions. Antipsychotic medications prescribed by a psychiatrist are much safer and more effective in reducing the symptoms than self-medication with addictive substances.

Genetics. Family and adoption studies show a higher rate of schizophrenia if another biological family member has the illness. This is true even when the child is adopted into a family with no history of schizophrenia. The closer and stronger the genetic link, the more likely the person is to develop schizophrenia. For example, if both biological parents have schizophrenia, the child has a 10 to 20 percent greater chance of having the illness. If an identical twin develops schizophrenia, the other twin has a 25 to 45 percent greater chance of developing the illness. These studies suggest that genetics play a role but do not necessarily determine who gets schizophrenia. Some people may carry a genetic *vulnerability* to the illness but may never develop it. Reducing stress, building coping skills, avoiding substance abuse, and learning good psychological skills can all provide a buffer against developing the illness. Many people who have schizophrenia have no family history, suggesting that there are also other causes.

Environment and stress. Stress can bring on the symptoms of schizophrenia. It appears, however, that the person must have a biological vulnerability (see chapter 1, "What Is Mental Illness?"). Many people experience high levels of stress and may develop other mental illnesses but never develop schizophrenia because they do not have the biological vulnerability. Many people who do show tendencies to the illness can reduce the likelihood of having an episode by learning to manage and reduce stress in their lives. There is no known cure for biological vulnerability. If that vulnerability is high, people may develop the illness regardless of how well they manage their life or how much social support they experience.

If you have a vulnerability to the illness, it is important that you take good care of yourself. Stress causes an increase of the chemical acetylcholine (which indirectly decreases dopamine and serotonin) in the brain. This explains how stress can cause symptoms in people who have a biological vulnerability.

Sometimes a person with biological vulnerability is exposed to abuse, neglect, or other painful events. These can increase the chance that the vulnerability will express itself. The stress of a dysfunctional, abusive, or chaotic family environment may increase the risk that the vulnerability develops into the illness. It is important, however, not to assume that all people who develop schizophrenia were abused or neglected as children. Loving parents in supportive families have raised children who developed schizophrenia. If the biological vulnerability is strong, good conditions cannot stop the onset of the disease (see chapter 1, "What Is Mental Illness?").

The same is true for many other diseases. People who eat in healthy ways may still develop diabetes. People who have never smoked may get lung cancer. Women who keep the commandments concerning chastity still may develop cervical cancer. Healthy living may provide some protection against these diseases, but it is not a sure guarantee of health.

How Is Schizophrenia Treated?

Early diagnosis and medical treatment is important in preventing brain damage from schizophrenia. Much of the damage to the brain occurs in the first few years after the onset of the disease. Research shows that medication slows that damage. In some cases, it can even rebuild brain tissue damaged by the disease. Getting help can be a challenge, however, because in the early stages, it may be hard to tell if the problems are caused by schizophrenia or something else.

If people have no insight into their illness, they may refuse to take medication. Many families hesitate to seek professional care because of stigma and misunderstandings about severe mental illnesses. The psychotic symptoms may be frightening to family members. They may feel overwhelmed by the possibility that their loved one has a serious illness. They may worry that they have caused the illness and feel ashamed. They should not let fear, disbelief, denial, and grief stop them from seeking appropriate help.

Treatment is best when a team of professionals work together to provide the best care for the complex problems associated with the illness. This team may include a psychiatrist, psychologist, social worker, rehabilitation specialist, and nurses. Each has a unique role in helping the person get help and care for some part of the challenge of schizophrenia. There are treatment centers that specialize in the diagnosis and treatment of psychotic disorders. Your family physician may be able to help you find such a center. Unfortunately, not all counselors and therapists are familiar with diagnosis and treatment of severe mental illnesses. It is important to seek help from professionals who have specialized training and can work with people with schizophrenia.

Treatment is much more effective when the family and others close to the person accurately understand the illness. This is one of the best protections against chronic relapses. Most people know little about schizophrenia. You may hear confusing myths and inaccurate information. National organizations can help you learn more and help you to get support in coping with this challenge. Three excellent sources are:

The National Alliance on Mental Illness (nami.org)
The National Mental Health Association (nmha.org)
The National Institute of Mental Health (nimh.nih.gov)

Medication is the cornerstone of treatment. Many older medications had severe side effects. Newer medications, however, are much safer and have fewer side effects (see chapter 3, "The Brain and Medical Treatment for Mental Disorders").

Abuse of substances like alcohol or drugs can interfere with the effectiveness of medications. It is important to tell your doctor what other prescriptions or over-the-counter medications you are taking. Because many of these medications have unpleasant side effects, you may be hesitant to take medications. Talk to your doctor about the side effects. Often a different medication or combination of medications may be better for you.

Do not stop taking your medication without consulting your doctor. Sometimes people start to feel better when medicated and believe they are *cured.* But like diabetes, schizophrenia is a lifelong illness. The symptoms may increase or decrease at times, but the illness will not go away. Most people need medication for the rest of their lives. Staying on your medication will reduce your risk for more psychotic episodes and further brain damage. Sometimes when people stop taking their medication and have a relapse, the medication does not work as well as it did before.

Behavioral and Psychological Therapies. Behavior therapy can help you learn how to change maladaptive behaviors. It can also help you recognize when your behavior might cause difficulties. You can learn how to replace ineffective behaviors with more effective ones. Social skills are difficult for people with schizophrenia. Social-skills training can help you to understand other people better and learn how to interact with them in healthy ways.

Cognitive therapy has also been shown to be helpful with schizophrenia. The illness makes it difficult to think clearly and rationally, but cognitive therapy can help you recognize irrational beliefs and improve your thinking skills.

Supportive therapy. Living with a severe chronic mental illness can be difficult. It is helpful to have an ongoing relationship with a therapist who knows you well and can provide a safe place to talk about your concerns and challenges. It is also helpful to see a counselor who is LDS or familiar and respectful of LDS teachings. An LDS therapist can help you strengthen your spirituality while recognizing what beliefs may be a result of the illness. Research shows the value of strengthening spirituality in people with schizophrenia. It is important to remember God's love for you. Support can help to restore self-esteem and identity, which are threatened by severe mental illness.

Family therapy. Strong and loving families can benefit from learning about managing and responding to their loved one's symptoms. If there are young children involved, it is important that they be taught that the family member is ill. This can help them not to be so fearful of bizarre or troubling behavior. Family therapy can also help members respond appropriately to problems created by the illness. Family education about the illness has been shown to help prevent psychotic relapses.

Career counseling and rehabilitation. Illness often interferes with people's ability to work as well as they did before they became ill. They may have difficulty thinking as clearly, and a stressful job can make their symptoms worse. It can be emotionally painful not to be able to do those things they easily did before. Career and job-rehabilitation counseling can help them discover what they can still do and what kind of work is best suited to their health limitations. Because schizophrenia is considered a real, disabling condition, many government agencies provide free counseling and job training for people whose symptoms are severe enough to make regular work impossible. If the illness is severe enough, they may not be able to work. By talking with a counselor, they can determine whether they qualify for disability benefits from Social Security. They may also qualify for Medicaid or Medicare to help pay for health care and medication.

Hospitalization. Sometimes people may become so ill that they are unable to safely care for themselves. They may also be delusional, and they may be a threat to themselves or others. Hospitalization may be necessary if medication needs to be adjusted. If people have little insight into their own illness, they may resist hospitalization. This can be difficult for families and loved ones. Family members may worry about their loved one's safety, as well as their own safety. Laws on involuntary commitment to a hospital vary from state to state. Most states allow involuntary commitment if people are a danger to themselves or others (see chapter 19, "Mental Health and the Law").

Some people with schizophrenia are unable to live independently. Families may care deeply about the ill family member, but it is not always the best solution to care for the person at home. Caring for a severely mentally ill family member can be difficult. If family members are targets of delusions and hallucinations, or if the person becomes violent, home care could even be dangerous. If keeping the person in the home is not the best option, many locations have supervised apartments, group homes, half-way houses, or crisis housing. Your local community mental health center is a good resource for finding housing options.

What Will Happen Over Time?

With treatment, support, and understanding, most people with schizophrenia can recover enough to control their symptoms. Medication helps about 70 percent of patients to improve. Many are able to live independently and have a family, a job, and a meaningful life. Medical science has made great progress in understanding and treating this disease. There is still much that is not understood, however. Some people continue to get worse despite good treatment. Relapse into psychosis can occur, and the illness often takes its own unexpected course. Setbacks are not necessarily signs of failure by anyone. Schizophrenia can be an unpredictable disease, but receiving early treatment, learning how to manage the illness, and working closely with a team of mental health professionals provide the best chances for a good outcome.

How Can You Help Yourself?

Some suggestions include the following:

Strengthen your spirituality. Believe that God loves you. Find spiritual strength through prayer, church attendance, and obedience to the commandments.

Keep your life simple and as stress free as possible. You are not required to do more than the illness will allow. Your life may be different than you had planned, but remember that God still has a plan for your eventual happiness.

Take good care of your health. Try to eat right, get enough sleep, and keep a regular schedule. Going for walks, doing yoga, and participating in other relaxing exercise can help you feel less anxious.

Do not use alcohol, illegal drugs, or other substances that could make your symptoms worse. Do not try to comfort the distress of the illness with addictive substances or pornography.

Get support from family, church, and wholesome social activities. Try to get out and around other people when possible. Some communities have support groups for people with chronic mental illness. Do not become alone and isolated from others. Find support from people who understand the illness and can provide empathy. Understand, however, that not everyone will understand what it means to have schizophrenia.

Write about your thoughts and feelings in a journal that you can share with someone who knows and cares about you. Sharing these thoughts and feelings can help your counselor to understand you better and know how to help you.

If you are unable to work, try some volunteer work, or take a class in something that interests you. It will help you to build social skills and give you a sense of accomplishment.

Focus on the things you can still do, and keep a written list of things to do. Enjoy satisfaction when you do get something done.

Keep a calendar or planner to help you remember appointments, tasks, and reminders for yourself.

Keep your surroundings as peaceful and distraction free as possible. Excessive noise and chaos can make you feel worse.

How Can You Help Others?

Some suggestions include the following:

Learn all you can about the illness. This can help you recognize which behaviors and problems are symptoms of the illness and which are not. It can also help you to have more empathy for what it is like to be ill.

Do not take psychotic symptoms, such as delusions, personally. Often family, loved ones, and others close to the person are targets of delusions and hallucinations. This can be painful and difficult for you to experience. Understand, however, that they are symptoms of the illness and are not your fault.

Learn skills for coping with and managing the person's difficult behaviors. The National Alliance on Mental Illness (NAMI) offers family education classes. There are also many good books that can help you know how to help. Examples are *How to Live with a Mentally Ill Person,* by Christine Adamec; *Coping with Schizophrenia,* by Kim T. Mueser and Susan Gingerich; and *Surviving Schizophrenia,* by E. Fuller Torrey (see Sources).

Recognize that the person may not always have the ability to truly understand and make choices. It can be difficult to tell where the limits of accountability exist. Rather than judging the person's behavior, you can trust that an all-knowing God will judge justly. Disease and disabilities will be taken into account in the final judgment.

Do not argue with delusions. This usually only upsets the person more. Gently and calmly ask about the person's thoughts and beliefs, or tactfully change the subject.

Boost the person's self-confidence and self-esteem by recognizing accomplishments.

Try to keep the environment calm. Noise, chaos, and other strong sensory stimulation make the ill person's symptoms worse.

Being a caretaker for someone with schizophrenia can be stressful. Take good care of yourself. Understand and respect your own limits.

Get support from mental health services, support groups, and other understanding people so you do not feel alone in caring for the ill person.

Seek help and comfort from the Lord. Building your own spiritual resources can help to keep you from becoming discouraged.

What Is It Like to Have Schizophrenia?

"Scott Hausey [not his real name] was the kind of young man who makes parenting seem easy. He was responsible and religious—an A student who did his homework without being prodded. He enjoyed camping with his parents and six brothers and sisters and planned to be a doctor. Admiring people in his ward would tell Brother and Sister Hausey, 'I hope my son will grow up to be like Scott.'

"Then, about a year into his mission for the Church, Scott became afflicted with a devastating illness. It attacked not his body, but his mind—disordering his thoughts and agitating him so much that he could not finish his mission.

"Scott began to hear strange voices in his head, voices no one else could hear. He couldn't finish his sentences. At times, he would pace for hours or simply sit in his room and rock. 'I can't describe our emotions when we saw

Scott like that,' recalls his father. 'We thought we'd failed as parents, but we didn't know how.'

"Scott had a number of counseling sessions and earnestly prayed for the Lord to heal him. Nothing seemed to help. Perhaps, some reasoned, he was possessed by an evil spirit. But Scott was not possessed. He had a serious mental disorder called schizophrenia.

"On a family vacation the year after he came home from his mission, Scott became violent and kicked his mother. The family called the police for help in calming him. Then Don Hausey called the local stake president for spiritual help. Fifteen years later, Brother Hausey still becomes emotional when he describes the 'miracle' that phone call brought about.

"'The stake president listened to our situation and said, "There's a member of our high council who may be able to help your son." The high councilor was a doctor who recognized Scott's problem and knew of a treatment that could help. With the medicine the doctor prescribed, Scott improved so significantly that his strange behavior disappeared.

"The road since then has not been easy for Scott or his family. For years, Scott refused to believe that he needed the medicine, and he had periodic 'breaks' that resulted in hospitalization. For a while, Scott wondered every day if this would be the day he would take his life.

"But today, at thirty-five, Scott has a wife and beautiful baby daughter who give him a reason to stay on the medicine that keeps his illness under control, much as insulin controls diabetes. For several months now, with proper medication and supportive therapy, Scott has kept a full-time job and has led a relatively stable life. Scott is not 'cured,' but with his symptoms under control, life looks brighter for him than it has for many years."

Note

1. Jan Underwood Pinborough, "Mental Illness: In Search of Understanding and Hope," *Ensign*, Feb. 1989, 52.

17

Eating Disorders

Marleen S. Williams, W. Dean Belnap, and John P. Livingstone

Young women in many modern cultures have more choices and opportunities than ever before in history. It is a wonderful time to be a woman and have chances to learn to use God-given agency wisely. These opportunities to grow and learn are one of the blessings of living in the latter days. Ironically, in these same cultures a dramatic rise in eating disorders has occurred. It is important to understand that eating disorders are mental illnesses that are not just about food and eating. Food is only the visible symptom of a much larger struggle to master the demands of living as an adult in a complex and challenging world.

Fortunately, one of the blessings of the restored gospel is an accurate understanding of the eternal purpose of the body (D&C 88:15). Our bodies are made in the image of God and have the divine potential to help us become like him (Alma 5:15; 11:43–45; 40:18–26). The gospel teaches us the value of caring for our bodies and of the wise use of the blessings of having a body (D&C 89; 59:19).

Women have eating disorders more frequently than men, but the number of men with eating disorders is also rising. Men are more socialized to desire a muscular body and are more likely to abuse steroids and bodybuilding substances than to focus on an overly thin ideal. Most of the research on eating disorders has been on women, but there appear to be some similarities in men and women who develop eating disorders.

As the media focus more on men's physical appearance, they also become more vulnerable to developing eating disorders. Why are so many people ignoring the body's natural signals that tell us when to eat and when we are full? How does a common, normal struggle to maintain moderation in eating and a healthy weight turn into a dangerous compulsion that is difficult to stop? How does our biological need for food turn into a life-threatening mental illness? To understand the answers to these questions, it is important to understand how eating disorders differ from healthy eating styles that can maintain health. It is also helpful to understand the undercurrent of struggles, concerns, and conflicts that drive dangerous eating behaviors.

Symptoms of Eating Disorders

Some warning signs that a person may have an eating disorder include the following:

Rapid weight loss of more than 25 percent of body weight, or a body-mass index (a measure of body fat based on weight and height) below 19 (121 pounds for someone 5 feet, 7 inches tall; 100 pounds for someone 5 feet, 1 inch tall).

Prolonged, excessive exercise despite fatigue, injury, or weakness.

Intense fear of gaining weight or insistence on dieting even though the person is slim.

Peculiar food habits or rituals.

Refusal to eat certain food groups, such as fats, carbohydrates, or proteins.

Loss of menstrual periods or, in young girls, failure to start menstruating.

Episodes of bingeing on food and then purging it. Purging can include vomiting, laxatives, diuretics, excessive exercise, or excessive fasting.

Withdrawal from usual activities that include food.

Retreating to the bathroom after eating; being secretive about eating.

Hair loss, fainting spells, intestinal disturbance, frequent sore throats, swollen glands or cheeks.

Types of Eating Disorders

There are different types of eating disorders.

Anorexia. Anorexia is resistance to maintaining body weight at or above a normal minimal weight for age and height. Despite being underweight, people with anorexia have an intense fear of getting fat or gaining weight. They experience their body as being much larger than it is, or they may deny that they are overly thin. Women may experience loss of menstrual periods for at least three months.

Melanie was 5-foot-7 but weighed only 110 pounds. She worried a lot about gaining weight and frequently complained that she was fat. She did not like to eat with her family. When forced to eat, she would cut her food into very small pieces and eat them very slowly. If no one was looking, she would spit the food out into her napkin. She ate very little, but whenever her mother offered her food, she said she was not hungry. She prided herself on her "discipline." If others commented that she was too thin, she told herself, "They are just jealous because I am thinner than they are." Melanie was fifteen, but she had yet to start menstrual periods. She had started controlling her food when she was twelve.

Bulimia. Bulimia is repeated episodes of eating large amounts of food, followed by purging the food. Purging can occur through vomiting, excessive exercise, fasting, or abuse of laxatives, fiber supplements, diet pills, or diuretics (water pills). People with bulimia eat more than is typically eaten in a short period. They feel out of control when eating and feel uncomfortable after bingeing. They may frequently try diets, and they worry excessively about weight and body shape.

Cindy turned to eating whenever she felt upset or sad. Sometimes she would eat a whole package of her favorite cookies in one sitting. She worried about gaining weight and hated the feeling of having so much food in her stomach. She learned that she could stick her fingers down her throat and force herself to vomit to get rid of the food. At first, she thought this was a solution to her episodes of overeating. She could comfort herself with food, indulging in her high-calorie favorites, and not gain weight. Sometimes she overate away from home. Other times, if she could not get to a bathroom to purge herself, she would force herself to eat nothing until twenty-four hours had passed. She also used over-the-counter diet pills. She liked feeling full of energy while not eating for long periods. When she began to experience medical problems from her eating disorder, she tried to stop but found that she needed more than willpower.

Binge-eating disorder (compulsive overeating). Binge-eating disorder manifests itself as periods of uncontrolled, impulsive eating beyond the point of feeling full. Eating is a way of soothing painful emotions, such as depression, anxiety, or loneliness. People with this disorder feel ashamed of overeating but are not able to control it.

Ruth had a naturally rounded figure. In high school, she felt comfortable in her curvy body. She was often told she was pretty. After she married, her husband traveled frequently with his job and became less attentive. She felt lonely and overwhelmed with caring for the children alone and keeping up with the housework. She loved to cook. Creating culinary masterpieces added to her self-esteem. She found it hard to stop eating once she sampled treats. They seemed to reduce her feelings of loneliness and depression. She began to gain weight. She felt ashamed that she could not control her eating. She tried to stop, but the episodes of overindulgence increased. When her husband complained about her extreme weight gain, she felt even more rejected and depressed. These feelings only made it easier to comfort herself with food.

What Causes Eating Disorders?

On the surface, it may appear that eating disorders are about food. It is important to realize, however, that they represent a struggle with deeper problems. You might think about the struggle with food, weight, and eating habits as the tip of an iceberg. The tip is visible. Below the surface, however, is a much larger mass of concerns that can be even more dangerous to the person's physical, emotional, and spiritual welfare. Eating disorders represent a struggle to master many complex challenges. Food and control of food are used to compensate for other problems that seem unmanageable to the person. Overeating, dieting, bingeing, and purging become ways of coping with problems.

When food and eating are used to manage emotional problems, it is easy to become trapped in a compulsive cycle that is hard to escape. We all feel painful emotions as part of our mortal experience. If you have few skills or resources for understanding and managing those emotions, you can feel overwhelmed. Many people confuse feeling bad with being bad. If you criticize and blame yourself for having painful emotions, you have even more pain.

It is easy to turn to a quick fix to calm and soothe the pain. A quick fix is anything that changes your emotions quickly but eventually causes more problems. A quick fix does not solve the original cause of your distress. Examples of things that can be used as a quick fix are food, mood-altering drugs, alcohol, pornography, inappropriate sexual behavior, compulsive spending, and other compulsive actions that may cause you even more problems. These things may make you feel better temporarily, but they will result in painful consequences. The quick fix does not solve the original problem, so the emotional pain continues. You began to feel helpless, out of control, inadequate, and unable to stop the compulsive behavior. Recovering from compulsive behaviors requires learning new skills, attitudes, and behaviors in

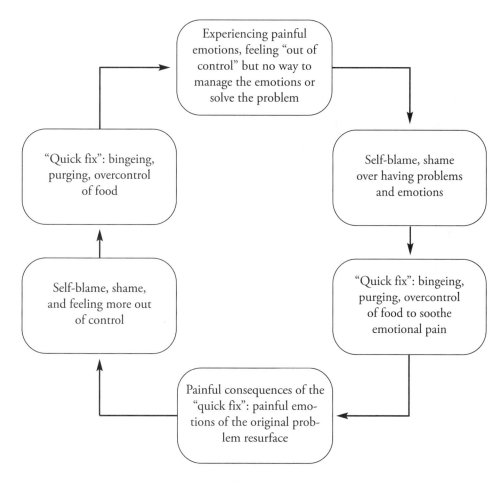

addition to stopping the quick fix. Willpower alone is usually not enough to change the behavior.

Many different challenges can contribute to being vulnerable to developing an eating disorder.

Biological. Chemicals in the brain help to control and regulate hunger, appetite, and digestion. It is important to have a physician rule out other medical problems that may interfere with normal eating and body functioning. Such problems include depression, inflammatory bowel disease, celiac disease, diabetes mellitus, hypothyroidism (insufficient thyroid production), neurological conditions, infections, and other chronic illnesses.

People with eating disorders have also been found to have disturbances in the serotonin systems of the brain. Dopamine in the limbic system and acetylcholine in the basal ganglia, for example, increase in people with eating disorders. These same chemical problems occur in the brains of people with other addictions. It is not clear whether poor nutrition associated with eating disorders causes the chemical imbalance or if it existed before the onset of the eating disorder. Constant starvation and irregular eating prevent the brain from developing normally and can impair the brain's ability to make healthy choices.

Neuroimaging also shows that some individuals with eating disorders have abnormalities in the parts of the brain that regulate hunger and fullness. These abnormalities may make it more difficult for the brain to process signals that you are hungry or full.

Some evidence also suggests that genetics may play a role in vulnerability to both anorexia and overeating. Eating disorders are more common in people who have family histories of eating disorders, depression, obsessive-compulsive disorders, and other mental illnesses even when these illnesses are not found in those they live with.

Eating disorders usually begin in childhood or adolescence. A technology called magnetic resonance imaging (MRI) shows that children's brains are not completely developed. They continue to grow and become more complex throughout adolescence. The frontal lobe of the brain that is used to plan, predict consequences, and manage emotional impulses is not fully developed and functional in children and adolescents.

Today's children and teens are bombarded by messages that they are fully capable of making adult decisions. In reality, they are not. Their brains still need more growth and *wiring* before they are ready to assume full responsibility for adult living. Exposing children and teens to adult information, roles, responsibilities, and decisions before they are developmentally ready creates more stress than they can handle. This exposure increases their vulnerability to managing that increased stress using food and dieting.

Stress. Many people with eating disorders use food to manage stress. Comfort foods—those high in sugar, fat, and calories—seem to calm the body's response to stress. Modern Western cultures often support a life that is fast-paced, competitive, and stressful.

Young people face intense pressure to accomplish many things, and they face many difficult decisions. They may believe that they must excel in everything they do, and many, despite pressure, aren't ready to choose what to pursue and what to let go.

Research shows that eating disorders often begin during a stressful change in young people's lives. Changes such as moving to a new school, loss of an important relationship through death or divorce, or difficulty achieving a goal that is important to their identity can be stressful.

Personality and psychological challenges. A strong relationship exists between developing an eating disorder and being a perfectionist (see chapter 12, "Mood Disorders"). Perfectionists often feel out of control if they cannot create a *perfect* life and perform *perfectly* in all they do. They want to feel in control and powerful. If you are a perfectionist, you may try to gain a feeling of being in control by controlling *food.* Perfectionists also tend to see life in all-or-nothing terms. Everything is either good or bad, success or failure, thin or fat. If fat is bad, then thin is the only way to be good. Being thinner is even better.

Problems managing emotions can lead to eating disorders. Our bodies are capable of feeling many powerful emotions. The ability to experience emotions is part of our divine inheritance (Jeremiah 9:24; Mosiah 11:22; D&C 56:1). The word *passion* is often used in the scriptures to describe strong feelings. We feel strong emotions in our bodies. We are not able to experience a fullness of joy without our bodies (D&C 88:15; 93:33–34). However, when emotions feel overwhelming, we may try to silence them by either eating or refusing to eat.

The scriptures teach us to "bridle all [our] passions" (Alma 38:12). This means that we must learn how to appropriately use and manage our emotions. It does not mean that we stop having emotions. Think about the purpose of a bridle in managing a horse. The bridle makes it possible to channel the direction of the horse. It helps the rider to stay in charge of the horse. The horse is not inherently evil or bad, but it must be managed. When properly bridled, the horse can be a means of power and joy. To bridle the horse does not mean we beat the horse, hurt it, or deny its potential blessings. This is also true of emotions. They are one of the blessings of having a body. Learning skills for emotional management is important in overcoming and preventing eating disorders.

Interpersonal relationships and social challenges. Earlier research showed that women with eating disorders tended to come from families that were overprotective and had rigid rules and poor problem-solving skills. It suggested that families that overvalued physical appearance and high achievement also increased the risk for eating disorders. Recent studies, however, show that many women who have problems with food come from loving, well-adjusted families.

Pressures from outside the family may be powerful even when you have a supportive, loving family. Peer pressure to be thin, belong to a particular social group, or excel in school and extracurricular activities all create strong social pressures. Young people may struggle as they try to become independent upon entering the adult world.

If you do not feel ready for these challenges, life can be stressful. When it is difficult to handle the challenges of becoming an adult, you may believe that being thinner or more attractive will solve your challenges. This can lead to eating problems. You lose weight, but the problems remain. Getting help to learn skills for adult roles and responsibilities can prepare you to handle your challenges better than trying to manage them through food.

The inability to solve interpersonal conflicts also contributes to eating disorders. Most relationships have occasional disagreements and differences. If these conflicts seem frightening and you have few skills for solving them, they may feel overwhelming. A young woman with an eating disorder commented, "Food is easier to manage than men. It is always around when you want it. You can just throw it up when you are sick of it. You never have to negotiate because you are always in control." This woman was struggling to understand how to have a relationship with a man but was comforting her distress with bulimia.

Cultural pressures and media messages. The media flood us with images, words, and messages. Many media messages are harmful, however. Successful women are usually portrayed as ultrathin and beautiful. The message is, "You must be thin and beautiful according to media standards to be happy." Many advertisements are designed to sell products by convincing people that they can achieve greater happiness by buying the product. Thin, media-beautiful people are used to sell the product, diet, or program.

The media often associate only one standard of beauty with success and happiness. That standard is thinner than most women can achieve and still be healthy. Many media messages suggest that you are not beautiful enough, thin enough, and acceptable enough as you are. You must conform to media standards in order to find happiness.

In reality, God created bodies in many sizes, shapes, and colors. There is variation in cared-for, healthy bodies. Real life presents examples of people who differ in their body type and appearance and still have happy, productive lives. The scriptures never mention physical beauty as a requirement for God's love or approval. Our eternal worth is not based on our outward appearance (1 Samuel 16:7).

Abuse and trauma to the body. An estimated one of every five women has an unwanted, abusive, or aggressive sexual experience in her life. This world is often not a safe place. Frightening and painful abuse to the body can lead to seeing it as an enemy and can contribute to eating problems. Chronic illness, injury, and other physical trauma also can contribute to such problems. Whenever your body is injured or abused, you may be afraid to trust it. You may even require help to learn how to care for your body following abuse, trauma, or serious illness. It is important to learn that you do not have to tolerate abuse. You have the right to protect and care for your body.

Spiritual concerns. It is important to have a correct understanding of spiritual truths related to our mortal experience, including having a body. People with eating disorders often have spiritual problems that prevent a correct understanding of important principles (see chapter 7, "Spiritual Sources of Support for Emotional Distress," and chapter 22, "The Role of Faith and Spirituality in Recovering from an Eating Disorder").

How Is an Eating Disorder Treated?

Eating disorders have the highest mortality rate of any mental illness. Death can be a direct result of the illness or a result of other health consequences of having an eating disorder. What may seem to be an easy solution to weight management and other problems is really a dangerous illness. Common medical problems associated with eating disorders include the following:

Heart arrhythmias and low blood pressure
Osteoporosis (softening of the bones)
Loss of muscle tissue
Kidney failure
Anemia
Liver disease
Reproductive and menstrual problems
Digestive problems

Tooth decay (from throwing up)

Electrolyte disturbances

These problems can be life threatening. It is important to seek treatment. Research shows that early intervention is more likely to result in full recovery of an eating disorder. As with other addictive and compulsive problems, recovery is often slow and may involve relapses. Do not get discouraged. Keep working toward full recovery. It may take time and strong effort to recover, but recovery is possible.

There are many different approaches to treatment. Each person with an eating disorder has a different combination of medical, psychological, social, and spiritual concerns. Treatment needs to be tailored to the individual. The most effective treatments involve a coordinated effort by a multidisciplinary staff of professionals. This can include medical management, psychotherapy, nutritional counseling, support groups, and medication.

Medical management. See a physician for a complete medical evaluation. It is important to rule out other medical conditions that may be contributing to the eating disorder. It is also important to get medical treatment for diseases caused by the eating disorder.

Counseling and psychotherapy. This can help you identify and solve the underlying emotional problems that contribute to the eating disorder. Some benefits of professional counseling include the following:

Learning skills for identifying, understanding, and managing emotions

Learning the difference between feeding the body and feeding emotions

Solving interpersonal problems

Correcting cognitive distortions and irrational beliefs (see chapter 12, "Mood Disorders")

Learning stress-management skills

Identifying and confronting false cultural and media messages

Resolving concerns related to abuse or trauma

Learning skills for adult living

Learning how care for your body

Improving communication and conflict-resolution skills

Nutritional counseling. A nutritionist or dietitian can help you learn healthy eating patterns. Learning healthy ways of managing your weight can reduce your vulnerability to dangerous solutions. A strategy called *intuitive eating* is also effective in helping you learn to recognize your body's natural ability to regulate eating. Intuitive-eating skills involve learning how to recognize hunger and fullness cues from your body. This can help you learn not to binge or starve. Intuitive-eating skills also help you recognize the difference between body sensations related to emotions and body sensations related to hunger and fullness.

Support groups. These groups can help you talk about your recovery with others who are also working to overcome eating problems. They can help you not to feel alone and ashamed of your struggle with food.

Medication. Your doctor may recommend medication as part of your treatment. Depression, obsessive-compulsive disorder (OCD), and other mental health problems often coexist with eating disorders. Sometimes failure to eat properly creates chemical imbalances in the brain that lead to the development of these other mental illnesses. If you have constant, intrusive thoughts of food that you cannot get out of your mind, medications called selective serotonin reuptake inhibitors (SSRIs) are often helpful (see chapter 3, "The Brain and Medical Treatment for Mental Disorders"). These and other medications are used to treat depression or OCD that may be part of the eating disorder.

Not all professionals are trained to work with eating disorders. It is helpful to find health care professionals who have experience and training in treating these disorders. Many people respond well to outpatient treatment. If the eating disorder is severe, life-threatening, or related to other severe mental health problems, inpatient hospitalization may be necessary. Some hospitals have specialized eating-disorder treatment programs. Specialized residential eating-disorder treatment clinics provide intensive treatment. These clinics usually use multiple approaches to recovery, such as those listed above. They also may include recreational therapy, music or art therapy, and other ways of helping you learn how to manage your life without an eating disorder. These inpatient treatment centers may require longer stays, ranging from weeks to months of treatment. With severe eating disorders, outpatient follow-up and aftercare is important to maintain the improvement made in the inpatient treatment center.

Spiritual recovery is also an important part of overcoming an eating disorder (see chapter 22, "The Role of Faith and Spirituality in Recovering from an Eating Disorder"). Learning a correct understanding of gospel principles can help you learn to have faith in God and to love yourself.

How Can You Help Yourself?

Some suggestions include the following:

Do not let yourself become convinced that an eating disorder is not a problem. The problem exists, but there is also hope.

Seek spiritual help from your Heavenly Father through prayer. He understands your struggle and he cares.

Learn to accept your limitations. Remember that "all have not every gift given unto them. . . . To some is given one, and to some is given another" (D&C 46:11–12). You are not required to excel in everything. You are also not required to "run faster or labor more than you have strength" (D&C 10:4; Mosiah 4:27).

Seek to understand your own unique personality, gifts, and mission in mortality. Do not compare yourself with others, but seek spiritual guidance through prayer, your patriarchal blessing, and inspiration from the Holy Ghost.

Honor your body's natural signals. If you are hungry, eat; if you are full, stop; if you are tired, rest; if you are stressed, relax. Your body's signals can help you keep your life balanced.

Learn about healthy eating and weight management. Get correct nutritional information rather than relying on fad diets.

Learn strategies for effectively managing stress, interpersonal problems, and painful emotions.

Learn the difference between eating to care for your body and eating to silence emotions or solve problems.

Be patient with yourself, but keep trying to overcome your eating disorder. It may take time and you may experience relapses, but you can eventually overcome an eating disorder.

For more help, see chapter 22, "The Role of Faith and Spirituality in Recovering from an Eating Disorder."

How Can You Help Others?

Some suggestions include the following:

Reinforce definitions of success that focus on personal qualities rather than on performance, achievement, and appearance. For example, being a good friend may be more important than winning a competition.

Honor diversity of appearance and body build. Beauty is found in many sizes, shapes, and colors.

Be aware of how competition and perfectionism can negatively affect a person's relationships and feelings of self-worth.

Be inclusive rather than exclusive. Provide a place of value and belonging for all regardless of abilities, talents, or appearance.

Keep conversations about eating supportive and confidential rather than being angry or controlling. Focus on concern for health rather than on weight or appearance. Do not engage in lengthy discussions about food and weight.

Do not try to change the person's behavior yourself. Seek help from God and appropriate Church leaders. Seek competent professional help if necessary. Do not get discouraged if change is slow.

Be supportive, be available, and listen with understanding. Show you care. Encourage the person to get help.

Do not take responsibility for the person's problems. Be open, honest, and caring, but recognize when to back off.

Be yourself. Share your own struggles and challenges. Be open and real.

Remember that a person with an eating disorder is just that—a person first and a person who has problems with food second.

Give nonjudgmental feedback about your concerns. Use "I" statements such as, "I worry about you when you never join us for dinner."

Model healthy eating and attitudes about the body.

How Can You Help Prevent Eating Disorders?

Some suggestions include the following:

Teach correct spiritual principles, and encourage young people to learn to govern themselves.

Teach young people to seek personal help through prayer, scripture study, patriarchal blessings, and listening to the Holy Ghost. Teach spiritual self-reliance.

Provide role models of personally empowered, competent women in all body shapes and sizes, reflecting multiple life experiences. Encourage young women to discover God's plan for them.

Teach skills for solving problems and, when necessary, speaking up.

Encourage normal, appropriate development. Protect children and teens from exposure to adult roles and responsibilities before they are ready. Do not push children to grow up too fast.

Help girls and young women learn adult roles and responsibilities.

Promote caring and cooperation instead of competition among women.

Counteract media messages. Help women see reality.

Teach the divine purposes and functions of a mortal body. A body is not just about physical beauty. Emphasize the function of having a body over its appearance.

Supply accurate information about eating, metabolism, genetic differences, and dieting.

What Is It Like to Have An Eating Disorder?

"Hi. My name is Francie. I'm twenty-six years old, and I'm anorexic. I have been this way for years. I started gymnastics at the age of six, and I competed until I was thirteen, when I switched to cheerleading. I was a cheerleader all through high school and for three years at college. I think that's where my issues with weight and food really started. We were weighed every day, and everybody knew how much you weighed and how much body fat you had. Since I was one of the tinier girls, I was a flyer, and it was even more important to be light. The lighter and skinnier you were, the better cheerleader you were. That's when I decided that being skinny meant being good enough. And so I started starving. I tried every diet there was. The cheerleaders taught each other dieting tricks: water pills, diet pills, starve yourself for six days and eat for one.

"I come from a perfectionist family. In high school during my sophomore and junior years, I'd go to my father's office for help with writing a paper. By

11:30 or 12 at night, I would be on the couch falling asleep, saying, 'I don't care what grade the teacher gives me. I just want to go home. I'm tired.' I was sixteen. But my father would hold my paper up to the light, making sure that all the page numbers lined up on top of each other and that the first lines and the last lines of each paper lined up right on top of each other. 'Just one more time,' he'd say. 'Let's print it out just one more time. Let's just change three words in this last paragraph. Just one more minute. It will just take a minute.' I think that's where I learned to expect perfection from myself. I'm either number one or I have failed. There is no second place for me. There is no third place. There is no average.

"My mother has struggled with food all of her life as well. When we went out to dinner, she never ordered her own meal. She only ate off my dad's plate. She didn't hit a hundred pounds until I was a senior in high school, and by then I weighed 105. I was giving her pants I had grown out of. I think I learned my eating habits from her."[1]

Note

1. Green, Anderson, and Dalton, eds. *Hearts Knit Together,* 215–16.

18

Cognitive Disorders

Marleen S. Williams and Erin D. Bigler

Many mental illnesses create problems in thinking and processing information. This chapter will help you understand the relationship shared by brain function, emotion, and cognitive (thinking and information processing) problems. To introduce these topics, a few assumptions need to be discussed, along with a bit of philosophy, because this information about behavior and cognitive disorders and their relationship to brain dysfunction may be different than what many people may think. This chapter is written from a perspective that will focus on how current scientific understanding helps us see various disorders of cognitive impairment related to mental health.

Most problems we call mental illnesses are related to problems in how the brain functions. Problems with mood, anxiety, stress, schizophrenia, autism, and learning disabilities all involve difficulty in thinking and processing information. This chapter, however, focuses on problems that are often referred to as cognitive disorders. To understand cognitive disorders, it is important to understand how the brain differs from other organs in the body.

Brain Function and Cognitive Disorders

The brain is not just a pumping station like the heart, with mechanical valves that move the blood. With seemingly infinite complexity in its healthy state, the brain is unlike any other organ system. To grasp this complexity, think how our mortal life begins with an egg being fertilized at conception, with a combination of the father's and mother's genetic blueprint being combined to begin life's journey. At the beginning of this nine-month stay in the womb, the fertilized egg begins a wonderful process of dividing and duplicating to become a fully formed, viable fetus in less than six months.

If the adult brain contains somewhere around two hundred billion cells (scientists still debate how many cells there are, but all agree it is in the billions), and at birth we generally have a full complement of brain cells that will carry us through life's journey, how many cells have to be generated per minute during early brain development? The answer is astonishing. At some point early in fetal brain development, somewhere in the neighborhood of one hundred thousand new brain cells are formed every minute! While this is a huge number, it does not match the complexity of what occurs next.

Each cell has to link up with countless neighboring cells—in some cases, doing so more than ten thousand times. Synapses have to occur in an orderly fashion, and their function depends in large part on the role of genetics and how the brain interacts with its environment. As soon as a neuron is formed, it begins to make its synaptic connections with other neurons. While these cells initially follow their predestined course, their ultimate functions are affected and determined by experience and repetition.

The brain *learns* from mortal experience as these synaptic connections are laid down, but if there are billions of brain cells, how fast do synapses develop in the formative years? The answer is another astounding fact. Early in fetal development, tens of thousands of synapses develop every minute. Some researchers estimate that even through late childhood and adolescence, synaptic formation occurs at a rate of twenty thousand to forty thousand synapses per minute!

The brain's complexity is more easily understood when one looks at the numbers of *things* that make up the brain. The neuron is the cell where much of the action occurs in the brain. No neuron actually touches another; rather, neurons communicate to other neurons by release of chemicals known as neurotransmitters (see chapter 2, "A Look at Your Brain").

A neuron is said to *fire,* or release, its chemical messenger, a neurotransmitter, which starts an electrochemical reaction that triggers the next cell in line. There are many ways a neuron can be either helped or hindered in its ability to fire and communicate with other neurons. When a neuron gets out of its normal balance or rhythm and fires too much, as in a seizure, dramatic changes in behavior and thinking can occur. On the other hand, when there is too little firing of a neurotransmitter, neurons cannot communicate effectively. In such cases, significant changes occur, such as with Parkinson's disease. Therefore, both overactivation *and* underactivation are bad.

The Principle of Homeostasis

Biological systems constantly attempt to be in balance, a state called *homeostasis.* When brain homeostasis is not achieved and maintained, abnormal behavior and thinking may occur.

The principle of homeostasis is a universal feature of all body systems and, as such, understanding how brain homeostasis controls behavior and emotion is critical to developing new and effective treatments. For example, when the heart is at rest, blood pressure to the brain and other vital organs is lowered. So the moment you stand, your heart rate and blood pressure rise in order to keep the proper amount of blood flowing to your brain.

Homeostasis is also the reason you get hungry and thirsty, and why your eyes get used to light. If, according to the description above, homeostasis is critical to the normal functioning of all body systems, and if mental and emotional functioning are also biologically based in the brain, then homeostatic functions of the brain are critical to mental and emotional well-being. In other words, our brain is constantly seeking stability, or equilibrium, to maintain emotional balance. This undoubtedly relates to how neurotransmitters are used and kept in balance in the critical regions of the brain. When that balance is disrupted through injury, disease, or mental illness, it typically affects one or more of the critical structures.

When a normal functioning brain is damaged or injured, predictable changes occur that reduce, or even eliminate, the range of behavior or potential that an individual had before the injury (or onset of a neurological disease or disorder). Likewise, if something genetic, physical, or biochemical does not develop properly in the brain, predictable problems in behavior and function may occur. In fact, understanding how these brain regions maintain a homeostatic balance one with another is probably one key to understanding normal and effective emotional regulation and is currently the focus of intense research.

Various types of brain scans, such as magnetic resonance imaging (MRI), are excellent for showing the *structure* of the brain. In addition, the *function,* or workings, of the brain can be shown with a functional MRI, known as an fMRI. There are also functional neuroimaging methods that measure blood flow or the uptake of a radioactive tracer, best shown by what is called positron emission tomography (PET).

Homeostasis and the fight-or-flight response. One final concept related to homeostasis, and critically linked to brain structures and mental health, is the brain's fight-or-flight response. The fight-or-flight regions of the brain represent a basic part of the brain that make up what is called the limbic system, or the emotional brain (see chapter 2, "A Look at Your Brain"). The brain must perceive danger and be able to react in order for us to survive. These brain regions have been described as fear centers, activation of which causes a fear response and a perception of a negative emotion.

For example, showing the picture of a menacing snake will activate these centers in most individuals. In the natural world, the appearance of something that is potentially threatening—like a menacing snake—requires a response. This means that the body must mobilize its resources to respond (fight or flight), which begins in the brain. Once the threat goes away, homeostasis returns the brain and body back into balance.

However, what happens if there is an excessive and continuous response within the limbic system? What does a fear overreaction do to the brain? Obviously, homeostasis is disrupted. Such disruptions become associated with many mental disorders. The key to understanding this is that it is a brain response that produces psychological reactions (emotions), and there is no such thing as a psychological reaction without the brain first processing and responding to either its internal and external environment. In other words, the brain is the seat of behavior. Behavior does not occur independent of the brain. When the brain malfunctions, it may be difficult or even impossible to make choices about behavior.

The sections that follow will briefly describe some of the major cognitive disorders as we currently understand them. Three excellent Web sites offer additional insights into cognitive disorders:

The National Institutes of Health (NIH): nih.gov

The Centers for Disease Control and Prevention (CDC): cdc.gov

The National Alliance on Mental Illness (NAMI): nami.org

Common Cognitive Disorders

Aging and dementia. Ronald Reagan, the forty-first president of the United States, was later diagnosed with Alzheimer's disease (AD). Because of President Regan's public struggle with the illness, awareness of AD was greatly increased, and most people now know that Alzheimer's affects memory. MRI pictures from someone with Alzheimer's disease show atrophy or shrinkage of the brain, particularly in the frontal and temporal lobes. In Alzheimer's, this type of atrophy leads to problems with memory, planning, and intellectual processes—hence the term *dementia,* or loss of cognitive ability.

Dementia is a *symptom,* merely reflecting the decrease of cognitive ability from a previous higher level of functioning. Alzheimer's is a specific type of dementia. There are numerous types of dementia. Each type has its own unique features, but central to all of them is some loss of cognitive ability because of degeneration in the brain.

What is less known about AD and most forms of dementia is that all kinds of behaviors can change depending on the stage of the disorder. Common symptoms of Alzheimer's include the following:

Loss of short-term memory
Loss of the ability to initiate and organize behavior (executive functioning)
Changes in personality
Changes in temperament

Other degenerative diseases, such as Pick's disease (named after the neuropathologist who first described the brain problem), may initially show only changes in personality as the primary clinical problem.

A well-respected minister started to use inappropriate and coarse language and to neglect his personal hygiene. He was later arrested for inappropriate sexual behavior with a parishioner. The members of this man's family were beside themselves and horrified by what had occurred, thinking that the minister had experienced some type of nervous breakdown. They assumed that he had succumbed to the pressure of running his ministry and inexplicably had lost his faith. The truth, however, is that he had a degenerative disease of the brain, which turned out to be Pick's disease, a particular type of dementia linked to these types of personality changes.

How Is Dementia Diagnosed?

Neuroimaging of brains with these disorders will typically show various forms of cerebral atrophy (shrinkage). Neuropsychological testing will typically show impaired cognitive function. These tests can determine if ability levels have fallen below what would normally be expected for an individual.

Neuroimaging in individuals with suspected dementia also should include functional neuroimaging. An MRI provides exquisite detail of the brain, but it represents a static anatomical image, like a picture. It does not show how the brain is functioning. Functional neuroimaging, however, can show if the brain is functioning correctly. Techniques like positron emission tomography (PET) provide a way to also examine glucose (sugar) or oxygen uptake in the brain, which shows whether the brain is metabolically normal or not.

Treatment for Dementia

More and more treatments are being developed for those with dementia. Currently dementia cannot be cured, but medications can slow the process, as well as manage the symptoms. The key is getting the proper diagnosis, which will typically require a neurologist to head a diagnostic and treatment team. On its Web site, the National Institute on Aging (NIA) provides detailed information on these disorders and their diagnosis and treatment (nia.nih.gov).

Traumatic Brain Injury (TBI)

Before the advent of modern medical care, most individuals with moderate to severe brain injury soon died from their injury. With sophisticated trauma centers now located in every major metropolitan area of the industrialized world, that is no longer the case.

The CDC estimates that each year 1.5 million people suffer a traumatic brain injury. In its latest estimates, the CDC reports that about 2 percent of the U.S. population has some degree of disability from having suffered a TBI.

MRI and fMRI pictures can show three-dimensional reconstruction of the typical effects of a TBI. The more severe the brain injury, the greater the likelihood for diffuse (general) brain damage, in particular in the white matter of the brain, where the axons that interconnect the brain reside. Disruption of these connections often results in slowed processing speed, one of the common problems associated with moderate-to-severe TBI.

Symptoms of Traumatic Brain Injury

The most common cognitive problems in TBI are the loss of short-term memory and/or the inability to initiate and organize behavior (executive functioning).

Sherrie was a bright, ambitious, university student. She had always earned excellent grades. While walking to class, she slipped on the ice and hit her head hard on a nearby metal bench. She was unconscious for a time and received treatment in the emergency room of the local hospital for a large gash on her head. When she returned to school, she noticed that it was hard to remember what she had just read. She frequently forgot assignments unless she wrote them down immediately. Her family also noticed that she lost her drive to get her homework done. She just could not seem to organize and plan sufficiently. Her once easygoing personality frequently erupted with angry outbursts or tearful episodes.

Treatment of Traumatic Brain Injury

Various forms of treatment may be helpful to those with TBI. Treatment is usually first orchestrated by a neurologist or psychiatrist. Neuropsychological testing helps define the presence and type of cognitive deficits. *Cognitive rehabilitation* is a therapy that focuses on training noninjured parts of the brain to take over functions that have been lost from damage to the brain. The Brain Injury Association of America (biausa.org) and the North American Brain Injury Society (NABIS: nabis.org) both have detailed information about TBI and its diagnosis and treatment on their Web sites.

Cerebrovascular Disorder and Stroke

The brain contains hundreds of miles of blood vessels. Remember that each of the billions of brain cells has to receive its own individual supply of oxygenated and glucose-laden blood. Both blood and oxygen have to be transported to the cell body so the cell can function. No cell in the brain has the capacity to store glucose or oxygen, so this has to be delivered every living moment to the billions of cells that make up the brain. With aging and disease, blood vessels lose their elasticity and often, because of high blood pressure and the buildup of cholesterol and other plaque-forming factors that can clog blood vessels, a cerebrovascular accident (CVA), or stroke, occurs. CVAs can also occur as a result of trauma, abnormalities of blood vessel development (such as an aneurysm), or malformation or a blood vessel. The location of a stroke in the brain will determine the type of cognitive effects it has on the individual.

An eighty-six-year-old man had been a high-functioning manager of a large business that had hundreds of employees. He had serious problems with congestive heart failure and hypertension and had suffered so-called ministrokes. As these small strokes accumulated, he became more and more cognitively impaired. He never suffered what would be considered a major stroke, but the effects of these small strokes accumulated and caused problems that were just as serious as a large stroke. A brain scan verified the damage.

Small strokes in strategic places can also produce dramatic changes. For example, a small stroke involving the hippocampus (see chapter 2, "A Look at Your Brain") can produce amnesia, preventing the sufferer from forming new memories. The person can remember events that occurred before the stroke but has no ability to form memories for events after the stroke.

The American Heart Association (americanheart.org) and the American Stroke Association (strokeassociation.org) have more information on their Web sites.

Epilepsy

Epilepsy is a neurological disorder that covers a broad range of conditions. The basic problem in epilepsy is an abnormal firing rate of neurons that overrides otherwise normally functioning neurons. This causes seizure or seizure-like activity. When most people think of a seizure, typically they think of a grand-mal type seizure with generalized tonic-clonic movements (generalized shaking). Such seizures are common and debilitating, but they represent only one form of epilepsy. Some seizures may not produce these kinds of obvious outward manifestations and may primarily affect thinking and behavior.

Sara's mother was the first to recognize her seizures. Sometimes when she was talking with her daughter, Sara would briefly stop and stare with a blank look. Her eyes would flutter slightly, and she would smack her lips. These episodes lasted only a few seconds. Sara would then resume her normal conversion with no memory that she had experienced a seizure. These episodes happened with no warning. Sara's mother later learned from the neurologist that Sara was having petit mal seizures.

Cognitive problems associated with epilepsy often come in the form of inattentiveness that may also affect learning and memory. The type of cognitive problem associated with epilepsy depends on the type of seizure disorder and the brain region or regions involved, particularly the areas most active in producing the seizures. For example, if someone has post-traumatic epilepsy, then cognitive problems may come from the regions of the brain directly injured, as well as from the actual seizure activity.

Treatment

Neurologists head treatment teams working with patients who have epilepsy and epilepsy-associated cognitive and behavior problems. Medication is often used to control seizures. In some cases surgery helps. The Epilepsy Foundation Web site (epilepsyfoundation.org) is a wonderful resource for patients and families with epilepsy.

Cerebral palsy

The term *cerebral palsy* is a generic term, merely reflecting impairment in motor control—or palsy—associated with some type of brain damage, injury, or poor development of the immature brain in an infant. Depending on how and where the brain is injured, in part, predicts the degree of cognitive impairment.

A student at a large university had severe, generalized cerebral palsy. She was confined to a wheelchair and could only control her wheelchair with a mouth-held joystick. She was unable to control the muscles of her mouth and tongue to be able to speak. She used a communication board to "speak." Despite these profound motor impairments, she was able to complete a master's degree.

Obviously, presence of motor problems does not necessarily mean impaired cognitive functioning; however, the presence of cerebral palsy is typically associated with some form of cognitive impairment, often significant learning disabilities. Brain imaging can help identify where abnormalities may be in the brain.

Treatment

Using neuropsychological tests, doctors should evaluate children with this disorder on a regular basis to measure their cognitive development. Families, schools, and others can maximize the development of the cognitive abilities of a child with cerebral palsy if they know the child's levels and types of cognitive impairment. Therapy and education can then target cognitive and educational goals with rehabilitation therapies. A good Web site is cerebralpalsy.org.

Addictions

Numerous recent studies have demonstrated the biological basis of addiction. If you stop and think about it, something powerful must be going on in the brain of those with an addiction. Individuals with addictions have a difficult time stopping their addictive behaviors even when there are serious consequences.

A woman had throat cancer from smoking. She had attempted to quit smoking for decades. She knew she needed to quit, and she had tried all types of psychological and medical therapies, but she was never successful. Eventually, the cancer had to be surgically treated. Extensive chemo and radiation therapies failed to stop the spread of the cancer. She could no longer talk because of multiple cancer operations on her throat, and she had to communicate through gestures and writing. She could only breathe through a tracheotomy tube. Finally, the cancer spread to her brain. After she had brain surgery to treat the metastasized cancer, a neuropsychological examination was performed to check on her cognitive status.

Throughout all of this she had not been able to quit smoking. She smoked by plugging her tracheotomy tube with a lit cigarette and inhaling. It was traumatic to witness her doing this, but it was a clear demonstration of the power of an addiction and how the addicted can resist rational thinking. While her cognitive deficits were minimal from the brain cancer and surgery, no amount of rational-based therapies could seem to help this lady quit her habit.

From the standpoint of the brain, it does not matter what the addiction may be. Whether the addiction is drugs, alcohol, pornography, or tobacco, the same brain areas are involved. These relate to the basal forebrain and limbic system. When these areas are activated, rational thinking and behavior may take a backseat. The terribly intense addictive cravings come from these regions of the brain. So often in addiction, there is a disconnect between the individual's ability to recognize and understand the addiction and the ability to stop the addictive behavior.

Individuals with alcohol and drug addictions may also suffer long-term cognitive effects of their addictions because of their direct adverse effects on the brain. For example, chronic alcoholism can lead to cerebral atrophy and dementia. Stimulants like amphetamine and cocaine can cause small *and* large strokes. Certain illicit drugs can permanently alter how some neurotransmitters are released in the brain.

Treatment

Treatment for addictions may be one of the most challenging of all therapies (see "Dual Diagnosis" in chapter 1, "What Is Mental Illness?"), but significant community resources are available as well. In many areas, LDS Family Services offers addiction-treatment groups. Many people do recover. Strengthening spiritual resources can be helpful in recovery. Two major government agencies offer information on treatment: The National Institute on Drug Abuse (nida.nih.gov) and the National Institute on Alcohol Abuse and Alcoholism (niaaa.nih.gov). Likewise, most states have various agencies that provide information and services.

Conclusions

This brief review demonstrates that what we have labeled as mental illnesses in the past are really closely related to disorders of the brain. This chapter provides only a partial and limited overview of cognitive disorders and only touches on the most significant disorders. In each disorder discussed, various brain regions related to problems in cognitive functioning and the behavioral and emotional expression of the disorder have been described. As we begin a new millennium, let us take a fresh look at these disorders, realizing that as we better understand how the brain regulates emotions and behavior, we will likely see improved treatments and outcomes.

Section IV
Coping with Mental Illness

19

Mental Health and the Law

Robert F. Williams

Individuals and families struggling with mental disorders have important consumer rights. Among these is the right to legal confidentiality of protected health information. *Confidentiality* means that in most cases, patients (often called consumers) have the legal right to decide who has access to their mental health records and information concerning diagnosis and treatment. By law, mental health providers and institutions must take care to guard the confidentiality of records regarding consumers of mental health care.

Consumers, or the parent or guardian of an underage minor, normally have the right to examine and obtain copies of records that concern them. Permission to view or release this information to a third party, such as a bishop, insurance company, employer, friend, family member, or anyone else ordinarily requires that the consumer (or parent if the consumer is under legal age) sign a release form. This legally protects your privacy. There are some notable exceptions:

> In most states, mental health providers are required to inform child-protection authorities if they have knowledge of abuse of a child.
>
> In some cases, a provider may have a legal obligation to break confidentiality in order to warn another person of clearly identifiable danger to that person.

If a person alleges in a lawsuit that he or she has suffered emotional damage or disability, the mental health records of that person may be subject to subpoena by the opposing side. In such a situation, the court can require that the records be presented in court.

When a person accused of a crime claims mental incompetence or insanity, the court will open the mental health records of that person.

The sensitive nature of mental health records is recognized by the laws of most countries. For example, in many countries, a mental health care consumer is not required to disclose the existence of a mental disorder to an employer. A person may choose not to disclose this information because of fear of potential bias or stigma. Or a person may choose to allow others to know in order to seek support and understanding regarding the nature of the disability.

Under the Americans with Disabilities Act (ADA) in the United States, persons with mental disorders are entitled to "reasonable accommodations" to assist them to do their job properly. Such accommodations may include time off in which to keep appointments for mental health care, an adjustment in scheduling or work pace, or a leave of absence to allow recovery from an episode of illness. Under the ADA, exceptions to normal work policies in order to accommodate an employee are not designed to allow the employee to take advantage of the system but rather to enable the employee to produce at the level at which the employee is truly capable of performing.

Children and adults in educational settings are also covered by the ADA. When a person's mental disorder prevents him from fully benefiting from school, the person is legally entitled to seek reasonable accommodations, such as front-row seating, additional time to complete tests, use of a calculator, or a setting free from distraction while taking tests. Nowadays most colleges and school systems have a person or office responsible for administering the provisions of the ADA and assisting mental health consumers to get the most possible from their educational experience.

Provider Responsibilities

Training. Mental health care providers must complete academic and practical training as required by state law for licensure. They must practice only within their particular area of competence. They must obtain continuing education to update their knowledge in their area of expertise as required by state law. They must observe legal and ethical standards appropriate to their particular profession.

Licensure. Different professions, such as psychiatry, clinical psychology, and social work, have different education, training, and licensing requirements. It is important to understand that some therapists and therapies are *not* regulated or licensed by government. For example, in some places, the practice of hypnosis is not restricted by law. A wise consumer will be cautious before seeking care from a practitioner who offers a form of mental health care not recognized and regulated by law.

Confidentiality. Providers must also observe legal guidelines for keeping records and maintaining confidentiality of records, such as those required in the United States by the Health Insurance Portability and Accountability Act of 1996 (HIPAA). These regulations are more strict and comprehensive than in the past and have required providers to take additional steps to safeguard protected health care information.

Duty to warn. U.S. court decisions have defined an additional duty for therapists termed the "duty to warn." The courts have held that a therapist has an obligation to protect the "foreseeable victims" of a client's violent action. This means that when a therapist recognizes (or should have recognized) that a client is a serious threat to cause physical harm to an identifiable victim, the therapist must make efforts to warn the potential victim of the possible danger.

Duty to protect. It is generally accepted that the mental health care provider has an obligation to protect the client from harm when it is within the therapist's power to do so. However, this duty is less well defined by the law. It is usually understood to exist when the client is perceived to be at urgent and immediate risk for severe psychological trauma, serious bodily injury, or death. The most typical example is when a client makes a believable threat of suicide and has an immediate plan to carry out the suicidal act. In such circumstances, the therapist may be required to tell others in order to take steps to protect the client, such as notifying the spouse, a parent, or the police.

Inpatient Admission

Reasons for psychiatric admission. A mental health client may become so disabled that the treatment team recommends admission to an inpatient psychiatric facility. Reasons for psychiatric hospitalization include the following:

To provide a protected environment until the person becomes better able to care for himself or herself.

To monitor the person's condition and response to medication and other treatments.

To stabilize the person's most serious symptoms.

To allow greater intensity of treatment in a controlled setting.

Voluntary admission. Many people are surprised to learn that most admissions to psychiatric inpatient facilities are *voluntary*. That is, most of those experiencing a mental health crisis recognize it and voluntarily enter the psychiatric unit upon recommendation of an admitting physician. The support and reassurance of family members is vital in helping those who are experiencing a crisis to understand the necessity and appropriateness of accepting a recommendation for admission to the hospital.

A voluntarily admitted person may leave the hospital voluntarily, although the person may be asked to sign a form acknowledging that he or she is leaving the hospital "against medical advice." Or, if the attending physician believes that discharge would seriously endanger the person or someone else, the doctor may place the person on a seventy-two-hour hold and ask the court to order an *involuntary* commitment. Sometimes this is necessary when the person is deemed to be so ill that he or she cannot rationally make the decision to leave.

Involuntary commitment. Contrary to popular belief, it is not easy to commit a person for inpatient mental health care without the person's voluntary consent. Laws protecting persons from exploitation and unfair treatment have become strict, and it can be frustrating to get help for a psychiatrically disabled person who resists voluntary admission. In the United States, the general criterion for involuntary commitment to a hospital is that the person be mentally ill *and* present an "immediate" or "substantial" danger to self or others. "Danger to self or others" might mean that the person has—

Exhibited violent or suicidal behavior in the recent past

Made credible, believable threats of suicide or violence toward
   others

Been living on the streets without money or means of support

Become so disabled that the person is unable to meet personal basic
   needs for food, shelter, and self-care

Been victimized and continues to be exposed to further danger

In an emergency situation, the law may authorize a peace officer to detain a person when the officer has a reasonable basis for belief that the person is mentally ill. For example, the individual may be observed to be behaving in a bizarre manner that threatens the safety of others. The officer will then detain and transport the person to a hospital emergency room for evaluation by someone authorized to do so by law.

Then, depending upon the outcome of the examiner's evaluation of the patient, he or she may or may not be admitted to an inpatient facility. The admission may be voluntary if the person agrees to accept hospitalization, or the examiner may recommend a seventy-two-hour hold if the legal criteria for "danger to self or others" have been met. This allows time for scheduling of a commitment hearing while the person is being held in a protected setting. Often, however, when the person's symptoms have been stabilized somewhat in the hospital, he or she will then accept voluntary admission, and the commitment hearing will not be necessary.

In the United States, proceedings for involuntary commitment are defined by state law. At a commitment hearing, the person may be represented by an attorney, introduce evidence, call witnesses, or testify in his or her own behalf. The judge may release the person or may order further evaluation or treatment in an inpatient facility, such as the state mental hospital.

So what do you do when a loved one is admitted to the hospital for mental health care?

Provide information to the treatment team. Family members of a person admitted to a psychiatric inpatient unit have a great deal of valuable information about the history and background of the patient. Do not hesitate to offer such information to assist in the diagnosis and treatment of the loved one. Sometimes concerned persons—even the parents of a child of legal age—may not be able to get information about the condition of the hospitalized patient without the patient's written consent. Remember, however, that confidentiality regulations do not prevent you from *giving* information to the mental health care team.

Offer support to the hospitalized person. Admission to a psychiatric facility can be a frightening experience in which the patient feels cut off from outside sources of support. Sometimes family members feel intimidated or embarrassed about being in a psychiatric hospital unit. To help their loved one, family members should do the following:

Learn about visiting hours and rules for the hospital unit.

Visit in small numbers—one or two at a time—so as to avoid overwhelming the patient and the facility.

Find out from the hospital staff what kinds of materials you might bring that would make the patient more comfortable.

Encourage the patient to participate as fully as possible in the programs and activities available during the hospital stay.

Be involved in the aftercare plan. Inpatient stays have become shorter because of the high cost of inpatient treatment, pressure from insurance companies to limit their financial liability, and stricter standards of care. As a result, even a severely ill patient may be stabilized and discharged within a few days or a week. This means that family members need to be involved from the beginning in developing the plan for the patient's care following discharge from the hospital:

Learn the names and functions of the treatment providers, such as the attending physician, the assigned therapist, and the case manager.

Understand what medications and dosages have been prescribed, what each medication is intended to do, and what side effects might arise.

Know what follow-up appointments have been made for outpatient care, such as appointments with a counselor or psychiatrist.

Ask about the patient's legal status and responsibilities to the court.

Find out about community resources that may assist the patient and the family.

Become better informed about the nature and treatment of mental illness through the local chapter of the National Alliance for the Mentally Ill (NAMI).

Warning Signs of Suicide

Sometimes a person who commits suicide has been careful to avoid giving any indication that he is planning his own death. In such cases, family and friends are taken completely by surprise, and they may feel guilt and blame because they failed to foresee what was about to happen. This is difficult for loved ones because none of us can claim to be a mind reader who can infallibly predict another person's behavior. Family and friends should not blame themselves for what they could neither predict nor control.

In other cases, it may be well known to the family and the treatment team that the person had strong suicidal tendencies. Nevertheless, they were unable to monitor the person twenty-four hours a day every day of the week to prevent suicidal behavior. A determined person can always be clever enough to escape detection and complete a plan for suicide. Try to remember that in the final analysis, each of us is individually responsible for our own survival.

Often a suicidal person *does* give warning signs that should not be ignored. Many people believe that "a person who talks about suicide isn't likely to do it." But this is simply *not* true. In fact, talking about suicide or expressing the wish to die is one of the most important signs that the person may be actively considering suicide. Other warning signs include the following:

Seeking access to firearms, pills, or other means of self-harm

Talking or writing about death and dying

Making a will or giving away possessions

Seeing no reason for living or having no purpose in life

Expressing feelings of hopelessness

Increasing alcohol or drug use

Feeling intense rage or desire to punish others

Experiencing a loss or crisis without seeing a way out

A person may be severely depressed but not suicidal. However, when an individual is also agitated and experiencing unbearable psychological pain, he or she may wrongly believe that suicide is the only solution available. In such a state of agitation, the individual may not be able to think clearly, make rational decisions, sleep, eat, or work. The individual may even think, "Everyone else will be better off when I am gone." You can help by doing the following:

Talk directly and openly with the person about suicide. Don't be afraid that talking about it will cause the person to do it.

Get involved, become available, and show interest and support.

Listen without judging and avoid preaching.

Offer hope that realistic alternatives to suicide are available.

Remove access to weapons or other means of self-harm.

Don't be sworn to secrecy. Get help quickly.

Seek professional guidance and assistance from a mental health agency or provider.

In urgent circumstances, do whatever is necessary to persuade the person to go with you to the emergency room of your local hospital.

The Mental Health System and the Criminal Justice System

Many people incarcerated within the criminal justice system have mental health problems. In fact, it has been estimated that about one in six prison inmates has some sort of diagnosable mental disorder. Mental illness is not against the law, and a person cannot be jailed simply for being mentally ill. Nevertheless, those with mental disorders often exercise poor judgment that leads to arrest and jail. Mental health care in jail facilities varies greatly and may be virtually nonexistent in some rural areas.

Some jurisdictions provide a *mental health court,* where minor law violations are handled. In this system, a person may be able to avoid going to jail by adhering to the requirements given by the court, such as taking medications as prescribed, attending therapy sessions, and reporting regularly to the court. This innovative system allows the court to supervise the person's compliance with treatment, which is often the best insurance against further violations of the law, as well as further episodes of illness.

Competency and insanity play key roles in the mental health and criminal justice systems.

Competency. The law provides that persons who are not competent to participate in their own defense cannot be prosecuted. Definitions of legal competency vary by state but revolve around the notion that people must have both a *factual* and a *rational* understanding of their legal situation.

For example, to have a factual understanding, persons must know the charges against them, the penalties they face, and the roles of the judge, prosecutor, and defense attorney. To have a rational understanding, they must appreciate the seriousness of the charges against them and the possible punishments, and they must be able to make reasoned decisions regarding their defense with the assistance of legal counsel.

When people are found incompetent by court-appointed examiners, they are ordinarily committed to a secure treatment facility, such as the forensic unit of a mental hospital. After they are successfully treated, they are then required to return to court to face charges.

Insanity is a legal term rather than a mental health diagnosis, and state statutes define what constitutes legal insanity. A few recent notorious cases in which there was a perceived abuse of the insanity defense have led state legislatures in the United States to tighten the legal definition of insanity. Partly as a result, insanity defenses are often unsuccessful in achieving an acquittal. In some states (such as Utah), the definition is so strict that even a person acting under the influence of a frank delusion may still be found guilty under the law.

Other pleas. Other pleas may be available to criminal defendants with mental disorders. For example, some states allow a plea of "guilty and mentally ill." This is still a guilty plea, not a defense. With this plea, the person admits guilt but asks the court to recognize his or her need for mental health care. The person may receive such care through the prison system or may be transferred to the state mental hospital during periods of severe mental illness. After being stabilized, the person is then returned to the prison system.

When a Mentally Ill Family Member Is in Jail

In the United States, there has historically been a lack of coordination between the mental health system and the criminal justice system. Mentally disabled people caught between these two systems may be confused and unable to understand how to work with the systems. As a concerned family member, you can help by doing the following:

Find out if the jail has a medical department. Ask to talk to the nurse or social worker assigned to the case. In smaller jails, you may need to talk to the jail administrator.

Offer information to the jail personnel regarding the inmate's symptoms, diagnosis, medications, and mental health history.

Ask if the inmate will be psychiatrically evaluated and receive prescribed medications while in jail.

If you can't afford an attorney, have one assigned through the public defender's office.

Acquaint the attorney with the inmate's mental health history. This may alert the attorney to the need to request a court-ordered competency evaluation and the possibility of a mental illness defense.

Ask the inmate's attorney whether a mental health court (described above) exists in the jurisdiction.

This information primarily relates to the legal system in the United States. If you live in another country, it is important to check the laws that govern mental health in that country.

20

How Does Serious and Persistent Mental Illness Affect Families?

Dawn Fox and Jay Fox

When mental illnesses such as schizophrenia, bipolar disorder, depression, and the various anxiety disorders strike, families face serious financial, emotional, and spiritual challenges. Sometimes it is easy to see the difficulties those with mental illness are having, but we often forget about the impact on the family, even though families are the primary caretakers for most people with mental illness. Elder Alexander B. Morrison has insightfully said, "Among the most painful and often protracted ordeals an individual or family may face is that of mental illness. . . . Unfortunately, the suffering of the mentally ill may . . . extend outward—like ripples in a dark pond—to engulf others. Family members, caught up in pain and even despair, may echo the anguish of the primary victims."[1]

To help you empathize with what families go through, try to think of some event or time in your life that was traumatic. Perhaps you were in an earthquake or an accident, perhaps someone you love suddenly died, or perhaps you were diagnosed with a serious illness. Can you remember the feelings you had of your world slipping out of control, of not knowing what was going to happen next, of not knowing how to cope? Do you remember the initial fear, anxiety, and disbelief? People who become afflicted with mental illness and their families may face just such a traumatic event.

Besides the initial, primary trauma of facing a mental illness, families experience other traumas that occur because of the illness. Perhaps an afflicted father who has always been the provider for the family cannot work, or perhaps a mother may no longer be able to care for her children. Often insurance companies do not cover treatment for mental illness the same way they cover treatment for other illnesses, leading to a great financial burden.

Bizarre and frightening behaviors, including drug and alcohol abuse, may follow that lead to trouble with the law. Relationships can become strained in a family dealing with mental illness. Often it is difficult for the ill person to even attend church because of depression or anxiety. In this chapter we want to examine these stressors facing families and then discuss some of the resources that can support families as they lovingly try to care for their ill loved one.

Why Do Mental Illnesses Cause Such Difficulty for Families?

Mental illness affects complex behaviors. Mental illness affects behavior, thought processes, and moods much more than other illnesses do. Behaviors that may be strange, frightening, or even bizarre may be symptoms of illness, as is thinking that is illogical, grandiose, exaggerated, or delusional. Moods may range from severe depression to euphoria. Normal controls on behavior may seem to be missing. For example, a person in a manic phase may sometimes spend money wildly, be sexually promiscuous, or engage in other self-destructive behavior. Families usually do not know how to respond. For most of them, nothing in their past experience has prepared them to deal with symptoms such as hallucinations or delusions.

Because of strange and even illegal behavior, many people with severe mental illness end up homeless or in legal difficulties. In fact, there are more people with mental illness in jail and prison than in treatment facilities. The fact that some people are in denial about being ill and reject treatment increases the problem. Denial may actually be one of the symptoms of the illness; this can leave the family feeling that there is no place to turn for help.

Mental illness can impair the freedom to choose. Mental illness is difficult for families (and all of us) to understand because in traditional "philosophy, religion, and psychology, the 'brain' has traditionally been interpreted as the 'mind,' which is controlled by a 'thinker' whose character is primarily shaped *by nurture,* but whose destiny is self-directed as a function of 'free-will.'"[2] Because of this view, it is difficult for us to accept the fact that the brain itself, like any other organ of the body, can be diseased. It is hard for us to admit that perhaps, in the severely mentally ill, the ability to choose and accept accountability for choices might be impaired because of brain disease, even though we allow for that in cases of retardation or dementia. We do not want to admit that those affected might not be able to *will* themselves out of hearing voices or out of a severe depression or manic episode. It is difficult for families to determine which behaviors are symptoms of illness and which behaviors are willful.

Managing severe mental illnesses for life. Mental illnesses such as schizophrenia, bipolar disorder, depression, panic disorder, and obsessive-compulsive disorder are difficult for families because, although effective treatments exist and much progress is being made in discovering the causes of these illnesses, often they have to be managed for life. Admitting that one has an illness; finding effective treatment with doctors, medications, and therapy; and enduring years of stigma and perhaps disability is a daunting process. Those afflicted must somehow "rebuild their lives *despite* their illness, but also in *light* of their illness."[3] They may have to adjust their expectations, finding ways to protect themselves from stress that might cause a relapse. Families also have the task of readjusting their expectations and dreams for their loved one, usually going through a grief process as they do this.

Reciprocity with others may be difficult. Because of a brain that is not working right, people with mental illness may have great difficulty carrying out normal activities and maintaining normal relationships. In fact, mental illness can disrupt family relationships. Sometimes mental illnesses can affect what we call *reciprocity*, the normal give and take required as we try to support each other emotionally. A mentally ill person may use up so much time, finances, and emotional resources that the needs of other family members are not met. Often illness interferes with the ability to fulfill normal roles, such as caring for children or supporting a family financially. These difficulties can greatly affect a family.

Lucy grew up in a family in which the mother had undiagnosed schizophrenia. The father had died when Lucy was about thirteen, and her mother became increasingly ill, withdrawn, and more and more fanatic about food and religion. By the time Lucy was fifteen and her younger siblings were thirteen, eleven, and eight, they had assumed the work of their mother. They milked the cow, fed the farm animals, and did the cleaning, cooking, ironing, and dishes. When something came up at school with the younger children, Lucy would take care of it. Their mother would allow no white flour or sugar in the house, and the family lived on raw peanuts, oatmeal, and raisins. They did not think of their mother as mentally ill; she was just mom.

The children lived this way for some time until Lucy was asked to the prom. She had no dress. She managed to get material and make her own dress, completing everything but the hem. She came home from school the day of the prom to find that her mother had taken the dress apart. Her younger sister was tearfully trying to sew it back together, but they couldn't complete it on time. Her date and those they were going with had to wait. Rumors started about her mother's strange behavior, which led to the children being sent to live with older brothers and sisters and the mother being placed in the state hospital. Later on, as a young married woman, Lucy lovingly took care of her mother until her death.

Imagine the burden of this young girl trying to complete her high school education while caring for her ill mother and three younger siblings. Roles can become mixed up with mental illness.

For the severely ill, even self-care may be compromised. Many have difficulty holding jobs and attending church. Imagine going to sacrament meeting if you believe you are in danger because of a delusional fear of being infected with germs. Shaking hands with other people, sitting near someone who has a cough, taking the sacrament, which has been prepared by someone else's hands, all fill you with overwhelming fear (see "Obsessive-compulsive disorder" in chapter 11, "Anxiety Disorders").

Or imagine being unable to screen out overly intense visual or auditory stimuli, which often happens to people with schizophrenia. Imagine the sound of people talking, the organ playing, children crying, the heating or air-conditioning system running, chairs scraping, and even the pages of the hymnbook being turned—all greatly amplified and coming at you in waves of sound. Add to that condemning and critical voices in your head. Is it any wonder that withdrawal and isolation are common? (See chapter 16, "Schizophrenia and Other Psychotic Disorders".)

All of these and other symptoms make it difficult for some people with mental illness to attend Church meetings or participate fully in ward activities. Perhaps we could do more to take the Church to them. Families appreciate teachers who reach out to their ill loved one by coming to their home with mini lessons or handouts, or priesthood leaders who arrange to bring the sacrament. In these cases understanding and compassionate home and visiting teachers can be a lifeline between the ill person and the Church. If an ill person is able to attend church meetings, the Church website on disabilities suggests that we "include the person in Church activities and appropriate service opportunities. Consult with the person, family members, and others who know the person well to identify limitations as well as strengths."[4]

Another problem reported by people with severe depression is that it is difficult for them to feel the Spirit. The Spirit speaks to our thoughts and feelings (see D&C 8:2), and these can be the very things that are distorted in mental illness. It is hard for those who are ill to break through feelings of hopelessness, despair, and worthlessness. Imagine having to watch a family member suffering like this!

Stigma is a barrier to treatment. Another cause of major difficulty for families and those with mental disorders is the pervasive stigma against those with mental illness in our society. *Stigma* is defined as that negative label we give to those with mental illness—that "mark of disgrace or infamy; a stain or reproach, as on one's reputation . . . a mental or physical mark that is characteristic of a defect or disease: as in *the stigmata of leprosy.*"[5]

Nothing can be so terrifying as having a brain that is not working correctly. Traditionally, people with mental illness have been ridiculed, isolated, shunned, and blamed.

U.S. Surgeon General Satcher in his well-researched and well-documented 1999 report on mental health concludes that stigma is one of the main reasons those with mental illness do not seek treatment.[6] Many of our perceptions and misconceptions about mental illness come to us from the media. Dr. Edward Hannin, of the American Psychiatric Association, summarizes media representations of those with mental illness this way: "Unfortunately, these depictions are too often distorted, outmoded, or just plain wrong. They perpetuate stigma and add to human suffering."[7]

During the October 2003 general conference, Elder M. Russell Ballard called us to action: "The time has come when members of the Church need to speak out and join with the many other concerned people in opposition to the offensive, destructive, and mean-spirited media influence that is sweeping over the earth."[8] Inaccurate media portrayals of mental illness have increased the lack of understanding of mental illness. Many people's knowledge of mental illness is limited to extreme, dramatic portrayals in film and television. This adds to the misunderstanding, fear, and stigma against those with mental illnesses. Because of stigma, families are often reluctant to disclose that a loved one has a mental illness and often do not try to get treatment for them. Because of embarrassment, they may cut themselves off from sources of emotional support, such as extended family, neighbors, or church leaders.

Families often encounter system failure. Because of the stigma directed against the mentally ill, it has been difficult to get funding to set up effective programs to help them. Despite the efforts of advocates, many insurance companies still do not adequately cover treatment for mental illness. Many companies limit the number of visits they will cover, refuse to cover hospitalization, or cover treatment at a lower rate or not at all. Medicaid funds to provide treatment for those with few resources are sometimes cut, and many uninsured people are denied coverage. This leaves them with no way to pay for medication or treatment.

Effective medications can be expensive but are still much less costly than putting a person in the hospital or in jail because of lack of effective treatment. The medications for schizophrenia in some cases can cost more than three thousand dollars a month. A family may love and care for an adult child, but a person with mental illness may tax a family's financial resources tremendously, especially if the family does not have sufficient private insurance or qualify for Medicaid.

The genetic component. Of great concern to those with the illness and to their families is the question, "What caused the illness?" Research has shown that genetics, although not the single cause, does influence whether a person may get a mental illness. If mental illness runs in the family, it is still impossible to predict which children will develop an illness. This creates difficult decisions.

James and John are brothers who have recently married. Their mother has schizophrenia. Both of their wives are now pregnant with their first children. These young couples are wondering if their babies will be healthy or if they will develop schizophrenia. Because the illness usually does not develop until late teens and early adult life, they have no way to know if any or even all of their children will develop schizophrenia.

Larry married without disclosing to his wife that his brother had schizophrenia. His wife became pregnant and then found out about his brother. She and her family were so afraid of mental illness that they had the marriage annulled, even though Larry did not have the illness. The baby was born, grew up without his birth father, and developed no illness.

Dual diagnosis complicates treatment. Another difficulty faced by many families with a mentally ill loved one is what we call *dual diagnosis.* About 50 percent of people with mental illness also have a substance abuse problem. This creates a second, or dual, mental health problem. (See chapter 1, "What Is Mental Illness?")

The threat of suicide. Finally, a heart-wrenching problem that many families face is the constant worry about suicide. Fifty percent of those with schizophrenia will attempt suicide at some point in their lives. Those with bipolar disorder and depression also have a much higher rate of suicide than the rest of the population, and those with anxiety disorders have the highest rate of *attempted* suicide.[9] If the worst does happen, it is helpful for families to think of losing their loved one to an illness. Just as we lose some people to heart attacks or cancer despite our best efforts, we sometimes lose people to mental illness (see chapter 1, "What Is Mental Illness?"). Families who lose a child to suicide often have difficulty seeking support from others because of the stigma of mental illness. This makes their grief even harder to bear.

Helpful Resources Are Available

What we have been describing is a somber but real picture; however, resources and support are available. Families probably cannot prevent serious mental illness from occurring, but there are many resources to help them as they struggle with the effects of serious and persistent mental illness.

Education

One of the major helps in overcoming the difficulties of mental illness is finding out as much about it as possible. Educating families about diagnosis, prognosis, symptoms, and medications can help them know what they are dealing with and can reduce guilt and blame. Sources of information include

Web sites, classes, books, and pamphlets. A valuable resource for many families is the free twelve-week Family-to-Family class and the monthly support group offered by the National Alliance on Mental Illness. One of the valuable insights from the class is that families go through predictable emotional stages as they try to understand what is happening to them. Information on these stages follow and is taken from the *NAMI Family-to-Family Education Program Teaching Manual.*[10]

Stages of Emotional Response

Following is a chart depicting the three principal stages of emotional response to serious challenges (adapted from Burland, *Family-to-Family,* 1.19–20).

PREDICTABLE STAGES OF EMOTIONAL REACTIONS

I. Dealing with Catastrophic Events

Characteristics: Crisis/Chaos/Shock/Denial/Hoping against Hope

Families in this stage need the following: Support/Comfort/Empathy for confusion/Help finding resources/Crisis intervention/Prognosis for the illness/Empathy for pain/NAMI

II. Learning to Cope

Characteristics: Anger/Guilt/Resentment/Recognition/Grief

Families in this stage need the following: To vent feelings/To keep hope/Education/Self-care/Networking/Skill training/To let go of unrealistic expectations/Cooperation from the system/NAMI

III. Moving into Advocacy

Characteristics: Understanding/Acceptance/Advocacy/Action

Families in this stage need the following: Activism/To restore balance in life/Responsiveness from the system/NAMI

Stage I: Dealing with Catastrophic Events

The first stage of emotional response is "Dealing with Catastrophic Events," which puts families in a state of crisis, chaos, fear, and shock. In the case of mental illness, this might be a psychotic episode in which a loved one has lost touch with reality, is hearing voices when no one is present, is unable to work or communicate, attempts suicide, or enters a manic phase of illness.

One father said the initial psychotic break which led to a diagnosis of schizophrenia for his previously very-high-functioning son was more traumatic to him than anything which happened to him in his service in Vietnam.

Another cherished son had his first psychotic break in front of his friends and their parents while bearing his testimony at his seminary graduation. This was a boy who had been a star soccer player, had passed AP classes in chemistry, biology, and calculus, had a scholarship to BYU, and because of his kindness was the one all the younger girls in the ward wanted to marry. At the time the parents thought, "This can't really be happening. He is just having a bad day. It is not as serious as it appears. Things will soon be back to normal."

Imagine the shock of this event to his parents sitting in the audience. Imagine their pain and grief as they learned what a diagnosis of schizophrenia might mean in their son's life. In this first stage of the crisis, there is often denial on the part of both the ill person and the family as they try to assimilate what has happened to them.

Families feel as if they are being turned inside out and upside down as their loved one's mental illness escalates. They do not know what is happening. Often they blame the ill person for the trouble the family is facing. They blame themselves, searching their hearts and past for something they might have done or not done to cause such difficulties. They often seek family counseling from a counselor unfamiliar with severe mental illness, only to be told the symptoms arose because they did not establish rules with consequences for their family. This and other child-rearing techniques work well for people who are not severely mentally ill, but they are usually not as effective for children with serious mental illness and do not *cure* or prevent the disease.

Often Church members go to their ward leaders for help. Depending on their understanding of mental illness and their familiarity with resources, leaders can be a great support and help to those families. Not all leaders, however, are equally familiar with mental illness, its causes, and treatments.

Sometimes parents may feel blamed by leaders who may imply that if they had just been better parents, they would not be having the problems. Families are often embarrassed and do not want their neighbors to know what is happening. They feel isolated, feeling that they have no one to talk to who will listen without judging. They sometimes feel as if they are hostages to the illness, unable to leave their family member alone—especially if the loved one becomes violent. Sometimes home is not a happy place, and the other children may not want to be there. Families are sometimes so caught up with trying to deal with the mentally ill person that they become blinded to some of the needs of other children in the family. This can cause problems for the other members.

Needs. Families in Stage I need support, empathy for their confusion and pain, help in finding resources, an understanding that they did not cause the illness, and someone to listen without judging.

Ward members should not be embarrassed or afraid to reach out to families in a mental illness crisis just as they would in any other illness. A listening ear, nonjudgmental responses, encouragement, help with the necessities of food, child care, and other temporal needs, can greatly help a family in Stage I.

Stage II: Learning to Cope

The second stage of emotional response is "Learning to Cope," recognizing that the illness is real and is not going to just magically go away. In this stage, families and those with the illness often feel anger and frustration. They may feel angry as they struggle with spiritual concerns and try to understand why God would let this happen. They may feel angry toward mental health professionals who diagnose and try to treat the illness. They may even feel angry toward the person with the illness. They also may feel tremendous guilt, thinking if they had only been better parents or had family prayer or family home evening more faithfully, their loved one would not be ill. This guilt is often an attempt to find out what they did wrong so they can *fix* it and undo the illness. This only makes them feel worse and does not make the illness go away.

Sue struggled with terrible, unrelenting depression. The illness became worse after the birth of her last child. Over the years this child had overheard people say that her mother became ill when she had been born. In her little mind, she somehow felt that if she had not been born her mother would not be ill. One day they found her lying in the middle of the road, hoping that a truck would run over her. She was so consumed with guilt that at five years of age, she did not want to live any longer.

Elder Alexander B. Morrison, emeritus member of the First Quorum of the Seventy, counsels that rather than getting caught up in guilt and blame, families would do better to spend their time and energies learning about the illnesses, finding good treatment, and trying to develop understanding, compassion, empathy, forgiveness, and patience.[11] Families in Stage II often go through a grief process as they come to terms with what the illness might mean in their lives and in the life of their loved one.

Needs. Families in Stage II need someone to listen to them, to acknowledge their feelings, and to say to them, "In light of what you have been through, your feelings (of anger, guilt, frustration, grief) are perfectly understandable." They also need education about the illness so they can know the prognosis, diagnosis, treatment options, and symptoms, which will allow them to differentiate symptoms from willful behaviors. They need help in letting go—not of loving and caring but of unrealistic expectations for themselves and their loved one. They must come to terms with the fact that life might now be very different from what they had thought it would be. They often have to let go of the idea that if they just work hard enough, they can fix things. In addition, they need a plan for the care and treatment of the family member with the illness. They need to widen their support system by including extended family members and others to help meet the needs of the ill person and other family members. They need to know what help is available and how to access it.

One family reported:

Something that helped us move from Stage I and helped us through Stage II began when a caring psychiatrist suggested to us that we attend the local support group of the National Alliance on Mental Illness. We had never heard of it before, but we were desperate to try anything. The first time we attended the meeting was like coming home. We were surrounded by people who had been through what we were going through, who understood our pain and our needs, and who knew about resources to help us. That support group and the NAMI Family-to-Family Education Program saved our emotional lives.

The needs of families in Stage II can vary widely depending on the diagnosis, severity of the illness, and the age of the ill person. If a father or mother is ill, the bishop and Relief Society President will need to determine, for example, if the family is in financial difficulty because a breadwinner cannot work or because of high medical expenses, or if a mother cannot adequately care for children. Then appropriate help can be extended.

Families in Stage II may have spiritual concerns that need to be addressed. They may be struggling with unwarranted guilt, or anger, or grief. They may be asking such questions as, "If God loves us, why did He allow this terrible illness to happen? Why doesn't He answer our prayers for it to be taken away?

Why aren't priesthood blessings 'working'?" Church leaders need to consider each less-active Church member under their stewardship to see if mental illness might be a factor so that those needs can be met. Elder Alexander B. Morrison counsels: "A primary role of a bishop, then, is to ascertain whether a deeply distressed member of his congregation is suffering the effects of sin, or of mental illness. . . . If the bishop understands the nature and symptoms of mental illness and discerns that the member's problems lie in that area, he should refer the individual to a properly qualified mental health professional."[12]

Stage III: Moving into Advocacy

The third stage of emotional response, "Moving into Advocacy," is the stage in which one gains an understanding of the illness and accepts it. It is like saying, "Yes, bad things do happen to good people, but life is still worth living. We will go on, and we will use the experience and understanding we have gained to help others." As families come to clearly understand their situation, they begin to feel a tremendous respect for those struggling with illness. They understand the heroism involved as they see loved ones try to manage their illness and keep going.

Needs. Family members in Stage III need to try to restore a balance in their lives as they try to care for their loved one and still meet their own needs and goals. They need to take time for themselves to fill their own reservoirs of strength. They often then get involved in teaching classes, advocating at state legislatures, and becoming involved in other activities that help those with mental illness and their families.

Families in Stage III who have weathered mental illness can be a valuable resource to bishops and Relief Society presidents trying to help others in the ward with these afflictions. They can educate ward members in ward councils, fifth Sunday meetings, etc., and will often know about available resources and how to access them. They can be great stigma busters and lead other ward members toward understanding and compassion.

These stages are not just something someone made up. They reflect the actual experience of many families.

One family reported:

The first time we saw a chart of emotional stages, it was as if we saw a map of where we had been and where we could go. Knowing about these stages increased our understanding and compassion for people experiencing the trauma of mental illness in their lives. We found that if we could determine where a person or family was in this process, it helped us to know what they needed and how we could help them.

Sometimes people get stuck in one of the stages, such as anger or denial, and they stay there until they get what they need before they can move on. But it is important to realize that whenever a new crisis or relapse happens, it can throw families right back to Stage I. People go through these stages in their own way and in their own time frame, but knowing about them can give insight and understanding.

Professional Help

In addition to gaining education about and understanding of mental illness, getting professional help and treatment is of paramount importance to families struggling with an ill loved one. (See chapter 3, "The Brain and Medical Treatment for Mental Disorders," and chapter 4, "Finding the Right Therapist for You and Your Family.")

Empathy

Besides seeking education and professional help in trying to survive the difficulties of mental illness, families need to shift from being judgmental to being empathetic. Empathy can be defined as "the intimate comprehension of another person's thoughts and feelings, *without imposing our own judgment or expectations.*"[13] Most people with serious mental illness quickly become discouraged as they see their life plan and goals disrupted. They have to try to rebuild their lives, often "without the tools of insight and emotional balance" that have been affected by illness.[14] True empathy can lead to understanding, forgiveness, patience, kindness, and love as families try to live the teachings of the Savior and nurture each other through the difficulties of mental illness.

Spiritual Resources

The final, and probably most important, resource for finding our way through the difficulties of serious mental illness is, of course, the help we can get from Heavenly Father, our faith in his eternal plan for each of us, and comfort from the Holy Ghost. Because of our beliefs, we know that adversity is a part of this life for everyone and that our Savior will heal all afflictions, if not in this life, then in the next. We will all be resurrected with perfect bodies, including a brain healed of all structural and functional problems.

Notes

1. Morrison, "Mental Illness and the Family," address to Families under Fire, conference held at Brigham Young University, 4 Oct. 2004; available online at familiesunderfire.byu.edu

2. Burland, *Family-to-Family,* 5.1.

3. Burland, *Family-to-Family,* 7.13.

4. Available online at disability.lds.org

5. *Random House Dictionary of the English Language,* 2d edition.

6. David Satcher, "Overcome Stigma," in *Mental Health: A Report of the Surgeon General.*

7. Hannin, "An Introduction," in *Mental Illness Awareness Guide for Image Makers,* 5.

8. M. Russell Ballard, "Let Our Voices Be Heard," *Ensign,* Nov. 2003, 17.

9. Burland, *NAMI Provider Education Program,* 4.22.

10. Burland, *Family-to-Family,* 1.19–1.20.

11. Alexander B. Morrison, "Myths about Mental Illness," *Ensign,* Oct. 2005, 33.

12. Morrison, "Mental Illness and the Family," 4 Oct. 2004; available online at familiesunderfire.byu.edu

13. Burland, *Family-to-Family,* 7.1.

14. Burland, *Family-to-Family,* 7.5.

21

Resilience, Healing, and Growth in Adversity

Richard A. Heaps and Lisa J. Fox

Many unwanted events happen in our lives. We all experience adversity in one form or another. Some of these may be daily challenges, and others may be unusually difficult. These events can be physical, emotional, or social. Some examples include the following:

Death of people or pets

Loss of finances, home, or independence

Disability (our own or that of someone close to us)

Rejection by peers, friends, or family

Divorce

Abuse by others (emotional, physical, or sexual)

Assault or violence (observed or personally experienced)

Natural disasters

Wartime traumas

Some of these unwanted events bring threats to our safety or well-being. All are potentially traumatic, distressing, or hurtful.

There are as many different ways of responding to adversity as there are people. How we respond is often based on our experiences and learning. These may influence our perceptions of events and the choices we make surrounding them. Epictetus said, "People feel disturbed not by things, but by the views they take of them."

Some of us learn to deal with these dilemmas as we gain experience and maturity. We respond with healthy coping behaviors that maintain our normal functioning and guard against stress. This is often referred to as *resilience.*

However, some painful events are so deeply and personally hurtful, prolonged, or repeated that our reactions go beyond our normal ability to cope and fix things. We may respond with intense, even unhealthy reactions that disrupt or interfere with healthy personal, social, or family living. This often requires that we learn *recovery* or *healing* skills in order to reestablish healthy functioning.

On the other hand, there are people who have a unique ability to view adversity, even in a severe form, as an opportunity to learn and become better than they were before. A variety of religious and spiritual philosophies support this idea. This process has been referred to as *adversarial growth.*

Let's look a little closer at each of these responses. As we do, it is important to understand that each is a normal process with different purposes and outcomes.

Resilience, Recovery, and Growth

Resilience, recovery, and growth in adversity are not independent, all-or-nothing processes. They might be considered as existing on an overlapping line from unhealthy reactions to recovery to resilience to growth. We will begin with resilience because it is probably the most common of the adult reactions to a painful event.

Resilience is easy to understand. It is the ability to cope with adversity, endure its stress, and maintain our strength in the process. Normal functioning continues despite difficulties or emotional pain.

Resilience is a practical approach to dealing with adversity. It includes adjusting to misfortune by finding practical solutions so one can return attention to normal living.

This response promotes problem solving and maintains supportive social interactions. It is an encouraging approach in which one does not dwell on misery, yet does not avoid thinking about it. Resilient people have the courage, willingness, energy, and ability to face and move successfully past potential bad effects of life challenges. They often refuse to yield or become a victim of life's traumas.

It has been suggested that this capacity to adapt may be related to having a positive view of ourselves and our ability to influence our circumstances. This optimism and hope sustains us in our search for solutions.

Resilience requires many things. Among these is something we might call *emotional stamina*—a hardiness or staying power that allows us not only to endure but also to maintain our energy for life in the face of difficult circumstances. It is interesting to think of resilience as emotional stamina—a form of emotional endurance. Just as cardiovascular exercise builds endurance for physical challenges, developing and practicing healthy coping skills builds endurance for emotional challenges.

An important message here is that resilience can be learned! We will discuss *how* later.

Recovery is a healing process. It is needed if our capacity for resilience becomes exhausted or overwhelmed and if we succumb to the stress of adversity. The purposes of recovery are to help us regain our emotional strength, change unhealthy reactions, face our adversity, and return to healthy functioning.

We are all different in how much stress and what types of stress we can endure. Abrupt, violent loss or tragedy is especially difficult. For some of us, the strain of intense, repeated, or prolonged stress from adversity disrupts or interferes with our normal, healthy functioning. It can do this in several ways.

For example, we may experience unwanted reactions, such as panic, fear, shock, anger, or grief. We also may experience sleep problems, anxiety, suspiciousness, concentration difficulties, repeated worries, guilt, shame, and depression.

If these reactions remain with us for very long or become intensified in unhealthy ways, we may begin viewing our world as a dangerous, unhappy place that we are helpless to change. We may lose our sense of capability and our confidence that we can influence circumstances in our lives. We may begin to feel *helpless.*

Such beliefs and feelings often distort healthy ways of thinking. We may personalize what happened to us and give it unhealthy meaning, such as "I'm worthless," "I'm unlovable," "People can't be trusted," "I can't recover from this," or "My life is over."

These distressing beliefs may cause us to worry that something is wrong with us, that we can't be happy, that the world and its people are dangerous, and that things probably can't be fixed. We do not like or want to have these intrusive feelings and thoughts. As a result, we may work hard to avoid them or other circumstances in order to survive or protect ourselves against the pain of what we have experienced.

Avoidance can take many forms, from simply not wanting to think or talk about *it* to avoiding certain activities or people, keeping ourselves too busy to think, numbing our emotions, developing eating problems or addictive behaviors, or injuring ourselves. (Sadly, some even view suicide as an ultimate avoidance to relieve their suffering.)

Unfortunately, avoidance only works for a short while, and then we begin having upsetting, intrusive reactions again. These hurt, so we go back to avoiding. This leads to a vicious cycle of avoidance and intrusion that prevents us from thinking about, understanding, and dealing with our misfortune. It interferes with healthy coping in a way that may eventually create more serious emotional and interpersonal difficulties.

When this cycle between avoidance and intrusive distress becomes a recurring feature of our experience, we need a way to get past this emotional trap, which stops our progress. This need also helps define and suggest where the recovery process begins. We need help moving out of this cycle, bouncing back from adversity, and returning to healthy functioning.

The recovery process does this by helping us face the things that have been so hurtful, learn how to endure the discomfort of unwanted reactions, understand our misfortune, challenge and change our unhealthy beliefs, develop confidence and appreciation for our capabilities, and return to approaching life with all its possibilities—positive and negative.

This is not an easy process. It can be difficult to do alone. It often requires support and help from others who care, understand, and know the nature and pitfalls of the process. It may or may not take a lot of time. The important thing to know is that it can be done. There is hope and there can be healing.

Adversarial growth is a response to adversity that goes beyond the recovery that restores healthy functioning and beyond the simple resilience that maintains healthy functioning. Some of us manage to gain greater insight and positive life change following painful events.

When this happens, we seem to learn from our adversity and become stronger or better in some way. Our view or perspective is enhanced. We see new, broader possibilities. In our minds, our adversity is transformed into a challenging growth opportunity.

Adversarial growth seems to include a willingness and ability to see beyond our own personal hurt in the moment. We are more able to do this if we learn to tolerate discomfort and delay here-and-now gratification. This allows us to work for goals that take longer to achieve and that go beyond immediate needs.

Another characteristic that can facilitate adversarial growth is the learned ability to look *outside ourselves* to the suffering of others. We become aware of and sensitive to their plight. This empathy for others can help in several ways. Understanding their suffering may help us realize we are not alone, become more accepting of our own misfortune, and gain the courage to go on. Understanding may also motivate us to look past our adversity and help others—*lose ourselves* and our immediate desires in the service of others.

People who experience adversarial growth frequently report the need to make growth decisions earlier rather than later, if possible. They suggest that it is important to adjust to their challenge quickly so they do not wallow in discouraging self-pity or dwell on their misery and the opportunities lost from their adversity.

This may include changing or adjusting plans and moving into what athletes sometimes call cross-training. For our purposes, this may mean involving ourselves in something new or different that is satisfying and may accomplish goals similar to ones we had before our adversity but will also accomplish new goals that are different from those lost through our adversity.

As we adjust by developing expanded perspective, greater purpose, new goals, and empathic service, we have an unusual opportunity to enhance rather than lose feelings of personal strength and self-worth through our adversity.

Learning How

There is hope, even if we have had problems responding to life's difficulties in the past. Most mental health workers believe we can learn processes that help us respond better to both daily and unique challenges.

Anything that promotes optimistic thinking, effective problem solving, adaptive coping skills, and supportive relationships can enhance one's resilience, ability to recover, and adversarial growth. In general, doing these things helps us:

Protect against the effects of adverse stress
View bad situations and events more accurately
Develop support resources among friends and family members
Generalize learning across many different situations in life

Enhance a positive view of ourselves and of our capacity to influence how we react to life

Resilience in the face of difficult events can be learned. There are things we can do before, during, and after painful misfortune to increase our capacity for a resilient response to adversity—our ability to maintain healthy functioning. We can enhance this capacity by learning, developing, and maintaining methods of coping and managing our own emotions. Some of these overlap and may include the following:

Good social and communication skills

Healthy social interaction patterns

Relationships with healthy people who can support and model resilience

An ability to see more solutions than the obvious

Skills of assertiveness (speaking out), negotiation, and decision making

Relaxation and other calming procedures

Strategies to identify and challenge negative or unhealthy beliefs

Ways of ignoring irrelevant or less important distractions or problems

An ability to return to disrupted, familiar roles and routines

Tolerance for change and ambiguity (confusing situations)

A continued sense of purpose or direction

Achievements in school, family, work, and other settings

Feelings of competence, confidence, and self-esteem

An optimistic belief that solutions are possible, even in dire circumstances

Patience and the ability to endure discomfort while solutions are found

Resilient people seem to develop the personal strength and resources to go through adversity or trauma with normal support and little additional or outside help. They have used self-regulatory and coping strategies often during daily living. They are well practiced and know how to use their resources when unusual difficulties occur.

Example of resilience. The rescue effort following the September 11, 2001, terrorist attacks and collapse of the World Trade Center towers was heroic and exhausting. A respite center was set up in an elementary school next to the debris pile at ground zero. Rescue workers (firefighters, police, and others) used it to get sleep, eat a hot meal, and find changes of clothing so they could continue their dangerous work uninterrupted.

Every day two high school girls showed up at the respite center in the morning and did not leave until the early evening. After about a week, they were complimented on the amazing job they were doing organizing and distributing donated clothing, boots, and toiletries to the rescue workers.

They lived in a nearby apartment and attended the high school directly around the corner. In fact, when the first plane struck one of the towers, they were in a gym class on an upper floor looking out of the south-facing windows directly at the World Trade Center. These girls witnessed the terrifying events firsthand.

As the school was being evacuated, the girls saw people falling, the collapse of the towers, and the cloud of debris racing toward them. Upon further questioning, they exhibited no evidence of traumatic problems in their reactions. They were willing to talk about their experiences in a healthy manner. They were simply doing what they thought was needed and would be helpful. They had a sense of purpose and were functioning well.

Recovery is different from resilience in that it typically requires assistance from knowledgeable, experienced sources. This is due to the overwhelming, personalized impact of the adverse circumstances that require it. These negative consequences often lead us to feeling unsafe, overwhelmed, or unworthy of finding or trying solutions to our downward spiral. This is what begins our avoidance behaviors.

The complex and personal nature of these negative consequences and behaviors are what require the healing process of recovery. Careful, sensitive support is usually needed to help deal with these personal complexities. Recovery is normally intended to help accomplish a number of goals:

Stop avoiding and start thinking about our suffering and what led to it.

Think about or tell our *story* to an understanding source.

Allow ourselves to experience the feelings we had been trying to avoid.

Identify the unhealthy beliefs and behaviors resulting from our adversity.

Rethink and decide more accurate and healthy beliefs.

Forgive ourselves and forgive innocent others.

Define who we are in more healthy ways—see ourselves with real capabilities and confidence.

Learn new skills, behaviors, and ways of solving problems.

Learn how to see differences between what caused our pain and other similar, but different circumstances.

Begin safely approaching people and doing things we were avoiding (provided they no longer remind us of our pain or feel threatening).

Learn and practice skills needed for resilience.

The beginning of the recovery process can pose a serious problem. Thinking about and telling the *story* of our hurtful experiences can prompt us to reexperience our pain in a way that could make us feel as if we were being revictimized. This can prompt a return to avoiding such reminders. Remember, avoidance doesn't work long term. It is usually followed by unwanted reactions of stress.

In other words, if not done with sensitivity and in appropriate ways, thinking about and telling our *story* can push us back to the unhealthy cycle that required recovery and healing in the first place. This is one of the reasons assistance from knowledgeable, experienced sources can be so important in the recovery process.

When offered properly, help with accomplishing the steps outlined above can assist us with healing and being in a better position to face future adversity. Healthy recovery can help with building the skills and attitudes needed to face future adversity with resilience rather than with an overwhelming sense of pain.

Example of recovery. On a tragic day one May, a terrible tornado touched down near Oklahoma City. It left in its wake what appeared to be a giant, flat landfill half a mile wide and nineteen miles long through what had been thriving neighborhoods of brick homes, schools, and shopping centers.

A single mother of five young children was referred to a service center for help. She stared blankly when the caseworker asked basic questions. She was not able to function well enough to get the help she needed. Noticing this, a mental health volunteer walked over, knelt beside her, and reflected how hard her predicament must be for her. With tears in her eyes, she shook her head and mumbled, "Yes, it is."

They exchanged names, but when asked about her children (two of whom were with her), the mother looked puzzled and said softly, "Isn't that strange. I can't remember their names." She was informed how short-term forgetfulness often follows traumatic experiences. Her eyes got bright and she said, "Is that right? I thought maybe I was going crazy!"

She was asked, if she could remember, to tell her *story* during the tornado. She recounted how she had gathered her children just in time to run into an interior closet, shut the door, and huddle closely together as the full force of the tornado began pulling her little house apart. As the closet began to peel open, she held on tightly as one of her daughters was lifted into the air; just as quickly, the daughter was released back into the mother's arms.

She talked about walking out of the rubble and not being able to recognize anything. Then she looked up and said, "I know their names now" and began naming all five of her children, along with their ages. Her story finished, she went on to get the help she needed without further difficulty.

Adversarial growth is different in that it goes beyond recovery and resilience. In many ways, it is more attitudinal or a way of thinking. It builds on the processes needed to heal or maintain functioning in adversity.

Life happens. Adversity happens. We may be able to prevent some misfortunes, but others are beyond our capacity to prevent. Adversarial growth begins with a belief that we have the ability to choose how we react to the circumstances around us. Such growth also results from an active rather than a passive process. We choose to approach rather than avoid thinking about our misfortune and our reactions to it. We understand that the most helpful way out of our painful or stressful dilemma is through it. This means we need to tolerate our discomfort in order to understand and resolve it.

Approaches to adversarial growth often change our perception of adversity. We begin to see it as a challenging growth opportunity with meaning and purpose. This does not necessarily mean that we view the misfortune as having a planned purpose. Such a view might lead to an unhelpful belief that all bad things are what we deserve and are desirable or good for us.

Growth in adversity, rather, may come from seeing value and purpose in how we respond to the adversity—what we do with it. This gives us opportunity to learn important things about ourselves and our strengths. These become the purpose of, and provide the meaning in, adversity.

How do we develop this growth? By discovering ways to enhance personal strength, self-worth, perspective, purpose, goals, power to choose our response, and empathic service. We may do this by—

Searching for positive role models who serve as examples of how to
react well

Practicing positive self-evaluation—learning to like ourselves and
what we do

Learning to calm anxiety and tolerate discomfort

Learning to delay immediate needs to achieve later goals

Accepting our misfortune as something that can be resolved with
time

Looking for alternative, more helpful ways of responding

Changing behaviors we do not like

Making growth decisions early during our misfortune

Adjusting to the challenge quickly

Not dwelling on our misery or wallowing in discouraging self-pity

Developing new strengths and interests

Finding alternative ways to accomplish or replace lost goals

Looking for comforting and encouraging sources of support

Looking around and noticing the plight of others

Developing empathy for the suffering of others

Helping relieve the pain others experience

Losing ourselves in the service of others

Thinking about what we can learn from our experience

Reading and praying

Those who do these things often report that their adversity and what they learned from it were life-changing experiences. They may even report that they feel renewed strength, purpose, and direction for daily living.[1]

Examples of growth. The news story is told of a local high school athlete who collapsed of sudden cardiac arrest during a team practice. He was not breathing and had no pulse. His coaches performed CPR and used a portable defibrillator to shock his heart into beating. His gratitude for a second chance at life changed his thinking. He began looking outside himself. He discovered that other athletes had died from a condition like his. His life goals changed, and he set a new goal of having automated external defibrillators (AEDs) in every school. He decided to give his life greater meaning and purpose by beginning a campaign to save the lives of others.

During most winter or summer Olympic Games, the sports reports in newspapers and in the broadcast media regularly recount stories of top athletes severely injured in training or other accidents. Many of these reports are of serious injuries, but the stories also tell of intensely painful dedication to rehabilitation. The athletes speak of developing a new view of life that has expanded meaning and purpose beyond their sport. They have become not only better athletes but also better people.

Notes

1. Hurtful or abusive experiences are typically beyond the capacity of most children to choose a growth response. In such circumstances, children often come to painful conclusions that their world is not safe, that others cannot be trusted, that they must do extraordinary things to make others happy, and that their pain is their own fault. This requires recovery and healing. Nurturing role models can help them understand the hurtful events, how to deal with the source of the adversity, and how to choose healing or growth responses.

22

The Role of Faith and Spirituality in Recovering from an Eating Disorder

Randy K. Hardman, P. Scott Richards, and Michael E. Berrett

When you realize that you or someone you love may be struggling with an eating disorder, naturally you want to know more about it. You may already know that anorexia and bulimia are complex and confusing illnesses. Now that you are past the initial shock of discovery, you may be experiencing feelings of anxiety, guilt, anger, and frustration—all understandable reactions. Suffering from an eating disorder, or seeing a loved one suffer from an eating disorder, is frightening and difficult.

Understand that the illness did not develop overnight and that recovery will not happen overnight. Know also that there is reason to have hope. With dedication to treatment, recovery is possible.

Use the Resources of Your Faith and Spirituality

We have found that for many of our clients, faith in God and personal spirituality have been a source of great strength in their healing journeys. When people with eating disorders affirm their faith in God and seek to grow spiritually, their strength and capacity to cope with and overcome the problems and challenges of life improve, regardless of whether their challenges are emotional, physical, relational, spiritual, or educational.

Spiritual Consequences of Eating Disorders

We believe that eating disorders are both an emotional and a spiritual problem. Almost all people with eating disorders have distorted views of themselves and have lost touch with their sense of identity and worth. This identity loss is so encompassing that they lose touch with virtually every healthy aspect of their identity until their identity *is* their eating disorder. They no longer are capable of seeing themselves as people, daughters, sons, mothers, fathers, artists, creations of God, and so on, but they see themselves exclusively *as* an eating disorder or as the expression of an eating disorder. A patient named Emily wrote:

"My eating disorder robbed me of my relationship with God. I was in a personal anguish that shredded my soul and threatened my spiritual and mortal life. I felt no love and saw no mercy. Anger consumed me. I felt abandoned and worthless. . . . My heart turned bitter and hard. I cut God out of my life completely. It was a downward spiral that almost led to my death."

One of the most significant consequences for those who have forgotten or who have lost their ability to listen to their hearts is that they lose their ability to feel love and to recognize spiritual feelings. For many, to lose that connection to love is a loss of their spiritual relationship with God. They feel distant and far removed from God's influence and love. They also lose their ability to feel connected to family and friends. They can feel lonely and empty, even in the presence of those who genuinely love and care for them.

When they do experience feelings in their heart or spirit, they are most often painful ones. Because they feel distant from their hearts and experience their heart as a source of pain, people with eating disorders often conclude that their heart or spiritual self is unacceptable, bad, or flawed.

Another spiritual consequence of eating disorders in the lives of those who suffer from them is that rather than trusting God and having faith in his healing power, they come to believe that their eating disorder will provide the solutions to their emotional and spiritual problems. They place their faith in their eating disorder rather than in divine influence. In this shift of faith, they begin to worship God and Christ less and their eating disorder more.

Most people with eating disorders are women, but more men are beginning to struggle with eating disorders. Many of the spiritual problems in men appear to be similar to those in women, on whom most research on eating disorders has been done. (We use the term *women* because of that fact.)

Satan is the author of all lies, and he would like women to believe that their eating disorder is the solution to their problems and pain. Eating disorders are based on false beliefs and lies that become counterfeits for what will truly bring happiness into a woman's life. Below are ten of the false beliefs or lies that women with eating disorders often come to believe.[1]

1. An eating disorder will give me control of my life and emotions.
2. An eating disorder will effectively communicate my pain and suffering.
3. An eating disorder will make me exceptional.
4. An eating disorder will prove that I am bad and unworthy.
5. An eating disorder will make me perfect.
6. An eating disorder will give me comfort and safety from pain.
7. An eating disorder will give me a sense of identity.
8. An eating disorder will compensate, or atone, for my past.
9. An eating disorder will allow me to avoid personal responsibility for life.
10. An eating disorder will give me approval from others.

We have observed that women with eating disorders often take up one or more of these ten false beliefs at the expense of their relationship with God, with themselves, and with other individuals. These unhealthy beliefs become the objects of their faith and attention, adding to their feelings of alienation from God's healing influence and from the supportive influence of other people.

Another spiritual consequence of eating disorders is that they cause women to lose hope. It is often difficult for LDS women who have been suffering with an eating disorder to believe that recovery is really possible.

During the course of their illness, many women come to feel that their faith is powerless to help them overcome the negative messages, obsessive fears, and constant thoughts of the eating disorder. They reach a point where the eating disorder dictates to them not only what they should do and not do but also who they are as a woman. The adversary takes full advantage of these messages and whispers to those afflicted that they are unacceptable and out of the healing reach of even God.

A patient named Laura wrote:

"At the lowest point in my eating disorder, I saw no hope. I had resigned myself to a life of despair and darkness, a life filled with obsessions of food and weight, but never satisfying myself. I felt shameful and worthless before others and God. I told myself how undeserving I was of anything good in my life. I knew my life was not pleasing to God, and that only intensified my feelings of shame and guilt. I felt I did not deserve to get help, but a little something inside of me did not want to live like I had been. I actually did not know how much longer I could live like that.

"Slowly through the course of treatment, I realized how my life could be without an eating disorder. And even more pivotal, when I realized and decided that that was what I wanted (life without an eating disorder), I started to let people in. I let God in. I took steps forward and backward and started to learn how to forgive myself for the steps backward. . . . I can say that my relationship with God has been the foundation. I came to know my divine and eternal worth as a daughter of God. Now I know that I am of worth and that I have a life worth living."

One of the important beginnings of recovery for Laura was that she began to have faith again that life could be better than the one she had been experiencing through her eating disorder. She had faith that God would help her, and she began to act on that faith. She began again to put faith in herself and in God.

Healing Power of Faith and Spirituality

Facing the pain and difficulties of an eating disorder, and having the stamina and courage to recover from that disorder, requires a great deal of spiritual faith and hope. It will require, in many ways, all of the energy of one's heart. One of the powerful messages repeated over and over again in the Book of Mormon is to come unto God with full purpose of heart and he will help you, he will heal you, and he will extend his mercy toward you. Jacob 6:5 reads:

"I beseech of you in words of soberness that ye would repent, and come with full purpose of heart, and cleave unto God as he cleaveth unto you. And while his arm of mercy is extended towards you in the light of the day, harden not your hearts."

Having faith and full purpose of heart means we don't hold anything back. We give all for the righteous purpose of recovery and healing of an eating disorder. Nephi talked about giving his heart to God in prayer when he said, "I did cry unto the Lord; and behold he did visit me, and did soften my heart" (1 Nephi 2:16).

By exercising faith, we can go to the Lord in prayer, and we can begin to ask for the specific help that we need to overcome the addictions, the inner conflicts, and the struggles of an eating disorder. This is possible because our hope is in Jesus Christ. One of the great miracles we have witnessed over the years in the treatment of LDS women with eating disorders is that often in the course of their treatment, they return to the faith they had given up during the development of their eating disorder. In a general conference talk, Elder Jeffrey R. Holland stated:

"I speak to those who are facing personal trials and family struggles, those who endure conflicts fought in the lonely foxholes of the heart, those trying to hold back floodwaters of despair that sometimes wash over us like a tsunami of the soul. I wish to speak particularly to you who feel your lives are broken, seemingly beyond repair.

"To all such I offer the surest and sweetest remedy that I know. It is found in the clarion call the Savior of the world Himself gave. He said it in the beginning of His ministry, and He said it in the end. He said it to believers, and He said it to those who were not so sure. He said to everyone, whatever their personal problems might be:

"'Come unto me, all ye that labour and are heavy laden, and I will give you rest. Take my yoke upon you, and learn of me; for I am meek and lowly in heart, and ye shall find rest unto your souls.'"[2]

The "lonely foxholes of the heart" metaphor is an accurate description of the sad state of those suffering from an eating disorder, just as it describes those suffering from the other disorders discussed in this book. We agree that the "surest and sweetest remedy" is the Savior. In a sense, the Savior holds out his merciful arms to those women suffering with eating disorders and asks them to come unto him because he is the true solution to their pain and sorrows, and he is the hope who can heal them. There is hope in knowing that Christ is the true light at the end of any eating-disorder tunnel, that he knows the way out of an eating disorder, and that he knows the way back to his arms and tender mercies. A patient named Sarah stated:

"A few months ago I realized that I needed to seek medical help for my eating disorder, bulimia, but the more I thought about it, the more impossible it seemed that anyone could help me. I had no hope and absolutely no faith that I could overcome my eating disorder. After all, I had wasted and ruined the last four years of my life, hadn't I? I had been so obsessed with myself and trying to escape my problems with a temporary solution that I was so unhappy. I was addicted to my eating disorder and thought that there was no hope in anyone being able to help me. I would be a terrible, miserable, worthless sinner forever.

"Then something changed. One night as I was feeling so depressed and so alone, a dear friend encouraged me to pray and to read my scriptures. I thought to myself, 'No way. Like this will really do anything for me.' But then I decided it could not hurt me, so I knelt on my knees and cried to God. I told him how worthless and hopeless I felt, and that I did not know what to do with myself. Then I pleaded with him to comfort me. I asked that if there was any way I could find someone to help me, to please let me find them. I expressed the feelings of doubt and hopelessness I felt about the possibility, but I did know that he knew all things.

"For the first time I had a slight ounce of hope and faith that night. I was totally relying on God and Jesus to save me from my darkness and hopelessness. Before I even ended my prayer, I started to feel a warm and comfortable feeling, and I strangely knew that there was hope, that everything would turn out okay, and that I would find help to overcome my bulimia. I thought that maybe there really would be a light at the end of the tunnel. The darkness would soon be gone.

"Now that I have been going through therapy and eating-disorder treatment, I have learned that you have to have hope and faith in yourself and in God and Jesus. It is the only way to win the battle. Without it you can never overcome any kind of obstacle. It is essential to have hope and faith in order to find true happiness. Believe in yourself. Believe in God and Jesus Christ. If you do that, you can overcome anything that stands in your way. I have been doing that, and because of that I have found the light at the end of the tunnel. And now I must venture into the light to continue my journey with the hope that brings happiness."

Satan will tell women with this illness that there is no hope, but that is a lie. Hope begins in the quiet but profound desires and intents of one's heart. As women begin to act on their heartfelt desires and have faith, they will progress toward recovery. One of the great powers motivating women toward recovery is feeling again in their hearts that they are not lost to God, that they are still precious in his sight, and that this is true despite their mistakes and the difficulties of their eating disorder.

Another thing that has helped many LDS women in recovery is letting God's love back into their hearts and souls, and trusting that they are not an exception to, or undeserving of, his love. By opening their hearts to receive the love of God, women are able to know through the power of the Holy Ghost that Christ's love for them is real and that it is available to them every day.

As we work with LDS women who have eating disorders, we know they need the power of God to help them overcome the powerful negative messages and compulsions—the addictive focus—of the disorder. We try to help them recognize that to defeat this enemy, they will need the same help and power from God that Ammon the missionary needed to protect King Lamoni's sheep and to fight against the Lamanite thieves (Alma 17:25–39). Overcoming an eating disorder requires similar hard work and courage.

It takes a strong and enduring fight against the fears and false beliefs of anorexia and bulimia, but it is achievable because God has all power, and he loves you and wants you to live again without the eating disorder. As you seek to get your life back in harmony with the principles of the gospel, he will strengthen you, help you, and keep you safe within the arms of his love as you make the necessary changes to eliminate the eating disorder from your life.

Messages of Hope and Guidance

The following words of hope come from women in our treatment center who have made progress in recovery. They offered their words for women who are beginning their journeys toward recovery:

"Know that there is One who understands with a perfect knowledge of how you feel."

"Forgiving yourself and being free of shame is an essential part of moving on and having a full recovery."

"Be humble. This is so hard because it takes admitting that we have a problem."

"Know that you are precious, beautiful, and loved."

"God heals."

"Thank your Heavenly Father for the gift of life and for your body—especially if you have a bad body image. At least you have a body!"

"You are a creation, a daughter of God. Don't ever forget the divine nature that is in you."

"God will never stop loving you! Don't be afraid to ask for his help."

"Never lose hope no matter how difficult things seem. Always hold on to the hope that there is a God who loves you, who knows your pain, and who will never leave you."

"Sometimes you can't do it on your own. That's when you must turn your pain and struggles over to Heavenly Father and let him carry your burdens for you."

"Don't be afraid to honestly speak to God—tell him your pains, fears, and rage. Tell him about your thankfulness, and love and trust him."

"When we lose being able to be in tune with our hearts, it is as if we have lost our compass. Things become dark, and we soon begin to wander in the darkness. Learn to listen to your heart, and never lose sight of that 'compass' again."

"If there seems to be nothing left to believe in, believe that there is a God and that he loves you. Try to let that love in."

"Knowing that God loves you is so much more fulfilling than worrying about other people liking you."

"Be brave! Gaining your faith back and accepting God's love is immensely hard, but it is worth it in the end."

"Dare to dream! God gives us dreams to help push us forward. God will help us find a way to accomplish every good thing."

"Count your blessings, look for the good things, and be grateful for each and every thing in your life. When we express gratitude, we will receive more."

"Forgive the people who hurt you. This is not easy, but it must be done. This does not mean that you have to let them back into your life. You need to go through all of the stages of forgiveness; feel the anger and hurt."

"Forgive yourself. As you do this, you will see that you are not bad."

"Trust God, not your eating disorder. God loves you so much, and he wants to help you so much. But you need to do your part and ask. I promise you that if you take that leap of faith and call on God for some help, he will help you get through this."[3]

Resources for LDS Women and Their Families

amcap.net

centerforchange.com

gurze.com

ldscounselors.net

mentalhealthlibrary.info

nationaleatingdisorders.org

Notes

1. Adapted from Richards, et al., *Spiritual Approaches in the Treatment of Women with Eating Disorders,* 47.

2. Jeffrey R. Holland, "Broken Things to Mend," *Ensign,* May 2006, 69.

3. Adapted from Richards, et al., *Spiritual Approaches,* 272–73.

23

Living with Serious, Persistent Mental Illness

Sherri D. Wittwer

John was an active young man with a great future. He was a great student and a gifted athlete who enjoyed skiing. John had many friends and was an active member of the Church. When he turned nineteen, he chose to serve a mission for the Church. He and his family made the preparations, and John received his call and looked forward with great anticipation to serving.

At first, John's mission went well. He got along with his companion and enjoyed teaching the gospel. As time went on, however, John started to experience some difficulty. Those around him noticed some strange behaviors. He started to become irritable and was difficult to get along with. He became nervous and uneasy around people and began to think that people were following him and his companion. John ate and slept little. Eventually, he did not attend to his personal hygiene and looked exhausted. Before long, after trying to get John to a physician, his mission president had to send him home from his mission. John then began a new phase in his life—a phase that would always include the diagnosis of schizophrenia.

Like John, Ben was a gifted little boy. Always a leader in school and at home, Ben had friends and was fun and playful. Still, Ben had difficulties with change and was inflexible. Sometimes simply being told "no" would cause him to have a tantrum.

Eventually, Ben's behavior seemed to worsen, and his thoughts became more distorted and his moods more volatile. He had periods of time when he had grandiose thoughts and wild ideas that did not make sense. During these times, he would be disrespectful, take unnecessary risks, and behave in irrational ways. Ben was only in the second grade, but eventually he was hospitalized and diagnosed with early-onset bipolar disorder. As Ben grew, it became evident that his illness would be serious and possibly have a great impact on the rest of his life.

Both John and Ben have been diagnosed with serious and persistent mental illness. While difficult and requiring long-term interventions, both embarked on a path to recovery and have found rich, meaningful lives.

Mental illness runs along a spectrum. As with other illnesses, mental illness can range in symptoms that are relatively mild and eased with basic interventions to serious and persistent illness that may require a combination of therapies and can be a lifelong battle.

"Mental disorders fall along a continuum of severity. The most serious and disabling conditions affect five to ten million adults (2.6–5.4 percent) and three to five million children ages five to seventeen (9–13 percent) in the United States."[1]

Serious and persistent mental illness can profoundly disrupt a person's thinking, feeling, moods, ability to relate to others, and capacity for coping with the demands of life. Serious and persistent mental illness can be traumatic and rob a person of identity while navigating the road to recovery. Left untreated, these illnesses are among the most disabling and destructive illnesses known to humankind. Millions of Americans struggling with severe mental illnesses, such as schizophrenia, bipolar disorder, and major depression, know only too well the personal costs of these devastating illnesses.

Stigma

Unfortunately, stigma is a serious issue associated with mental illness that can have many serious consequences. Because of stigma, many individuals and families affected by mental illness are reluctant to seek lifesaving treatment. Others who seek and obtain treatment often suffer in loneliness and shame, too embarrassed to share their experiences with anyone for fear of judgment and further isolation. Stigma affects the way the public views people with mental illness, often reinforcing negative images and misconceptions. Stigma can make it difficult for people with mental illness and their families to get treatment, find employment, and locate housing. Public policy affecting individuals and families is even influenced by stigma.

Stigma occurs because many myths surround mental illness. While many factors, including genetics and environment, can affect a person's overall mental health, mental illnesses are not the result of personal weakness, lack of character, lack of intelligence, or sin. Angst, guilt, and torment associated with sin or other parts of the human experience should not be confused with serious and persistent mental illness. Sin *does not* cause bipolar disorder or schizophrenia. Serious and persistent mental illness can affect persons of any age, race, religion, or income.

One of the most damaging myths is that mental illness is not treatable. This myth is damaging because early identification of mental illness and treatment is vital. By getting people the treatment they need early on, recovery is accelerated and the brain is protected from further harm related to the course of the illness. The best treatments for serious mental illnesses today are highly effective.

Between 70 and 90 percent of individuals who receive a combination of medication, psychosocial treatments, and supportive counseling experience a significant decrease in symptoms and an improved quality of life.[2] Therefore, most people with serious mental illness need medication to help control symptoms but also need to rely on supportive counseling, self-help groups, assistance with housing, vocational rehabilitation, income assistance, and other community services in order to achieve their highest level of recovery.

Treatment

Mental health treatment works and gives people with mental illness (consumers) hope for recovery. Still, treatments for mental illness can be difficult for consumers for many reasons. The cost of mental health treatment is often more than they can afford. Even with the best health insurance coverage, the ability to access mental health services may be limited. Lack of transportation can also be a barrier to treatment. Medications for mental illness can pose a variety of problems as well. Newer medications are effective and have fewer side effects, but they are far from perfect. Side effects can make the consumer unwilling to take medication. More research is needed to find more effective treatments with fewer side effects, which will make compliance with the treatment easier and more likely.

Relationships

The toll mental illness can take on relationships can be significant. Many individuals with serious and persistent mental illness and their families spend countless difficult years trying to deal with the illness and understand one another. Sometimes consumers feel that their family and friends do not understand them or understand that the consumer's aberrant behaviors are symptoms of mental illness.

As family and friends start to understand the seriousness of mental illness and go through their learning and grieving process, some consumers may feel that their loved ones are giving up on them. Many consumers want their families and friends to become informed about mental illness so that they can have a true understanding of, and an empathy for, what it is like to experience it and live with it. This knowledge can bring together those struggling with mental illness and their families and friends. These bonds can be a critical element in providing a caring support system and in aiding the recovery process.

Spirituality

People who have a serious and persistent mental illness may struggle spiritually. It can be difficult to be in tune with the Spirit and feel open to spiritual ideas when the mind and emotions are affected by a mental illness. Ironically, some people may develop an unhealthy, overzealous religiosity. This may be an attempt to overcome the illness by trying to overcompensate for the limitations created by the illness, or it may be due to distortions in thinking or misunderstanding spiritual teachings. Still others feel that their illness is a result of not obeying the commandments, living the gospel, or fighting off Satan's influence. These false beliefs can bring a tremendous amount of guilt and shame to those struggling with mental illness. A person may still have real spiritual concerns or may need to change sinful behaviors, but it is important to separate these from problems caused by the illness.

Many of the things people take for granted as members of the Church can be difficult for someone living with serious and persistent mental illness. Because of problems with regulating emotions, thinking clearly, and managing behavior caused by the illness, attending church meetings, church activities, and the temple can prove to be challenging. Speaking in church and participating in church callings can also be difficult. Even shaking hands with people can be a struggle. Church leaders and members can help when they are aware of these kinds of challenges.

Interestingly, spirituality is seen as an important component in the recovery process by the mental health profession. Many mental health professionals understand and appreciate the role a supportive religious community can play in assisting people with mental illness. Furthermore, belief and faith in God (or a higher power) has been proven to help many people in their recovery process.

What Is Recovery from Mental Illness?

Recovery from mental illness does not necessarily mean that the symptoms of mental illness will completely go away—although for some they may.

Nor does it mean to simply *manage* those symptoms. Recovery is a process that has many steps.

Diagnosis. Learning about the illness and available treatments.

Empowerment. Getting the support of family and peers.

Advocacy. Moving to a point where there is a sense of being able to support and help others.

In the past, people with serious and persistent mental illness were often encouraged to live simple lives with low expectations. Today, however, they are encouraged to pursue their goals and dreams, though they may need to learn skills to manage their illness and adapt to their persistent symptoms.

Recovery may mean that individuals regain a sense of self and that they learn to see themselves as valuable and able to live full, meaningful, and productive lives. Recovery is possible and there is hope!

The road to recovery from serious and persistent mental illness can take many forms. The National Alliance on Mental Illness has a mental health education program titled Building Recovery of Individual Dreams and Goals through Education and Support (BRIDGES). The program, designed for mental health consumers, discusses the stages of recovery. These stages are similar to the stages experienced by families learning to cope with an ill family member. Recovery from mental illness is individualized—no two people are the same. And yet, there are some similarities in how people respond. The "Emotional Stages of Recovery"[3] in the BRIDGES program was developed through feedback from many consumers. These stages include the following:

Event 1: Crisis

The first event is a crisis brought on by mental illness. This crisis may have been brought on by psychosis, mania, panic attack, or attempted suicide. Some of the emotions experienced during this time may include shock, confusion, fear, anger, despair, numbness, guilt, horror, or denial.

Stage 1: Recuperation

The stage called recuperation follows a mental health crisis. This is a time when the consumer needs nurturing and acceptance. After the chaos and trauma of an episode of mental illness, many people who have major mental illness experience exhaustion—physically, mentally, emotionally, and spiritually. This is a time of many negative emotions, including denial, confusion, despair, and anger.

Needs during this stage may include a safe place to live, lots of sleep, nutritious food, personal hygiene, a caregiver, and medications. Those who have been through this stage offer the following descriptions:

"I had a hard time explaining to those around me what I was feeling and why."

"I needed a place where I had space that was safe and supportive."

"I just wanted to be in a place where there was no stigma and no pressure."

"I needed understanding and comfort—like a big, warm, fuzzy blanket wrapped around me."

"I needed aspects of control of myself and of my environment."

"I needed people to understand that I was struggling and trying my best to get better as quickly as possible."

"I needed a place where I felt safe to be myself and not feel like I was going to be judged."

"I needed the mental health professionals to slow down. I had a hard time thinking."

"I felt very isolated and alone."

Event 2: Decision

After a period of recuperation comes the decision to get going again. The timing for this event is different for every individual. For some, it may take a couple of months; for others, it may take a couple of years.

Stage 2: Rebuilding

After the decision to get going has been made, a desire to start rebuilding life and independence follows. The individual takes responsibility to get the help needed and to learn and practice living and working skills. Setbacks as well as successes will happen during this stage, and there will be mixed emotions—grief, doubt, hope, anxiety, frustration, and pride.

Needs during this stage may include the need to be heard and the need to be accepted. In this stage there is a need to learn about mental illness and to understand it. Individuals with serious and persistent mental illness may need to learn or relearn people skills, problem-solving skills, and work or occupational skills. In addition, individuals may need to learn about financial planning and about general wellness, including nutrition, sleep, and exercise. Those who have been through this stage explain it like this:

> "I was glad to finally get the right help. It was a relief to me. I wanted to get better. Still, I struggled and felt like my brain was broken. I liked to stay close to home and did not like to go out much."
>
> "I feared I would never be myself again. I started to find myself again."
>
> "This is a time of trial and error."
>
> "I made progress a little bit at a time. Baby steps were necessary."
>
> "You need to take little steps to build your life again. You need to give yourself permission to do that."
>
> "I needed to feel that it was okay to have setbacks."
>
> "I needed to learn from the setbacks to move forward."
>
> "I needed to reevaluate my expectations of myself. I needed to take it slow and not try to conquer the world all at once."
>
> "I felt a need to feel useful, to get involved, and to be needed. You can only spend so much time by yourself at home."

"Education of the illness was important to me. I had a real need to
be informed so I could start understanding the process and
what was happening to me."

Event 3: Awakening

As a person rebuilds himself, there comes a sense of a new person emerging.
He starts to realize that there is more to him than his mental illness and that he
is a whole person. He is not better or worse, just different. He begins to dream
again about who he is and what he can be. This is the beginning of *recovery.*

Stage 3: Recovery

This is a stage of building healthy interdependence. There is an understanding of what is important to the individual—who the individual cares
about and who cares about the individual. Emotions during this time can
include acceptance of self and others, confidence, anger at injustice, and help-
fulness to others. Needs during this stage include the following:

A dream to strive for

Appreciation from people

Intimacy (emotional closeness and someone to love)

Meaningful work

Play and physical activity

To advocate for self and others (being able to educate, help, and
inform others with similar struggles)

Those who have been through this stage describe it like this:

"I joined a group for people who live with mental illness. I enjoyed
getting to know other people who also struggled with mental
illness—particularly those who had the same illness I did. It felt
good to know other people felt the same way. Before long, I was
eager to help other people with their illness."

"I became more compassionate, empathetic, and understanding."

"It felt good to learn about the illness and then to become an advocate."

"I needed some kind of meaningful work."

"Helping others along the road of recovery was healing."

"Getting back to playfulness, enjoyment, caring—to those things that have meaning in life."

"I am able to enjoy life and feel that I have a purpose."

"It feels good to be myself again, but I realize that things will not always stay perfect, and I will always have to work on it."

"I became a more empowered person than before."

The Components of Recovery

Again, recovery does not necessarily mean that the symptoms of mental illness necessarily disappear. Recovery means that people with mental illness are able to regain a sense of self, manage their illness and symptoms, and fulfill daily tasks and goals. People need many tools to successfully navigate the road to recovery. Medication is but one important tool of recovery. People struggling with mental illness may also need psychotherapy or supportive counseling and rehabilitative services to rebuild their life. In addition, they may need a strong support system, education about the illness, and housing and employment support. Recovery from mental illness, *with any diagnosis,* is possible, so there is always reason to have hope.

What We Should Learn from Those Who Live with Mental Illness

Mental illness can be complicated and confusing for everyone. Those who struggle with mental illness and their families, communities, and mental health professionals are always learning about these illnesses. The best way to understand these illnesses comes from the voices of those who live with them every day. When asked, "What would you like people to know about mental illness?" several individuals responded with the following:

"My illness is *just one part* of me. It is not me."

"Just be patient with me. Sometimes I just can't help how I feel."

"I don't want to feel judged."

"My mental illness is like any other illness. It should be looked at the same way as other illnesses."

"I worry about a lot of things. I worry about my future."

"I just want others to understand me."

"I want people to understand that it is a medical disorder."

"There is a conclusion to mental illness. There is an end to the chaos. The bad times are temporary. You move on."

"Judgment can be the most detrimental thing. No one can understand mental illness until you live it and walk in those shoes."

"Mental illnesses are a dramatic part of life. We are all affected by mental illness, and how we choose to view it is critical to the success of the treatment for those who struggle with it."

"Do not treat me like it is my fault or like I am lazy."

"Don't label me or judge me."

"Mental illness is not a death sentence. It is a manageable thing."

"There is hope. There are other people who are in the same place. You can recover."

"Serving other people really helps us grow. It helps to build our self-esteem, which has been ripped apart from mental illness. Being able to reach out to other people is really empowering."

"You can recover from mental illness!"

Living with a serious and persistent mental illness can be extremely difficult in a world that does not always understand the true nature of mental illness and its challenges. But a mental health diagnosis does not have to mean that life is diminished or destroyed. A full, rich, meaningful life can be achieved. Treatment works, recovery is possible, there is hope, and no one need feel alone.

Notes

1. NAMI, Oct. 28, 2006 (nami.org).
2. NAMI, Oct. 28, 2006 (nami.org).
3. BRIDGES Mental Health Education Program.

24

Caring for Someone with Dementia or Alzheimer's Disease

Mary Ellen Smoot

I never dreamed that my own sister would forget my name. But when I visit her care center, she doesn't even know who I am. For several years now, my sister Maurine has struggled with dementia and Alzheimer's disease.

The *American Heritage College Dictionary* defines dementia as the "deterioration of intellectual faculties resulting from a disorder of the brain and often accompanied by emotional disturbance." That same dictionary defines Alzheimer's as "a disease marked by progressive loss of mental capacity." While these definitions are technically correct, they do not describe the anguish or joy that can come to family members who care for victims with these conditions.

Perhaps we do not completely understand our Heavenly Father's plan for bringing His children through the tests of this mortal life. However, we can be assured that we will all be tested one way or another. It often seems that some people have far greater trials than others. Some are taken in the prime of their lives; others live in a mental world we cannot seem to penetrate. In such cases, we sometimes wonder who is being tested more—the victims of death and disease or the loved ones they leave behind?

In this chapter, I share a few insights and experiences that I hope will benefit those who care for loved ones who suffer from dementia or Alzheimer's.

This chapter is by no means comprehensive, but I hope it will help ease someone's burden or brighten someone's day.

"Clothe Yourselves with the Bond of Charity"

The Lord has commanded, "See that ye love one another; cease to be covetous; learn to impart one to another as the gospel requires. And above all things, clothe yourselves with the bond of charity, as with a mantle, which is the bond of perfectness and peace" (D&C 88:123, 125).

The initial stages of dementia or Alzheimer's can be devastating for the caregiver, especially if the caregiver is the spouse of the victim. Imagine the pain a husband must feel when his wife looks at him quizzically and says, "Who are you?" As painful as such disconnection can be, the best way to respond is with continuing connection—with "the bond of charity."

I once spoke with two sisters who frequently visited their ninety-three-year-old mother, an Alzheimer's patient at a care center. They were familiar with the challenges of this disease—their father had also suffered from Alzheimer's for ten years before he died of cancer. These sisters found that their father became more kind and loving when he had Alzheimer's. Their most memorable moments with their father occurred in assisting him during this time. Their secret for serving their parents—an expression of true charity—was simple: "We treat them as we would expect to be treated in the same condition."

Our devotion is put to the test when we become caregivers of someone affected by dementia or Alzheimer's disease. But when kindness abounds in all we do and say, we will feel more at peace. So will our loved one, whether he or she acknowledges it or not.

The sisters who cared for their mother tried various ways to keep her in her home forty-five miles away. At first they ran back and forth. Later they hired someone to live with her. Then they moved her to an assisted-living center until she broke her hip. While healing from this painful experience, the mother was brought into one of the sister's homes for a period of time and then moved to the home of the other sister.

Their mother was miserable and made life unbearable for all. Finally she was placed in an Alzheimer's hospital, where she regained her sweet personality and started walking with her walker again. One day we taped a conversation the sisters had with their mother. She reminisced about her youth for half an hour, vividly recalling her life on the family farm.

Find Strength in the Lord

The exultant Ammon declared, "I know that I am nothing; as to my strength I am weak; therefore I will not boast of myself, but I will boast of my God, for in his strength I can do all things" (Alma 26:12).

These are beautiful words, and we believe them. We have read of many miracles that prophets, leaders, and friends have experienced as they have depended on the Lord's strength in their lives. But sometimes we struggle to actually believe these words in our own lives. In our efforts to serve a loved one who suffers from dementia or Alzheimer's, one of the most important things we can do is trust that the Lord will help us and our family, just as he has helped others. We will never be able to do everything on our own, but combined with the Lord's strength, our efforts will be enough.

Work Together as a Family

The diagnosis that a loved one has dementia or Alzheimer's leads to life-changing decisions. In many cases, the patient's spouse begins by taking on care-giving responsibilities alone. Eventually, especially as the patient's health deteriorates, the spouse will need the help of extended family. Without such help, the daily strain, both physical and emotional, can affect the caregiver's health.

Some families immediately organize as soon as the diagnosis is given. Together they ensure that someone is with the ill person at all times. They take turns, perhaps accepting assignments for specific days of the week. This takes great support and devotion. When family members work together, they all witness the gradual changes in their loved one.

Because they cannot completely understand the causes of their loved one's agitation and confusion, this can be one of the greatest tests they face as a family. Depending on the support and love they have for one another, this test can either drive them apart or bring them close together. They can draw strength from one another as they fast and pray together, both for their loved one and for each other. Working together and exercising their faith together, they can better cope with the daily challenges of their care-giving responsibilities.

Seek Help from Qualified Professionals

Susan's example. I have a friend named Susan who became concerned when she saw signs that her mother's personality was changing. But her mother was still able to communicate, and her father cared for his wife valiantly and tenderly, even though his physical health was failing. Then Susan's father died, and Susan realized that she needed a doctor's opinion about her mother's condition. The doctor's diagnosis confirmed her suspicion. Her mother was suffering from dementia, and she eventually developed Alzheimer's disease as well.

Upon learning of her mother's condition, Susan enrolled in a class at a care-giving facility. She found it helpful to learn from experts in the field and from others who had gone through the same experience with their loved ones. As she learned more, she realized that she needed help adjusting to the responsibility of her mother's care. Susan placed her mother in an assisted-living center, where she enjoyed interacting with others. This was not an easy decision for Susan. However, she knew it was the right decision, and this assurance brought her inner peace.

Of this time, Susan recalled, "You are spiritually attuned to your parents, and as well as losing the precious mental and emotional connection, you have to be prepared for losing that spiritual connection with the parent that is suffering from dementia or Alzheimer's. You seek answers to your prayers on a daily basis."

Susan visited her mother often in the assisted living center. The more time the two of them spent together, the more Susan realized that there was only a small window of time in which her mother would be able to interact with others and express herself. At first, her mother always greeted her by saying, "There is my baby!" And Susan always replied, "Don't you ever forget I am your baby!" But as time went on, Susan became the "nice lady that brings me breakfast." Later, her mother stopped interacting altogether. And soon another difficult decision had to be made.

One day Susan's mother fell out of her bed and broke her hip, necessitating an extended stay in a hospital. Susan and her devoted husband prayed diligently to know what to do. They both came to know it was time to take her mother into their home. Susan admitted, "I understood that this was not going to be easy, realizing that it would be a journey and that I had to accept this calling."

Susan continued to seek help with meeting her mother's needs. She and her family hired a hospice service—experienced personnel who came to their home. Susan spoke of the care she and others continued to give her mother: "We would prepare her for each day. She would be showered, we would wash her hair and dress her special and do her nails, and we would prepare her for this experience so she would feel better. This made it easier to care for her."

My own experience. My family had a similar experience as we witnessed the gradual decline in the mental health of my sister Maurine. Her husband had already passed away, so when she was diagnosed with dementia, her children and siblings gathered to discuss her situation. We are a loving, compassionate group, and we determined that we would do all we could to care for her. Her children were especially determined to give her all the care she needed. In their minds, there was no other option; they were certain they could handle the constant care of their mother.

Maurine's children were devoted and diligent. They truly did all they could. A daughter took Maurine into her home for a time, and the family arranged for someone to be with her every day. A son moved his family to live closer to her, and finally, her oldest son moved into Maurine's home with his wife, who was a full-time nurse. They felt good about their efforts to care for her, but her difficulties became more and more challenging for them. Their own health began to fail under the stress of providing care.

When Maurine's oldest son died of a stroke, his wife carried most of the caretaking load for a time. She worked every day and came home to her struggling, needy mother-in-law every night. This was an overwhelming experience, especially for someone who had just lost her husband. Finally the siblings determined to move their mother to a nursing home. They saw that she was placed in an excellent facility and treated well, and they committed to take turns visiting her.

The facility has been just what Maurine needed. She has a lovely room, good food, and a bath every day. A beautician comes in once each week to do her hair, if she desires. The employees arrange special birthday parties for the residents, and they celebrate every holiday. Children's groups come to perform and brighten the lives of the residents. Latter-day Saint residents make up a small branch in the care center and are blessed by the service of a loving branch presidency. Women from neighboring wards conduct Relief Society there. My sister and her fellow residents do not understand everything that goes on, but they feel the Spirit as they hear the music and the messages that their visitors share.

Seek Help from Volunteers

A coordinator at a care center once expressed gratitude for volunteers, saying that there is "nothing like the human touch." She said that people in care centers who do not receive visits are like "abandoned babies" but that volunteers can help "keep the minds and the spirits of our patients high." Donating an hour or two each week, volunteers give valuable attention to those who suffer from dementia or Alzheimer's.

They might comb their hair or put nail polish and lipstick on them. They might put lotion on their arms and legs. They might read to them, write letters to their family members, sing to them, or take them on walks. One-on-one, a volunteer, whether a member of the family or a kind friend, can change darkness into light, despair into hope, and sadness into laughter.

Savor the Tender Moments

For Susan, the hardest tasks involved helping her mother with physical needs, such as showering and using the bathroom. But these responsibilities, difficult as they were, brought tender, memorable moments.

"Once as I was taking her to the bathroom," Susan remembered, "I had on my high-heeled shoes because I was getting ready for church. I slipped and fell, and she fell on me. I sat and cried, and she looked at me and said, 'I'm sorry.' These were the most sensible words she had spoken in days."

Susan recalled one especially tender moment that came as she cared for her mother's physical needs. "The first time I had to shower her," she said, "it was touching to me as a daughter." Their roles had reversed—she was now bathing her mother, who had done the same for her when she was a baby. "It turned out to be a sweet blessing," Susan said.

Record Special Memories

When persons affected by dementia or Alzheimer's can still remember the past and talk about it, family members or volunteers should consider recording their voice as they share experiences from their lives. This can leave a beautiful legacy for the family.

Create a Spiritual Haven

Referring to the time when she and her husband took her mother into their home, Susan said, "You feel incapable on occasions. We came to the conclusion that on a daily basis we needed to create a spiritual haven. That was our answer: thinking beyond that struggle and making things beautiful and pleasant."

One thing they did to create a spiritual haven was to play a CD of Primary songs. Her mother, who had spent many years serving in the Primary, often sang along. Seeing the comfort that came with music, they played beautiful, soft music throughout each day. Even in the spiritual haven they created, however, Susan's mother sometimes became unreasonable. But, Susan observed, "As long as I kept my mind on the spiritual side of this, it was just fine. When she would become angry and violent, we would have to remain calm and patient."

In addition to playing soft music, Susan found other ways to soothe her mother. Every day she read love letters that her father had written to her mother when he was serving in the military. His stories of faith and family were uplifting and sometimes humorous. She also read short stories and talks from general conference.

Take a Break

Soon after Susan took her mother into her home, she had a conversation with a neighbor who had spent her life as a caregiver to her disabled daughter. Susan's friend gave her the name of a local care-giving organization and insisted that Susan take a break periodically. Susan needed the rejuvenation that would come with a little free time, her friend explained.

Susan took her friend's advice and grew to appreciate the regular help the care-giving organization provided in her home. "They worked with me," she said, "and my mother's schedule never changed. We all had prayers in the morning and evening with her. There was a circle of people caring for her and doing the same things we had done every day."

In addition to the care-giving organization, Susan's immediate family often came to spend time with their loved one. This relieved Susan of her continual duties and gave her opportunities to go to the grocery store and take care of the home.

Don't Be Afraid to Laugh

Just as a little child will innocently say some of the funniest things, a loved one with dementia or Alzheimer's will occasionally say something that makes us laugh. It's okay to chuckle from time to time at the comments and antics of a loved one. One such story, my favorite, is told by Patricia MacLachlan, the author of the Newberry Award–winning novel *Sarah, Plain and Tall.* Ms. MacLachlan relates that her mother suffered from Alzheimer's. As the two of them were on a car ride one day, the mother asked, "Who are you?" Patricia replied, "I am your daughter!" Her mother responded, "I am so glad because I like you."

Stay Physically, Mentally, and Spiritually Awake

My friend Bill remembers the day his wife, Ellie, came to him with tears in her eyes and said, "Something is wrong with me." Afterward, day by day, Bill's family watched her change until she was diagnosed with Alzheimer's. At first, Bill was determined to keep her at home, and he did so for four years. Then one day she looked at him seriously and said, "Who are you?"

Ellie now lives in a care center. Bill visits her every day, and he fills the rest of his time keeping himself invigorated physically, mentally, and spiritually. He serves in the temple, works in his yard, exercises, reads, and writes.

Remember the Good Times

One day a hospice nurse approached Susan and said simply about her mother, "She only has a day or two [to live]." Susan recalled the sweet experience of her mother's passing: "She passed on with the whole family around the bed. It was a tender moment. It had been a process and a two-year journey, but we made it very special. The family was able to say good-bye to her with the knowledge of a special reunion on the other side."

However hard the experience had seemed at the time, Susan later said, "We miss the closeness, the peace, and the serenity we felt in our home during that care-giving process. Alzheimer's disease slows down life, but it makes you appreciate the moments so tender: the blue sky outside the window; the squirrels playing outdoors; the change of the seasons; beautiful, consoling music; scriptures, letters, and thoughts. The days when you have clarity are so special."

Enduring to the End

My sister passed away November 28, 2006, at the age of eighty-two. Just a few months before, her doctor had said she was physically healthy and could live for some time to come. At times we asked ourselves, "Are we doing enough?" Of course, we will never feel that we gave enough, but we loved her, visited her often, and always signed a guest book to keep track of her condition.

She knew no one. However, we would occasionally see a glimpse of recognition in her eyes. She was always excited to see us, and when we took her to Relief Society meetings, she would hum along as others sang familiar hymns.

Life goes on. We continue to love and serve one another and learn from our experiences. Day by day, we find ways to deal with each challenge we face during our sojourn on earth. We grow in our conviction that in the strength of the Lord we can do all things.

As I contemplate the struggles of those who suffer from dementia or Alzheimer's disease—and as I consider the tireless love of those who serve them—I am reminded of a verse from a song in the musical *Les Misérables:*

Do you hear the people sing?
Lost in the valley of the night?
It is the music of a people
Who are climbing to the light.
For the wretched of the earth
There is a flame that never dies,
Even the darkest night will end
And the sun will rise.[1]

Note

1. "EPILOGUE (Finale)" from the Broadway Musical *Les Misérables* by Alain Boublil & Claude-Michel Schönberg. Music by Claud-Michel Schönberg. Lyrics by Alain Boublil, Herbert Kretzmer & Jean Marc-Natel. © Alain Boublil Music Ltd. (ASCAP). Used by permission.

Sources

Articles in Latter-day Saint Periodicals

Ballard, M. Russell. "Let Our Voices Be Heard." *Ensign,* Nov. 2003, 16–19.

———. "Suicide: Some Things We Know, and Some We Do Not." *Ensign,* Oct. 1987, 6–8.

Benson, Ezra Taft. "'Come unto Christ, and Be Perfected in Him.'" *Ensign,* May 1988, 84–85.

———. "Do Not Despair." *Ensign,* Nov. 1974, 65–67.

Carmack, John K. "United in Love and Testimony." *Ensign,* May 2001, 76–77.

Faust, James E. "Refined in Our Trials." *Ensign,* Feb. 2006, 3–7.

Fox, Dawn and Jay Fox. "Easing the Burdens of Mental Illness." *Ensign,* Oct. 2001.

Groberg, John H. "The Power of God's Love." *Ensign,* Nov. 2004, 9–11.

Hinckley, Gordon B. "Of Missions, Temples, and Stewardship." *Ensign,* Nov. 1995, 51–54.

Holland, Jeffrey R. "Broken Things to Mend." *Ensign,* May 2006, 69–71.

———. "The Grandeur of God." *Ensign,* Nov. 2003, 70–73.

Hughes, Kathleen H. "Blessed by Living Water." *Ensign,* May 2003, 13–15.

"Light in Darkness." *Ensign,* June 1998, 16–21.

Maxwell, Neal A. "According to the Desire of [Our] Hearts." *Ensign,* Nov. 1996, 21–23.

Monson, Thomas S. "The Temple of the Lord." *Ensign,* May 1993, 4–5.

Morrison, Alexander B. "Myths about Mental Illness." *Ensign,* Oct. 2005, 31–35.

———. "Mental Illness and the Family." Address to Families under Fire, conference held at Brigham Young University, 4 Oct. 2008; available online at familiesunder fire.byu.edu.

Oaks, Dallin H. "He Heals the Heavy Laden." *Ensign,* Nov. 2006, 6–9.

———. "Powerful Ideas." *Ensign,* Nov. 1995, 25–27.

———. "Worship through Music." *Ensign,* Nov. 1994, 9–12.

Packer, Boyd K. "'The Touch of the Master's Hand.'" *Ensign,* May 2001, 22–24.

———. "Little Children." *Ensign,* Nov. 1986, 16–18.

Packer, Karen Athay. "The Broken Bowl." *Ensign,* Sept. 1992, 52–54.

Pinborough, Jan Underwood. "Mental Illness: In Search of Understanding and Hope." *Ensign,* Feb. 1989, 50–58.

Pingree, Carmen B. " 'So Near and Yet So Far': Living with Autism." *Ensign,* Aug. 1983, 56–59.

"Q&A: Questions and Answers." *New Era,* Jan. 1990, 14–18.

Richards, Franklin D. In Conference Report, Oct. 1970, 80.

Scott, Richard G. "The Path to Peace and Joy." *Ensign,* Nov. 2000, 25–27.

———. "Removing Barriers to Happiness." *Ensign,* May 1998, 85–87.

———. "To Be Healed." *Ensign,* May 1994, 7–9.

Simmons, Dennis E. "But If Not . . ." *Ensign,* May 2004, 73–75.

Thornton, Laurie Wilson. "The Hidden Handicap." *Ensign,* Apr. 1990, 44–48.

VanDenBerghe, Elizabeth. "Helping and Being Helped by the Intellectually Impaired." *Ensign,* Oct. 1993, 26–32.

Weight, David G. "Why Is My Wife (Or Husband) Depressed?" *Ensign,* Mar. 1990, 27–29.

Wirthlin, Joseph B. "Finding a Safe Harbor." *Ensign,* May 2000, 59–61.

Books

Adamec, Christine. *How to Live with a Mentally Ill Person.* Toronto: John Wiley and Sons, 1996.

American Heritage College Dictionary. 4th ed. Boston: Houghton Mifflin, 2002.

American Psychiatric Association. *Diagnostic and Statistical Manual of Mental Disorders,* 4th ed. Washington, D.C.: 1994.

Attwood, T. *Asperger's Syndrome: A Guide for Parents and Professionals.* Philadelphia: Jessica Kingsley Publisher, 1998.

Burland, Joyce. *NAMI Family-to-Family Education Program Teaching Manual.* 2d ed. Arlington, Virginia: National Alliance for the Mentally Ill, 1998.

———.*NAMI Provider Education Program.* Arlington, Virginia: National Alliance for the Mentally Ill, 1999.

Burns, David D. *The Feeling Good Handbook.* New York: Plume, Penguin Group, 1999.

———. *Feeling Good: The New Mood Therapy.* New York: Avon, Harper Collins, 1999.

Byrd, A. Dean. *Willpower Is Not Enough.* Salt Lake City: Deseret Book, 1990.

Church Handbook of Instructions. 2 books. Salt Lake City: The Church of Jesus Christ of Latter-day Saints, 2006.

Conroy, Pat. *Beach Music.* New York: Nan A. Talese, 1995.

Cook, Gene R. *Receiving Answers to Our Prayers.* Salt Lake City: Deseret Book, 1996.

Coping with Anxiety and Phobias. Boston: President and Fellows of Harvard College, 2006.

Diagnostic and Statistical Manual of Mental Disorders. 4th ed. Washington, D.C.: American Psychiatric Association, 1994.

Encyclopedia of Joseph Smith's Teachings. Edited by Larry E. Dahl and Donald Q. Cannon. Salt Lake City: Bookcraft, 1997.

Hannin, Edward. "An Introduction." In *Mental Illness Awareness Guide for Image Makers.* Washington, D.C.: American Psychiatric Association, 1993.

Hearts Knit Together: Talks from the 1995 Women's Conference. Edited by Susette Fletcher Green, Dawn Hall Anderson, and Dlora Hall Dalton. Salt Lake City: Deseret Book, 1996.

Hymns of The Church of Jesus Christ of Latter-day Saints. Salt Lake City: The Church of Jesus Christ of Latter-day Saints, 1985.

Integrating Spirituality into Treatment. Edited by William R. Miller. Washington, D.C.: American Psychological Association, 2003.

Kimball, Spencer W. *Teachings of Presidents of the Church: Spencer W. Kimball.* Salt Lake City: The Church of Jesus Christ of Latter-day Saints, 2006.

Klin, Ami, and F. R. Volkmar. "Treatment and Intervention Guidelines for Individuals with Asperger Syndrome." In *Asperger Syndrome.* Edited by Ami Klin, Fred R. Volkmar, and Susan S. Sparrow. New York: Guilford Press, 2000.

LDS Family Services: Agency Plan and Operations Guide. Salt Lake City: The Church of Jesus Christ of Latter-day Saints, 2003.

Morrison, Alexander B. *Valley of Sorrow.* Salt Lake City: Deseret Book, 2003.

Mueser, Kim T., and Susan Gingerich. *Coping with Schizophrenia.* Oakland, Calif.: New Harbinger Publications, 1994

National Institute of Mental Health. *Men and Depression.* Bethesda, Maryland: National Institute of Mental Health, 2005.

Neighbors, H., J. Jackson, P. Bowman, and G. Gurin. *Stress, Coping and Black Mental Health: Preliminary findings from a national study.* Newbury Park, CA: Sage, 1983. Quoted in Christopher Peterson and Martin E. P. Seligman, *Character Strength and Virtues: A Handbook and Classification.* Washington, D.C.: American Psychological Association, 2004.

Packer, Boyd K. *That All May Be Edified.* Salt Lake City: Bookcraft, 1982.

Peterson, Christopher, and Martin E. P. Seligman. *Character Strength and Virtues: A Handbook and Classification.* Washington, D.C.: American Psychological Association, 2004.

Random House Dictionary of the English Language. 2d ed. New York: Random House, 1987.

Richards, P. Scott, Randy K. Hardman, and Michael E. Berrett. *Spiritual Approaches in the Treatment of Women with Eating Disorders.* Washington, D.C.: American Psychological Association, 2006.

Richards, P. Scott, and Allen E. Bergin. *A Spiritual Strategy for Counseling and Psychotherapy.* Washington, D.C.: American Psychological Association, 1997.

———. *Handbook of Psychotherapy and Religious Diversity.* Washington, D.C.: American Psychological Association, 2000.

Smith, Joseph. *History of The Church of Jesus Christ of Latter-day Saints.* Edited by B. H. Roberts. 2d ed. rev. 7 vols. Salt Lake City: The Church of Jesus Christ of Latter-day Saints, 1932–51.

———. *Teachings of the Prophet Joseph Smith.* Selected by Joseph Fielding Smith. Salt Lake City: Deseret Book, 1976.

Smith, Joseph F. *Gospel Doctrine.* 5th ed. Salt Lake City: Deseret Book, 1939.

Smith, Joseph Fielding. *Doctrines of Salvation.* Compiled by Bruce R. McConkie, 3 vols. Salt Lake City, Utah: Bookcraft, 1955.

———. *Answers to Gospel Questions.* Salt Lake City: Deseret Book, 1960.

Torrey, E. Fuller. *Surviving Schizophrenia: A Manual for Families, Consumers, and Providers.* New York: Harper and Row, 1983.

Understanding Depression. Boston: President and Fellows of Harvard College, 2006.

Women's Mental Health. Edited by Susan G. Kornstein and Anita H. Clayton. New York: Guilford Press, 2002.

Yamada, Steven C. "Coping with Suicide." In *Helping and Healing Our Families.* Edited by Craig H. Hart, Lloyd D. Newell, Elaine Walton, and David C. Dollahite. Salt Lake City: Deseret Book, 2005.

Journals

"Ethical Principles of Psychologists and Code of Conduct." American Psychologist 47 (December 1992): 1599.

Gray, C. A. "Social Stories: Improving Responses of Students with Autism with Accurate Social Information." Focus on Autistic Behavior 8 (1993): 1–10.

Hallfors, D. D., M. W. Waller, D. Bauer, et al. "Which Comes First in Adolescents—Sex and Drugs or Depression?" American Journal of Preventive Medicine 29 (2000): 163–70.

Online and Other Resources

amcap.net (Association of Mormon Counselors and Psychotherapists)

americanheart.org (American Heart Association)

autism-society.org (Autism Society of America)

autismspeaks.org (Autism Speaks)

biausa.org (Brain Injury Association of America)

BRIDGES Mental Health Education Program. Tennessee Mental Health Consumer's Association. NAMI Tennessee: Sita Diehl, 2004.

cdc.gov (Centers for Disease Control and Prevention)

centerforchange.com (Center for Change)

cerebralpalsy.org

disability.lds.org

epilepsyfoundation.org (Epilepsy Foundation)

familiesunderfire.byu.edu

familiesunderfire.byu.edu.

gurze.com (Bulimia.com)

health.harvard.edu (Harvard Health Publications)

health.harvard.edu/special_health_reports/Coping_with_Anxiety_and_Phobias.htm

health.harvard.edu/special_health_reports/Understanding_Depression.htm

ldanatl.org (Learning Disabilities Association of America)

ldscounselors.net (LDS Counselors)

lds.org (The Church of Jesus Christ of Latter-day Saints)

mentalhealthlibrary.info (Mental Health Resource Foundation)

Morrison, Alexander B. "Mental Illness and the Family." 4 Oct. 2004. Available online at familiesunderfire.byu.edu

nabis.org (North American Brain Injury Society)

NAMI Grading the States 2006. "Mental Illness Facts." Retrieved Mar. 5, 2007, from nami.org/Content/NavigationMenu/Grading_the_States/Newsroom/Mental

nami.org (National Alliance on Mental Illness)

nationaleatingdisorders.org (National Eating Disorders Association)

niaaa.nih.gov (National Institute on Alcohol Abuse)

nia.nih.gov (National Institute on Aging)

nida.nih.gov (National Institute on Drug Abuse)

nih.gov (National Institutes of Health)

nimh.nih.gov (National Institute of Mental Health)

nmha.org (Mental Health America)

Satcher, David. "Overcome Stigma." In *Mental Health: A Report of the Surgeon General.* Department of Health and Human Services, U.S. Public Health Service (surgeongeneral.gov/library/mentalhealth/chapter8/sec1.html).

"Spirituality and Healing in Medicine." Conference held at Harvard University, December 2006.

strokeassociation.org (American Stroke Association)

Contributors

Grant Belnap and Carol Belnap are married to each other. Grant is a psychiatrist, and Carol has a doctorate in neuropsychology.

W. Dean Belnap, M.D., is a certified specialist in pediatrics and psychiatry. He and his wife, Mary Elen, have six children, twenty-nine grandchildren, and eleven great-grandchildren.

Michael E. Berrett received his Ph.D. in counseling psychology from Brigham Young University and is currently CEO and executive director of Center for Change in Orem, Utah.

Erin D. Bigler, Ph.D., is a professor of psychology and neuroscience at Brigham Young University and an adjunct professor of psychiatry at the University of Utah, where he is also a faculty member of The Brain Institute.

A. Dean Byrd, Ph.D., M.B.A., M.P.H., is the president and CEO of the Thrasher Research Fund and serves as a faculty member of the University of Utah School of Medicine.

Tina Taylor Dyches, Ed.D., is an associate professor and coordinator for special education programs in the Department of Counseling Psychology and Special Education at Brigham Young University.

Dawn Fox and Jay Fox are actively involved as volunteers with the National Alliance on Mental Illness. Dawn received her bachelor of arts degree from Brigham Young University, and Jay is the Nan Osmond Grass Professor of English at BYU.

Lisa J. Fox earned her bachelor of science degree in marriage, family, and human development from Brigham Young University. She is currently in a Ph.D. program in counseling psychology at BYU.

Randy K. Hardman earned his Ph.D. in counseling psychology at Brigham Young University and is clinical director and chief operating officer at Center for Change in Orem, Utah.

Richard A. Heaps, Ph.D., is a board certified clinical psychologist and professor of counseling psychology at the Brigham Young University Counseling Center and Department of Counseling Psychology and Special Education.

John P. Livingstone is licensed in Canada as a psychologist and is associate chair of the Department of Church History and Doctrine in Religious Education at Brigham Young University.

Carol P. Moody is a clinical supervisor in the Communication Disorders Department at Brigham Young University and a speech and language pathologist.

Richard A. Moody, a psychologist, is an associate clinical professor at Brigham Young University.

Christine S. Packard received her master of counseling degree from Arizona State University. She is a licensed professional counselor with a private practice in individual and family counseling in Mesa, Arizona.

P. Scott Richards earned his Ph.D. in counseling psychology at the University of Minnesota and is a professor of counseling psychology at Brigham Young University.

S. Brent Scharman is a licensed psychologist employed as an assistant commissioner of LDS Family Services.

Timothy B. Smith is a professor of counseling psychology at Brigham Young University. His research focuses on spirituality and multicultural psychology.

Mary Ellen Smoot served as general president of the Relief Society organization of The Church of Jesus Christ of Latter-day Saints from 1997 to 2002.

Wendy Ulrich, **Ph.D.,** holds degrees in education, business, and psychology from Brigham Young University, UCLA, and the University of Michigan.

Marleen S. Williams, who holds a Ph.D. in clinical psychology, is a clinical professor of counseling psychology at Brigham Young University.

Robert F. Williams, who earned his Ph.D. from Northwestern University, is a clinical psychologist in private practice in Orem, Utah.

Sherri D. Wittwer is the executive director of the National Alliance on Mental Illness–Utah.

Index

About the Editors

Marleen S. Williams, Ph.D., works as a clinical professor of counseling psychology at Brigham Young University and has served as president of the Association of Mormon Counselors and Psychotherapists (AMCAP). As a widowed mother of four children, she returned to school to complete a Ph.D. in clinical psychology. Her professional work includes research and writing on marriage and relationships, mental health and spirituality, disabilities, women's mental health, eating disorders, and psychological trauma. Her work has been published and presented nationally and internationally. She has written articles for the *Ensign* and the *Liahona* and has spoken frequently at Latter-day Saint conferences and workshops.

Sister Williams has served in the Church in stake and ward auxiliary presidencies, but her favorite calling so far was den mother. She is married to Dr. Robert F. Williams, a clinical child psychologist; they have a blended family of ten children and twenty-four grandchildren.

W. Dean Belnap, M.D., is a specialist in pediatrics and in child and adolescent psychiatry. He obtained his medical degree at the University of Utah, with postgraduate training at the University of Utah, Case Western Reserve, and Harvard University Schools of Medicine. He is a fellow of the American Academy of Pediatrics, the American Psychiatric Association, the Society of Behavioral Pediatrics, the American Society of Adolescent Psychiatry, and the American Neuropsychiatric Association.

Dr. Belnap has been in private practice and served as clinical professor at the University of Utah. He has been involved in local and state public health and community mental health agencies and has served as director of nationwide psychiatric hospitals. He has also been elected to local and state boards of education. His professional appointments include the School Health Committee of the American Medical Association and the Handicapped Children's Committee of the American Academy of Pediatrics. He has served as an officer of the National School Boards Association. During President Ronald Reagan's administration, he served on the advisory council of the U. S. Department of Health and Human Services. He has published many articles in medical journals and has also authored or co-authored several books on mental health subjects.

Church and humanitarian assignments have taken Brother Belnap to many parts of the world for extended periods of time. He and his wife, Mary Elen, are the parents of six children, grandparents of twenty-nine, and great-grandparents of thirteen.

John P. Livingstone, Ed.D., is a Canadian who joined the faculty of Brigham Young University in 1998 after his service as president of the Michigan Detroit Mission. A chartered psychologist in two Canadian provinces, he is a past president of the Association of Mormon Counselors and Psychotherapists (AMCAP). John began employment with the Church Educational System in 1972 and presently serves as associate chair of the Department of Church History and Doctrine at BYU. His interests lie in creating virtual tours of Church history sites, early missionary work in the Church, the Church's simplified basic unit program for developing areas of the Church, and in presenting mental illness issues to the general Church membership.

Brother Livingstone serves as president of the Orem College Second Stake (single students). He and his wife, Linda, became American citizens in May 2005. They are the parents of six daughters and one son and grandparents of an ever-growing number of grandchildren.